More praise for *Cases in Intelligence Analysis*

"*Cases in Intelligence Analysis: Structured Analytic Techniques in Action* represents very deep analytical work, written with vision and experience that only true specialists can bring. I recommend it highly to new and experienced practitioners, instructors, and students alike. This excellent book fully supports the instruction of structured analytic techniques, and the step-by-step methodology is easy to follow. Thanks to Beebe and Pherson, SATs are forever going to be easier to teach and learn. A mandatory book for any intelligence analyst's personal library."

—Arturo Fuenzalida P.
Rear Admiral (Ret.)—Intelligence Analyst-Chilean Navy

"The best way to teach students how to analyze and interpret crucial events in international affairs, this indispensable set of cases should be required reading in every political science department. *Experto credite.*"

—Edward M. Roche, PhD, JD
Professor (Affil.), Grenoble Ecole de Management

"*Cases in Intelligence Analysis* is a must-have practical text for intelligence practitioners and serious students of the field. With its companion text, *Structured Analytic Techniques for Intelligence Analysis*, by Richards J. Heuer Jr. and Randolph H. Pherson, the book masterfully guides readers through some of the most important analytical concepts and challenges. Its case studies, each clearly written and accessible, stimulate thinking beyond the instinctive guesswork of much traditional analysis into the sophisticated but satisfying realm of structured techniques. Its authors have made another significant contribution to the development of the discipline."

—Michael Mulqueen, PhD
Associate Professor and Head of the Department of Politics, History, Media, and Communication, Liverpool Hope University, Scotland

Cases in Intelligence Analysis

Structured Analytic Techniques in Action

Sarah Miller Beebe and Randolph H. Pherson

Los Angeles | London | New Delhi
Singapore | Washington DC

Los Angeles | London | New Delhi
Singapore | Washington DC

FOR INFORMATION:

CQ Press

An Imprint of SAGE Publications, Inc.

2455 Teller Road

Thousand Oaks, California 91320

E-mail: order@sagepub.com

SAGE Publications Ltd.

1 Oliver's Yard

55 City Road

London, EC1Y 1SP

United Kingdom

SAGE Publications India Pvt. Ltd.

B 1/I 1 Mohan Cooperative Industrial Area

Mathura Road, New Delhi 110 044

India

SAGE Publications Asia-Pacific Pte. Ltd.

33 Pekin Street #02-01

Far East Square

Singapore 048763

Acquisitions Editor: Elise Frasier

Production Editor: Gwenda Larsen

Marketing Manager: Christopher O'Brien

Typesetter: C&M Digitals (P) Ltd.

Cartographer: International Mapping Associates

Cover Designer: Paula Goldstein, Blue Bungalow Design

Printed in the United States of America

Library of Congress Cataloging-in-Publication Data

Beebe, Sarah Miller.

Cases in intelligence analysis : structured analytic techniques in action / Sarah Miller Beebe and Randolph H. Pherson.

p. cm.
Includes bibliographical references.

ISBN 978-1-60871-681-4 (pbk. : alk. paper)

1. Intelligence service—Methodology—Case studies. I. Pherson, Randolph H. II. Title.

JF1525.I6B44 2011
327.12—dc23   2011038815

This book is printed on acid-free paper.

11 12 13 14 15 10 9 8 7 6 5 4 3 2 1

Cover Image Credits: top to bottom: Oleg Zabielin/ Fotalia; Reuters/STR; David Wasserman; © Tetra Images/ Corbis

*To Sophia, Nora, Grant, Richie, and
Amanda—the next generation*

Brief Contents

Annotated Contents

1   WHO POISONED KARINNA MOSKALENKO?   7

*The poisoning of prominent Russian human rights lawyer Karinna Moskalenko captured worldwide media attention in the fall of 2008. It was regarded as yet another entry in a growing list of poisonings and assassinations allegedly carried out by Russia's government against its critics at home and abroad. This case employs the **Premortem Analysis**, **Structured Self-Critique**, and **Starbursting** techniques to help analysts examine the facts of this fast-moving story and develop a robust set of questions to guide a nuanced analysis of the case.*

Case Narrative   7

Who Poisoned Karinna Moskalenko? Structured Analytic
  Techniques in Action   16

2   IS WEN HO LEE A SPY?   21

In 1999, the New York Times *reported that China had used stolen US nuclear secrets to make rapid advances in its nuclear warhead development. Given the small community of US scientists with access to such data, investigators quickly focused their case on Taiwanese-American nuclear scientist Wen Ho Lee. Had Wen Ho Lee engaged in undetected* *nefarious activities for decades, or did the government narrow its gaze too quickly? Analysts use the **Force Field Analysis**, **Deception Detection**, **Premortem Analysis**, and **Structured Self-Critique** techniques to evaluate both sides of the case, test for deception, and troubleshoot the government's position that Wen Ho Lee was a spy.*

3   THE ROAD TO TARIN KOWT   43

*The US military in 2005 faced a pivotal decision about building a paved road through a Taliban stronghold to Tarin Kowt, a provincial capital in Afghanistan. The United States and other international donors saw the road as a critical element in efforts to stabilize, modernize, and democratize Afghanistan. With Afghanistan's first parliamentary elections since the overthrow of the Taliban on the horizon, the US Army considered embarking on a highly accelerated schedule to complete the road in time for the election. This case uses the **Key Assumptions Check**, **Devil's Advocacy**, and **Strengths-Weaknesses-Opportunities-Threats** techniques to structure a thorough assessment of the operating environment, the probable enemy response, and the potential impact on broader US goals for Afghanistan.*

4   WHO MURDERED JONATHAN LUNA?   61

*Jonathan Luna was a youthful and gregarious federal prosecutor whose mysterious death in December 2003 shocked his friends and colleagues and led to a multiyear, multistate investigation into how and why Jonathan Luna died. With multiple theories swirling amid a plethora of ambiguous and sometimes contradictory evidence, analysts use **Chronologies and Timelines**, **Simple Hypotheses**, the **Multiple Hypotheses Generator**, and **Analysis of Competing Hypotheses** to track and assess events, develop a range of plausible explanations, and rigorously evaluate evidence in this perplexing case.*

provides analysts with a framework to assess the evidence for and against the main suspect, and the **Multiple Hypotheses Generator** *assists in identifying other plausible perpetrators of the crime.*

8   THE DC SNIPER   137

In 2002, only a year after the 9/11 attacks, Washington, D.C., was again gripped with fear as men, women, and children were gunned down by sniper fire across the greater metropolitan area. As authorities raced to find the culprit, they were inundated with myriad eyewitness reports, call-in tips, and other data, but assessing this information proved difficult. This case uses a **Key Assumptions Check** *to help analysts uncover and challenge implicit assumptions that can color evaluation of the available evidence, and it employs the* **Multiple Hypotheses Generator** *and* **Quadrant Crunching** *to help systematically develop and assess a range of possible explanations.*

9   COLOMBIA'S FARC ATTACKS THE US HOMELAND   155

The Revolutionary Armed Forces of Colombia (FARC) is Latin America's largest, oldest, and most capable insurgent group. Its history of kidnappings, assassinations, and indiscriminate acts of violence makes it one of the most despised groups in Colombia, but it has never conducted operations in the United States. This case helps analysts to assess the possibility of such an attack against the homeland using **Red Hat Analysis, Structured Brainstorming, Multiple Scenarios Generation, Indicators,** *and the* **Indicators Validator** *to prompt creative thinking about the range of possible FARC attack scenarios and to identify specific signs that would tip off local officials of an impending attack.*

*Analysis, a **Decision Matrix**, and **Pros-Cons-Faults-and-Fixes** provide a robust framework for conducting a thorough assessment to support decision making in a crisis environment.*

Tables, Figures, and Boxes

MATRIX OF TECHNIQUES

	DECOMPOSITION AND VISUALIZATION		IDEA GENERATION			SCENARIOS AND INDICATORS			
	Chronologies and Timelines	Mind Maps	Structured Brainstorming	Starbursting	Quadrant Crunching	Simple Scenarios	Multiple Scenarios Generation	Indicators	Indicators Validator
1. Who Poisoned Karinna Moskalenko?			❖	✓					
2. Is Wen Ho Lee a Spy?									
3. The Road to Tarin Kowt									
4. Who Murdered Jonathan Luna?	✓		❖						
5. The Assassination of Benazir Bhutto	✓	✓							
6. Death in the Southwest			✓	✓					
7. The Atlanta Olympics Bombing									
8. The DC Sniper					✓				
9. Colombia's FARC Attacks the US Homeland						✓	✓	✓	✓
10. Defending Mumbai from Terrorist Attack					✓	✓		✓	✓
11. Shades of Orange in Ukraine						✓	✓		
12. Violence Erupts in Belgrade			❖						

✓ The technique is featured in the case.
❖ The technique is used implicitly in the case.

HYPOTHESIS GENERATION AND TESTING				ASSESSMENT OF CAUSE AND EFFECT			CHALLENGE ANALYSIS			DECISION SUPPORT			
Simple Hypotheses	Multiple Hypotheses Generator	Analysis of Competing Hypotheses	Deception Detection	Key Assumptions Check	Red Hat Analysis	Outside-In Thinking	Premortem Analysis	Structured Self-Critique	Devil's Advocacy	Decision Matrix	Force Field Analysis	Pros-Cons-Faults-and-Fixes	Strengths-Weaknesses-Opportunities-Threats
				❖			✓	✓					
			✓	❖			✓	✓			✓		
				✓					✓				✓
✓	✓	✓											
		✓											
	✓	✓		✓									
	✓			✓								✓	
	✓			✓									
					✓								
				❖	✓								
						✓							
										✓	✓	✓	

Foreword

Robert Jervis, Columbia University

Ever since Roberta Wohlstetter's pathbreaking study of why the United States was taken by surprise at Pearl Harbor 50 years ago,[1] both academics and members of the Intelligence Community (IC) have made significant progress in understanding intelligence failures. About how to correct these errors and do better we know much less, however, and it is to this subject that this volume makes a major contribution.

The fundamental problem, still unrecognized by most members of the general public and all too many government officials, is that intelligence can never be right all the time, even on the most important issues on which it concentrates the bulk of its resources. Others have said this better than I, so let me just draw on two quite different observers. Clausewitz saw that "many intelligence reports in war are contradictory; even more are false, and most are uncertain."[2] The only amendment I would make is to drop the modifier "in war." Samuel Butler put it even more broadly: "Life is the art of drawing sufficient conclusions from insufficient premises."[3] The world is too complex, evidence is too fragmentary and inconsistent, and our brains and organizations are too limited to allow us to completely understand the world and accurately discern others' capabilities and intentions. Indeed, in addition to the evidence being convoluted and often contradictory, people and states often behave in ways that are inconsistent (even leaving aside the fact that they and those who are trying to understand them may define *consistency* very differently).

In international politics, furthermore, deception is rampant. Adversaries usually wish to mislead others about at least some aspects of what they can and will do. Those who expect intelligence services to ferret out the truth should remember how often one—or even both—members of a couple are startled to eventually learn about the other's infidelity. In an additional nasty twist, the knowledge that deception is possible degrades valid information (something that can happen in marriages as well). One reason American intelligence was not disturbed by the paucity of solid evidence that Saddam Hussein's Iraq was actively pursuing WMD was the well-founded (but later proven incorrect) belief that it was employing an extensive deception and denial program.[4]

Deception sometimes adds to and sometimes competes with the enormous amount of misleading information that is generated in the natural course of events—the "noise" that disguises "signal," to use Wohlstetter's terms. Many items of information are true but not diagnostic. And often remarks by a foreign leader may tell us quite a bit, but then again they may not—they may be exceptions or aberrations; in other cases, the remarks may have been intended for domestic audiences, or they may have represented designs that were later abandoned or the views of the faction that did not prevail. Even apparently solid evidence may not be so. Iraq seemed to be building plants that produced potentially dangerous chemicals in amounts far in excess of the civilian needs, but it turned out that the country did need the products for innocent use.

Most evidence is then highly ambiguous. This makes our lives very difficult, both as individuals and as intelligence analysts. In fact, it would make our lives impossible if we were to form our conclusions only on the basis of particular bits of information as they are received. To act in a world filled with messy information, we have to come to conclusions fairly quickly, not be swayed by every stray bit of information that comes our way, and have the beliefs and theories that we have formed (partly on the basis of information) guide what we see and how we see it. This way of thinking may seem unempirical, unfair, and indefensible. It implies we are closed-minded and impervious to annoying facts. So we fail to understand that this is the way that we *do* think and, instead, believe that we are being fair to all the facts, which actually is impossible. We may think that it is a bit too suspicious to say, "I'll believe it when I see it," but few doubt that this is the right approach. But this is not the way we think, and cannot be.

Closer to the truth is to say, "I'll see it when I believe it." Our minds are hard-wired to make sense out of disparate goings-on, to see patterns and cause-and-effect relations in our environment, and to quickly make sense out of things. We probably could not survive as individuals or as a species otherwise; our ancestors would quickly have been devoured by predators had they not jumped to the conclusion that the rustling in the bushes might be a saber-toothed tiger. But the result is that when the picture that we have in our mind is wrong, the interpretation of evidence that we make, often easily and quickly, will not only be consistent with this picture but will reinforce the error. Indeed, alternative interpretations may be almost impossible unless we already have an alternative perspective.

Iraq again provides a telling example. In his speech to the UN, Secretary of State Colin Powell quoted Baghdad as telling officials at a military base that was about to be visited by the US inspectors: "We sent you a message . . . to clean out all the areas, the scrap areas, the abandoned areas. Make sure there is nothing there." The meaning seems—or seemed—self-evident. Now we know that it was not and that the Iraqis were just seeking to remove signs or bits of evidence that would in fact have been misleading. But as far as I know, no one suggested this at the time, even though in retrospect the specifying of "the scrap areas, the abandoned areas" could have been correctly read as indicating a fear that traces of old chemicals remained even though the weapons had been destroyed.

The reason was that almost no one understood Saddam's bizarre approach and outlook. More afraid of Iran, domestic opponents, and his own generals, he played a bizarre form of bluff. Compounded by the rivalries, corruption, and inefficiencies that characterized the regime, this made sense of a good deal (although not all) of the evidence. But one could not interpret the evidence in this way until one had first grasped what Saddam's regime was all about.[5]

Intelligence analysis then tries to make sense of the world, and it can only produce intelligible reports when analysts have some idea of what they are seeing. No analysts can be "true to all the facts"—not only is what constitutes a fact not objective, but many "facts" actually prove to be false. Ignoring them, or at least putting them aside, is a necessary part of the human endeavor; it is not antiscientific. To take just one example, recently scientists reported that meticulous analysis found particles traveling faster than the speed of light. If this is true, Einstein's laws of relativity must be thrown out. Doing so means discarding much of modern physics, and because that has been supported by so much theory and evidence, almost all scientists assume that the recent finding will eventually be shown to be mistaken.

Good scientists then are closed-minded—at least to a point. But it is impossible to specify rules by which we can tell that this point has been passed. In numerous battles over intelligence, each side thinks the other is being preposterously stubborn and for reasons of ego, politics, or worldview is sticking to a discredited hypothesis in the face of massive evidence to the contrary. Someone is right, but usually both sides are reasoning in a similar manner, and after the fact we often can continue the debate. Thus, while most people believe that there were no strong connections between Saddam's regime and terrorists, especially Al-Qaeda, and that analysts in the Office of the Secretary of Defense and the Office of the Vice President both clutched at straws and greatly exaggerated, if not lied, others claim that they were right and it is those who denied these links who were unprofessionally closed-minded.[6]

This is bad enough, but it gets even worse. Intelligence analysis, like other forms of understanding the world, is most convincing when it is most plausible in the sense of seeming to fit best not only with specific bits of evidence but with the general sense of how people and states behave that we have built up over the years. Almost by definition, this serves us well in most cases. But it makes us ill-suited to detect change or exceptions. Richard Betts shows that it is in just these circumstances that intelligence is particularly likely to go wrong.[7] The problem is not that we are overlooking facts, are too closed-minded, or are under great political pressure, although these forces are troublesome and can be present. But even when they are not, it is very hard to understand what others are doing when a correct answer does not make much sense. Sometimes the problem is that we are mirror-imaging and projecting our goals and beliefs onto others, sometimes others are being more clever than we are, and sometimes (as I believe is the case for Saddam) what others are doing is foolish and self-defeating. In all these cases, we will be misled.

Combating these and other impediments to good analysis is extraordinarily difficult. People have to be trained to think in counterintuitive ways. This is true in natural and social science as well, which is why my colleagues and I devote much of our teaching to forms (note the plural) of scientific reasoning in the treatment of evidence, something we would not need to do if this came naturally. But being aware of these problems, although an important step, is often insufficient.[8]

We need help, both as individuals and as organizations. And this is where *Cases in Intelligence Analysis* comes in. There have been other explications of structured analytic techniques, but they are hard to grasp in the abstract. Here they are brought to bear on specific cases. What is particularly telling is that when one reads several of the cases, some answers are likely to come too quickly to mind. These are very hard to shake, even though they are often wrong. I doubt if I am alone in thinking that I could not shake them intuitively. Rather, we need a set of tools to encourage or even force us to think about alternatives, to probe the evidence more deeply, to ask whether it really fits our conclusion and, even more, whether it contradicts alternative claims, and to think systematically about the next stages of our investigation. The cases are also interesting because when the mind does not immediately leap to a conclusion, the right answer—assuming there is one—is not obvious, and knowing the truth is a major barrier to fruitful thinking when we do most postmortems. Of course, there is no guarantee that these or other methods will lead us to the correct answer, even when there is one. Indeed, the techniques are disruptive, and that is their point.

Finally, we should note that it is not only analysts but intelligence consumers who may find the results disturbing. Policies are often built on intelligence and, in other cases, may produce confirming intelligence.[9] In any case, although coming up with new and even better ideas is appealing to academics, and occasionally to journalists, it is usually upsetting to policy makers. Policy is hard enough to establish; it is even more difficult to change. This assumes, of course, that better intelligence will come up with an answer that is better, if not exactly right. This will sometimes be the case, but even more annoyingly, better analytical techniques are likely to open minds to new alternatives without clearly indicating which one is correct.

Just as better intelligence on Iraq would have made policy makers less certain of Saddam's capabilities (assuming policy makers listened), so in many other cases good intelligence will ask them to think about several possibilities. This can be unsettling, especially to those with low tolerance for ambiguity. Better intelligence then requires strong policy makers who will not jump to conclusions but will be able to think about alternatives and ambiguities and nevertheless act as best they can.

This is a tall order, and helps explain why the policy-making community has not adequately pressed for a better intelligence system. The IC then has to look within its own resources to improve, and learning how to employ structured analytic techniques is a big step in the right direction.

NOTES

1. Roberta Wohlstetter, *Pearl Harbor: Warning and Decision* (Stanford, CA: Stanford University, 1962).

2. Carl von Clausewitz, *On War*, ed. and trans. Michael Howard and Peter Paret (Princeton, NJ: Princeton University Press, 1976), p. 117.

3. Samuel Butler, *The Notebooks of Samuel Butler: Selections*, ed. Henry Festing Jones (London: A. C. Fifield, 1918), p. 11.

4. For more on this and other topics touched on here, see Robert Jervis, *Why Intelligence Fails: Lessons from the Iranian Revolution and the Iraq War* (Ithaca, NY: Cornell University Press, 2010).

5. For fascinating evidence, see Kevin M. Woods, David D. Palkki, and Mark E. Stout, eds., *The Saddam Tapes: The Inner Workings of a Tyrant's Regime, 1978–2001* (New York: Cambridge University Press, 2011). This is not to say that there is agreement on the regime's motives, behavior, or likely course of actions had the United States allowed it to continue. As every historian knows, the passage of time and the opening of new archives does not always—or even usually—produce consensus.

6. See, for example, Christina Shelton, "The Roots of Analytic Failures in the U.S. Intelligence Community," *International Journal of Intelligence and CounterIntelligence* 24, no. 4 (2011): 337–55.

7. Richard K. Betts, "Theory Traps: Expertise as an Enemy," chap. 3 in *Enemies of Intelligence: Knowledge and Power in American National Security* (New York: Columbia University Press, 2007).

8. See the discussions of "de-biasing" and its limits: Philip E. Tetlock and Jae Il Kim, "Accountability and Judgment Processes in a Personality Prediction Task," *Journal of Personality and Social Psychology* 52, no. 4 (1987): 700–709; Tetlock, "Cognitive Biases and Organizational Correctives: Do Both Disease and Cure Depend on the Political Beholder?" *Administrative Science Quarterly* 45, no. 2 (2000): 293–326; Tetlock, "Social Functionalist Frameworks for Judgment and Choice: Intuitive Politicians, Theologians, and Prosecutors," *Psychological Review* 109, no. 3 (2002): 451–71. For the related and important finding that people who are more open to discrepant information make better predictions over the long run than those who are more strongly driven by powerful beliefs about how the world operates, see Tetlock, *Expert Political Judgment: How Good Is It? How Can We Know?* (Princeton, NJ: Princeton University Press, 2005).

9. Wesley K. Wark, *The Ultimate Enemy: British Intelligence and Nazi Germany* (Ithaca, NY: Cornell University Press, 1985); Joshua Rovner, *Fixing the Facts: National Security and the Politics of Intelligence* (Ithaca, NY: Cornell University Press, 2011).

Preface

There's an old anecdote about a tourist who stops a New Yorker on the street and asks, "How do you get to Carnegie Hall?" The New Yorker replies, "Practice, practice, practice." The humor in the anecdote highlights an important truth: the great musicians who play at Carnegie Hall have a lot of innate talent, but none of them got there without a lot of practice.

Really great analysts have a lot of innate talent too. Whether in government, academia, or business, analysts are usually curious, question-asking puzzle solvers who have deep expertise in their subject matter. Not surprisingly, they like to be right, and they frequently are. And yet, the Iraq WMD Commission Report shows that analysts can be wrong. Analytic failures often are attributed to a range of cognitive factors that are an unavoidable part of being human, such as faulty memory, misperception, and a range of biases. Sometimes the consequences are unremarkable. Other times, the consequences are devastating. Structured analysis gives analysts a variety of techniques they can use to mitigate these cognitive challenges and potentially avoid failures, *if* analysts know when and how best to apply them. This book is designed to give analysts practice using structured analytic techniques.

Improving one's cognitive processes by using the techniques discussed in this book can be challenging but also rewarding. The techniques themselves are not that complicated, but they can push us out of our intuitive and comfortable—but not always reliable—thought processes. They make us think differently in order to generate new ideas, consider alternative outcomes, troubleshoot our own work, and collaborate more effectively.

This process is like starting a fitness regimen for the brain. At the beginning, your muscles burn a little. But over time and with repetition, you become stronger, and the improvements you see in yourself can be remarkable. Becoming a better thinker, just like becoming a better athlete, requires practice. We challenge you to feel the burn.

Audience

This book is for anyone who wants to explore new ways of thinking more deeply and thoroughly. It is primarily intended to help up-and-coming analysts in colleges and universities, as well as Intelligence Community professionals, learn techniques that can make them better analysts throughout their careers. But this book is just as salient for seasoned intelligence veterans who are looking for ways to brush up on skills—or even learn new ones. The cases also are intended for teams of analysts who want to rehearse and refine their collaboration skills so that when real-life situations arise, they are prepared to rise to the challenge together.

Content and Design

We chose the case study format because it provides an opportunity to practice the techniques with real-life, contemporary issues. It is also a proven teaching method in many disciplines. We chose subject matter that is relatively recent—usually from within the last decade—and that comprises a mix of better- and lesser-known issues. In all cases, we strove to produce compelling and historically accurate portrayals of events, although for learning purposes, we have tailored the content of the cases to focus on key learning objectives. For example, we end many of the cases without revealing the full outcome. Several cases, such as "Who Murdered Jonathan Luna?," have no known outcome. But whether or not the outcome is known, we urge students to judge their performance on the merits of their analytic process. Like mathematics, just arriving at a numerical value or "correct" outcome is not enough; we need to show our work. The value of the cases lies in the process itself and in learning how to replicate it when real-life analytic challenges arise.

The twelve cases and analytic exercises in this book help prepare analysts to deal with the authentic problems and real-life situations they encounter every day. Taken as a whole, the twelve cases walk through a broad array of issues such as how to identify mindsets, mitigate biases, challenge assumptions, think expansively and creatively, develop and test multiple hypotheses, create plausible scenarios, identify indicators of change, validate those indicators, frame a decision-making process, and troubleshoot analytic judgments—all of which reinforce the main elements of critical thinking that are so important for successful analysis. Individually, each chapter employs a consistent organization that models a robust analytic process by presenting the key questions in the case, a compelling and well-illustrated narrative, and carefully chosen recommended readings. Each also includes question-based analytic exercises that challenge students to employ structured analytic techniques and to explicate the value added by employing structured techniques.

Instructor Resources

As instructors ourselves, we understand how important it is to provide truly turnkey instructor resources. The *Instructor Materials* that accompany this book are free to all users as a downloadable PDF, and graphics from both the case book and the *Instructor Materials* are available as free, downloadable JPEG and PowerPoint slides. We have classroom tested each case study and applied what we have learned to enhance the *Instructor Materials* and better anticipate the instructor's needs. Just like the cases themselves, the *Instructor Materials* employ a consistent organization across all cases that first puts the case and the analytic challenges in context, offers step-by-step solutions for each exercise, and provides detailed conclusions and key takeaways to enhance classroom discussion.

Acknowledgments

Both authors would like to thank Ray Converse, Claudia Peña Crossland, James Steiner, Mary O'Sullivan, and Roy Sullivan for their substantial contributions to the book. Both authors are grateful to many other individuals who helped review, test, and otherwise improve the cases, including Nigah Ajaj, Todd Bacastow, Milton Bearden, George Beebe, Mark T. Clark, Eric Dahl, Jack Davis, Matthew Degn, John Evans, Roger George, Joseph Gordon, Thomas Graham, Richards J. Heuer Jr., Georgia Holmer, Daryl Johnson, Laura Lenz, Austin Long, Frank Marsh, Richard Miles, Gregory Moore, Polly Nayak, Rudolph Perina, Marilyn Peterson, Kathy Pherson, Mark Polyak, Libby Sass, Marilyn Scott, Raymond Sontag, Leah Tarbell, Greg Treverton, and Phil Williams, as well as students of James Madison University, Mercyhurst College, the University of Mississippi, and the University of Pittsburgh.

Disclaimer

All statements of fact, opinion, or analysis expressed in this book are those of the authors and do not reflect the official positions of the Office of the Director of National Intelligence (ODNI), the Central Intelligence Agency, or any other US government agency. Nothing in the contents should be construed as asserting or implying US government authentication of information or agency endorsement of the authors' views. This material has been reviewed by the ODNI only to prevent the disclosure of classified material.

About the Authors

Sarah Miller Beebe began thinking about a book of cases during her career as an analyst and manager at the Central Intelligence Agency. A variety of broadening experiences, including an assignment as Director for Russia on the National Security Council staff and a position as a national counterintelligence officer at the Office of the National Counterintelligence Executive, drove home the need for rigorous and effective approaches to intelligence analysis. It became apparent to her that cases could not only teach important analytic lessons surrounding historical events but also give analysts experience using a question-based thinking approach underpinned by practical techniques to improve their analyses. Now, as owner of Ascendant Analytics, she helps organizations apply such techniques against their specific analytic problems.

Randolph H. Pherson has spearheaded teaching and developing analytic techniques and critical thinking skills in the Intelligence Community. He is the author of the *Handbook of Analytic Tools and Techniques* and co-author of *Structured Analytic Techniques for Intelligence Analysis* with Richards J. Heuer Jr. Throughout his twenty-eight-year career at the Central Intelligence Agency, where he last served as National Intelligence Officer for Latin America, he was an avid supporter of ways to instill more rigor in the analytic process. As President of Pherson Associates since 2003, he has been a vigorous proponent of a case-based approach to analytic instruction.

Together, Beebe and Pherson have developed and tested new analytic tools and techniques, created interactive analytic tradecraft courses, and facilitated analytic projects. In their work as analytic coaches, facilitators, and instructors, they have found the case approach to be an invaluable teaching tool. This book of cases is their most recent collaboration and one that they hope will help analysts of all types improve their analysis.

Introduction

For the past two decades, a quiet movement has been gathering momentum to transform the ways in which intelligence analysis is practiced. Prior to this movement, analysts generally approached their tradecraft as a somewhat mysterious exercise that used their expert judgment and inherent critical thinking skills. Although some analysts produced solid reports, this traditional approach was vulnerable to a large number of common cognitive pitfalls, including unexamined assumptions, confirmation bias, and deeply ingrained mental mindsets that increased the chances of missed calls and mistaken forecasts.[1] Without a means of describing these invisible mental processes to others, instruction in analysis was difficult, and objective assessments of what worked and what did not work were nearly impossible. Moreover, this traditional approach tended to make analysis an individual process rather than a group activity; when conclusions were reached through internal processes that were essentially intuitive, groups of analysts could not approach problems on a common basis, and consumers of analysis could not discern how judgments had been reached. Absent systematic methods for making the analytic process transparent, problems that required collaboration across substantive disciplines and geographic regions were particularly prone to failure.

The desire for change has been propelled by a growing awareness that analytic performance has too often fallen short. Former CIA Deputy Directors of Intelligence Robert Gates and Doug MacEachin did much to spark this awareness within the Intelligence Community during the 1980s and 1990s, criticizing what they regarded as "flabby" thinking and insisting that CIA analysts employ evidence and argumentation in much more rigorous and systematic ways. To address these problems, Gates focused on raising the quality of analytic reviews, and MacEachin established a set of standard corporate practices for analytic tradecraft, which were disseminated and taught to CIA analysts.[2] Subsequent investigations into the failure to anticipate India's 1998 nuclear test, the surprise terrorist attacks of September 11, 2001, and the erroneous judgments about Iraq's possession of weapons of mass destruction brought the need for analytic improvements into broader public view.

But simply realizing that improvements in analysis were needed was not sufficient to produce effective change. An understanding of the exact nature of the analytic problems, as well as a clear sense of how to address them, was required. Richards J. Heuer Jr., a longtime veteran of the CIA, provided the theoretical underpinnings for a new approach to analysis in his pioneering work *Psychology of Intelligence Analysis*.[3] In this, Heuer drew upon the work of leading cognitive psychologists to explain why the human brain constructs mental models to deal with inherent uncertainty, tends to perceive information that is consistent with its beliefs more vividly than it sees contradictory data, and is often unconscious of key assumptions that underpin its judgments. Heuer argued that these problems could best be overcome by increasing the use of tools and techniques that structure information, challenge assumptions, and explore alternative interpretations. These techniques have since come to be known collectively as structured analytic techniques, or SATs. He developed one of the earliest techniques, called Analysis of Competing Hypotheses, to address problems of deception in intelligence analysis. It now is being used throughout the community to address a variety of other analytic problems as well, helping to counter the natural tendency toward confirmation bias.[4]

Since the pioneering efforts of Heuer to understand and address common cognitive pitfalls and analytic pathologies, considerable progress has been made in developing a variety of new SATs and defining the ways they may be used. In 2010, Heuer joined one of the authors of this volume, Randolph H. Pherson, in publishing the most comprehensive work on this subject to date, *Structured Analytic Techniques for Intelligence Analysis*.[5] The book describes how structured analysis compares to other analytic methods, including expert judgment and quantitative methods, and provides a taxonomy of eight families of SATs and detailed descriptions of over fifty techniques. By including an in-depth discussion of how each technique can be used in collaborative team projects and a vision for how the techniques can be successfully integrated into the Intelligence Community, Heuer and Pherson challenged the analytic community to harness the techniques to produce more rigorous and informative analysis.

Why a Book of Cases?

The books published by Heuer and Pherson have familiarized analysts with the range of available structured analytic techniques and their purposes, but little work has been done to provide analysts with practical exercises for mastering the use of SATs. This book is designed to fill that gap. As such, it is best regarded as a companion to both *Psychology of Intelligence Analysis* and *Structured Analytic Techniques for Intelligence Analysis*. The cases in this book— vivid, contemporary issues coupled with value-added analytic exercises—are meant to bridge the worlds of theory and practice and bring analysis to life. They compel readers to put themselves in the shoes of analysts grappling with very real and difficult challenges. Readers will encounter all the complexities, uncertainties, and ambiguities that attend actual analytic problems and, in some cases, the pressures of policy decisions that hang in the balance.

We have chosen a case study approach for several reasons. First, the technique has proved an effective teaching tool in a wide variety of disciplines, fostering interactive learning and shifting the emphasis from instructor-centric to student-centric activity, while usually sparking interest in issues previously unfamiliar to students.[6] The use of the case study approach also allows students to tackle problems on either an individual or a group basis, facilitating insights into the strengths and weaknesses of various approaches to independent and collaborative analysis. While the twelve cases in this book are used to illustrate how structured analysis can aid the analytic process, they also can be used to catalyze broader discussions about current issues, such as foreign policy decision making, international relations, law enforcement, homeland security, and many other topics covered in the book. It is through these types of practical exercises and discussions that analysts learn to put problems in context and develop and execute a clear and effective analytic framework.

The cases cover recent events and include a mix of functional and regional issues from across the world. We strive to present compelling and historically accurate portrayals of events—albeit tailored for learning purposes—to demonstrate how SATs can be applied in the fast-breaking and gritty world of actual events and policy decisions. To discourage students from "gaming" their analysis, however, we end many of the cases without revealing the full outcome in the main text, and several—such as "Who Murdered Jonathan Luna?"—have no known outcome. But whether or not the outcome is known, the purpose of the exercises is not simply to arrive at the "correct" judgment or forecast contained in the *Instructor Materials* or to make the analysis mirror the actual outcome. As with exercises in mathematics, arriving at the proper numerical value or outcome does not demonstrate mastery; that can only be demonstrated by showing the math that led one to the proper outcome. The value of the cases lies in learning the analytic processes themselves and how to apply them against real-life problems.

Order and Organization

The order of the cases roughly mirrors the hierarchy of problems that analysts face when assuming responsibility for a new portfolio or account. Typically, when starting a new assignment, analysts are asked to familiarize themselves with past analytic reports and judgments on the topic. When done well, such a process will uncover preexisting mindsets and expose unsupported assumptions. The first cases in the book—"Who Poisoned Karinna Moskalenko?" "Is Wen Ho Lee a Spy?" "The Road to Tarin Kowt," and "Who Murdered Jonathan Luna?"—are designed to teach SATs that challenge prevailing mindsets and develop alternative explanations for events.

As analysts gain more familiarity with the issues for which they are responsible, they often encounter new developments for which no line of analysis has been developed. In such circumstances, analysts require techniques for developing and testing new hypotheses and for visualizing the data in creative and thought-provoking ways. "The Assassination of Benazir Bhutto," "Death in the Southwest," "The Atlanta Olympics Bombing," and "The DC Sniper" are designed with these goals in mind.

Finally, as analysts master their subjects, they are asked to tackle problem sets that are arguably the most difficult analytic challenges: understanding the perceptions and plans of foreign adversaries and forecasting uncertain future developments shaped by dynamic sets of drivers. In "Colombia's FARC Attacks the US Homeland" and "Defending Mumbai from Terrorist Attack," students put themselves in the shoes of the adversary and develop a range of plausible future outcomes, while in "Shades of Orange in Ukraine," students not only develop scenarios but also actively consider how exogenous forces could affect future outcomes. "Violence Erupts in Belgrade" rounds out the cases by placing students in a direct decision support role in which they must not only provide assessments about the forces and factors that will drive events but also develop a decision framework and troubleshoot their analysis.

Each of our case studies employs a consistent internal organization that guides the student through an analytic process. We begin each case study by listing several overarching *Key Questions*. These questions are designed as general reading guides as well as small-group discussion questions. The questions are followed by the *Case Narrative*, which tells the story of the case. This is followed by a *Recommended Readings* section. The final section, *Structured Analytic Techniques in Action,* presents focused intelligence questions and exercises to guide the student through the use of several structured analytic techniques and toward self-identification of the value added by SAT-aided analysis. The turnkey *Instructor Materials,* which are available to instructors via download, put the learning points for the cases in context, present detailed explanations of how the student can successfully apply the techniques, and provide case conclusions and additional key takeaways that may be used in instruction.

Technique Choice

The techniques are matched to the analytic tasks in each case. For example, in "Who Poisoned Karinna Moskalenko?" there are many unanswered questions that require the kind of divergent and imaginative thinking that Starbursting can prompt. In "Violence Erupts in Belgrade," Force Field Analysis helps the analyst make a judgment about the prospect of additional violence—an analytic judgment that will shape decisions about what to do to protect the US embassy. Each case includes at least three technique-driven exercises, and each exercise begins with a discussion of how the technique can be used by analysts to tackle the kind of problem presented in the exercise. Space constraints preclude the inclusion of all techniques that might be applicable for each case; we chose those that we felt were most salient and illustrative. For example, nearly two-thirds of the cases implicitly or explicitly include a Key Assumptions Check or Structured Brainstorming, but these core techniques could easily be applied to all the cases. Overall, we strove to include a variety of SATs throughout the book that are representative of each of the eight families of techniques. To help orient readers, we have included a secondary, matrixed table of contents that details the cases and the full complement of techniques that each utilizes.

How Can These Cases Best Facilitate Learning?

Whether students are working alone or in small groups, the cases are most effective when students and instructors view them as an opportunity to test and practice new ways of thinking that can help them break through the cognitive biases and mindsets that are at the core of so many analytic failures. Viewed this way, the techniques are a means by which analysts can practice robust analytic approaches, not an end in and of themselves. Our goal was to give analysts a fun and effective way to hone their cognitive skills. We hope we have hit the mark, and we welcome feedback on the cases and the techniques, as well as suggestions for their refinement and further development.

NOTES

1. See Rob Johnston, *Analytic Culture in the U.S. Intelligence Community: An Ethnographic Study* (Washington, DC: Center for the Study of Intelligence, Central Intelligence Agency, 2005), http://www.fas.org/irp/cia/product/analytic.pdf, 22–23. "What tends to occur is that the analyst looks for current data that confirms the existing organizational opinion or the opinion that seems most probable and, consequently, is easiest to support. . . . This tendency to search for confirmatory data is not necessarily a conscious choice; rather, it is the result of accepting an existing set of hypotheses, developing a mental model based on previous corporate products, and then trying to augment that model with current data in order to support the existing hypotheses."

2. See Jack Davis, "Introduction: Improving Intelligence Analysis at CIA; Dick Heuer's Contribution to Intelligence Analysis," in *Psychology of Intelligence Analysis*, ed. Richards J. Heuer Jr. (Washington, D.C.: Center for the Study of Intelligence, Central Intelligence Agency, 1999), https://www.cia.gov/library/center-for-the-study-of-intelligence/csi-publications/books-and-monographs/psychology-of-intelligence-analysis/PsychofIntelNew.pdf, xv–xix.

3. Richards J. Heuer Jr., ed., *Psychology of Intelligence Analysis*.

4. Richards J. Heuer Jr., "The Evolution of Structured Analytic Techniques" (presentation to the National Academy of Science, National Research Council Committee on Behavioral and Social Science Research to Improve Intelligence Analysis for National Security, Washington, DC, December 8, 2009), http://www7.nationalacademies.org/bbcss/DNI_Heuer_Text.pdf.

5. Richards J. Heuer Jr. and Randolph H. Pherson, *Structured Analytic Techniques for Intelligence Analysis* (Washington, DC: CQ Press, 2011).

6. See Richard Grant, "A Claim for the Case Method in the Teaching of Geography," *Journal of Geography in Higher Education* 21, no. 2 (1997): 171–85; and P. K. Raju and Chetan S. Sankar, "Teaching Real-World Issues through Case Studies," *Journal of Engineering Education* 88, no. 4 (1999): 501–08.

Key Questions

▶ Why is Karinna Moskalenko a target?

▶ What tactics has Russia used in the past to poison opponents?

▶ Are there any common features among the alleged poisonings?

▶ Why do most observers believe that the Russian government is responsible for Moskalenko's poisoning?

1 Who Poisoned Karinna Moskalenko?

CASE NARRATIVE

Karinna Moskalenko is a prominent Russian human rights lawyer whose work in the Russian courts and at the European Court of Human Rights (ECHR) has gained her fame both at home and abroad. Her representation of prominent Kremlin foes in recent years has only heightened her profile; among these cases are her posthumous representation of Anna Politkovskaya, a Russian journalist widely known for her critical coverage of Moscow's policies toward Chechnya, and her representation of jailed former oil tycoon Mikhail Khodorkovsky. In 2008, Moskalenko herself captured international headlines with news that she had fallen ill with mercury poisoning. Press reports indicated that she and her family—all of whom were living in Strasbourg, France, at the time of the incident in order to facilitate her work at the Strasbourg-based ECHR—were taken to a French hospital suffering from headaches, dizziness, and vomiting.[1] Moskalenko told reporters that the poisoning may have been an attempt to frighten her before a pretrial date in the Politkovskaya case,[2] noting that "people do not put mercury in your car to improve your health."[3]

Russia's Poisoned Past

Poison figures prominently in recent Russian politics. A rash of cases throughout the last decade in which Kremlin critics have suffered the effects of a range of toxins has added to an already long list of notable poisonings in Russian history (see Figure 1.1). While Russian government involvement in some of these recent cases has not been substantiated, allegations of Russian government–sponsored attacks against those who publicly criticize Moscow's policies have

7

Figure 1.1 ▶ Chronology of Alleged Russian Poisonings, 2000–2010

Year	Alleged Poisoning
2002	Ibn al-Khattab, a Chechen Sunni jihadist dies from a poisoned letter sent by the Russian FSB.
2003	Duma deputy and opposition newspaper editor Yuri Shchekochikin mysteriously dies. His family believes that he was a victim of poisoning—possibly with dioxin.
2004	Russian presidential candidate Ivan Rybkin goes missing for several days in advance of the election and later claims he was drugged by Russian authorities.
2004	Ukrainian presidential candidate Viktor Yushchenko is poisoned with dioxin; Yushchenko suspects a Ukrainian-Russian cabal.
2004	Russian journalist Anna Politkovskaya says she was poisoned on a flight she took to cover the Beslan School tragedy.
2006	Former KGB officer and later Kremlin critic Aleksander Litvinenko dies from polonium-210 radiation poisoning in London. The Russian government refuses Britain's request to extradite the prime suspect.

continued throughout the decade. The victims of the poisonings range widely from Russian journalists, lawyers, and businesspeople to foreign politicians and Chechen rebels.

In some cases the targets have been longtime, self-declared foes of the Russian government who aim to destroy Russian interests just as much as Moscow aims to destroy the targets. Such was the case of Omar Ibn al-Khattab, a symbol of Islamic extremism and notorious guerrilla commander in the second Chechen war against Moscow. Khattab's guerilla roots can be traced back to the 1980s when he fought against the Soviets in Afghanistan. He later participated in Muslim insurrections in the Soviet Central Asian republics. Khattab enlisted in the Chechen separatist movement in the mid-1990s and played a leading role in numerous attacks on Russian interests until his death in 2002. Press reports indicate that he was killed by a poisoned letter slipped to him by the Russian Federal Security Service (FSB), which had accused Khattab of links to Al-Qaeda.[4,5]

Prominent Russian and foreign political leaders have also been targets of poisoning. In 2004, then-Russian presidential candidate Ivan Rybkin mysteriously disappeared for several days ahead of the election. When he resurfaced, he first told a garbled tale of travel to London and the Ukrainian capital, Kiev, but eventually he revealed that he had been drugged, abducted, and forced to make a compromising video by the FSB.[6] He left politics after his ordeal. The

fate of other Russian politicians has been far worse. Duma deputy Yuri Shchekochikin's family suspects that his puzzling death in 2003 was a result of poisoning by the toxin dioxin because he suffered an unexplained skin rash while investigating a company owned by high-level former KGB officials just before his death.[7]

Ukrainian presidential candidate Viktor Yushchenko experienced a rapid transformation in 2004 after ingesting the toxin dioxin. The photo on the left shows Yushchenko before being poisoned; on the right, after.

Also in 2004, then-Ukrainian presidential candidate Viktor Yushchenko underwent a dramatic transformation that medical experts determined was the result of dioxin poisoning. The Ukrainian prosecutor general said that tests confirmed Yushchenko suffered from poisoning by highly purified dioxin that is manufactured only in Russia, the United States, and Great Britain.[8] Investigators received samples from all but Russia, which has kept "silent on the matter" despite two requests for a sample, according to the Ukrainian prosecutor general.[9]

The case remains unsolved, and as of August 2009, experts involved in Yushchenko's treatment said that scientific analysis had not provided any more clues as to who was responsible for the poisoning.[10] Nonetheless, many—including Yushchenko—speculate that the dioxin originated in Russia and was slipped to him during a 5 September 2004, dinner with the head of the Ukrainian security services—which has close ties to Moscow—most likely in order to complicate Yushchenko's bid for the presidency and to improve the chances of the Moscow-backed candidate Viktor Yanukovich.[11] Russian officials have denied any Russian involvement in the case, saying, "There is no evidence to support such claims," but former Soviet and Russian security services officers say that they believe the Russian security services may have been involved.[12]

Reknowned Russian journalists such as Anna Politkovskaya have claimed to be targets of poisoning as well. Politkovskaya was born into the Soviet elite but committed herself to chronicling alleged Russian abuses in Chechnya. In a 2004 interview with the London-based *Guardian* newspaper, she said,

> To this day there's torture in any FSB branch in Chechnya, like the so-called "telephone," where they pass an electric current through a person's body. I've seen hundreds of people who've been through this torture. Some have been tortured in such an intricate way that it's hard for me to believe that it was done by people who went to the same sort of schools that I did, who read the same textbooks.[13]

The same interview repeated her claims that that she nearly died in 2004 when she was slipped poison in a cup of tea while on her way to cover the Beslan school hostage tragedy. It also cited her claims of numerous death threats from Russian troops, noting that "the kidnappings, extrajudicial killings, disappearances, rapes and tortures she has reported on in Chechnya have left her convinced that Putin's policies are engendering the terrorists they are supposed to eliminate."[14]

Politkovskaya was gunned down in 2006 outside her apartment. The Russian government says that the murder was ordered from abroad by enemies of the state. Russian prosecutor general Yuri Chaika in 2007 said the killers hoped to "create a crisis situation and bring about a return to the old management system in which money and oligarchs decided everything."[15] Those who ordered the killing have not yet been identified.

Aleksander Litvinenko, a onetime Russian KGB officer whose public comments on KGB practices raised Moscow's ire, himself fell ill after the radioactive isotope polonium-210 was slipped into his tea at an upscale London hotel in 2006.[16] British officials traced a radioactive trail across London to Hamburg, Germany, and aboard British Airways planes that had flown to Moscow. [17] The trail coincided with the routes of Andrei Lugovoi, a former KGB bodyguard whom British authorities have identified as the prime suspect, and his

associate, Dmitri Kovtun.[18] Litvinenko alleged on his deathbed that he had been poisoned at the behest of then-Russian president Vladimir Putin.[19] The Russian government has denied British requests for extradition of Lugovoi, who claims that he is the scapegoat for a British intelligence plot executed with the help of self-exiled Russian tycoon Boris Berezovsky to create a political scandal.[20] All involved deny the allegations.

Aleksander Litvinenko's wife, Marina (third from left), announces the establishment of the Alexander Litvinenko Foundation in 2007 with, from left, the family's spokesperson Alex Goldfarb, human rights lawyer Louise Christian, and Russian billionaire Boris Berezovsky. Photos of Litvinenko before and after the poisoning appear above the presenters.

The Experts Concur

Although Russian officials either deny involvement in many of these cases or have simply ignored the allegations, several former KGB and FSB officers support the claims that Moscow has used poisoning as a tool of intimidation, coercion, and murder.

In addition to Litvinenko, Oleg Gordievsky is another prominent former KGB colonel who has spoken out about Russia's tactics. Gordievsky, who defected to the United Kingdom in the mid-1980s, has lamented the "gangster mentality" that he says has spread through the FSB since 2000 and has accused Russia of becoming "a terrorist regime."[21] He has claimed "with certainty" that

Politkovskaya's poisoning was the work of the FSB.[22] The same is true, he says, of Shchekochikin and Litvinenko.

Oleg Kalugin, a former chief of KGB counterintelligence who defected to the United States, is also confident of the FSB's use of poison to silence its opponents. In a book he published in 1994, Kalugin detailed the KGB's use of a ricin-tipped umbrella to murder the Soviet dissident Sergei Markov.[23] Litvinenko, he said in a 2006 interview, "fell victim to the Russian security services. They resort to murder, and poison is one of the weapons they have used for decades."[24] Vitaly Yurchenko, a KGB official who defected to the West in 1985, provides additional details to Kalugin's account of the KGB's role in Markov's murder, saying the KGB used "Special Lab 100" in Moscow to develop poisons for operational use, including the ricin used to kill Markov.[25]

Moskalenko Falls Ill

It was against this backdrop that reports of Moskalenko's poisoning surfaced in October 2008 (see Figure 1.2). On Sunday, 12 October 2008, Moskalenko's husband discovered a dozen small pellets of mercury on the floor of the passenger and driver's side of their car as he, Moskalenko, and their three children arrived at church. Moskalenko's husband is a chemist and understood the pellets to be out of the ordinary. Moskalenko lodged a formal complaint with French authorities on 13 October. The French prosecutor's office deemed the discovery to be serious and opened an investigation.[26]

Moskalenko and her family did not immediately note any symptoms at the time of their discovery of the mercury, but by Tuesday, 14 October, Moskalenko and her family complained publicly of nausea, headaches, and vomiting.[27] They were transported to a French hospital at the request of French officials for examination. By 16 October, press reports indicated that toxicology tests confirmed the substance in the car was mercury.[28]

Figure 1.2 ▶ Chronology of the Karinna Moskalenko Poisoning

Date	Events
12 October 2008	Moskalenko's husband finds pellets of mercury in the family car.
13 October 2008	Moskalenko files a complaint with French authorities, who open an investigation.
14 October 2008	Moskalenko is taken to a French hospital with dizziness, headaches, and vomiting.
15 October 2008	Moskalenko misses a pretrial hearing in Moscow in the Anna Politkovskaya case.
16 October 2008	Press reports indicate that toxicology tests confirm mercury as the substance found in the Moskalenko vehicle.

The French Investigation

French officials did not immediately comment on the exact cause of the poisoning; neither did they explicitly rule in or out Russian involvement or any other cause. In public comments during the investigation, French authorities remained circumspect about both the physical effect that the amount of mercury found in the car could have on the family and the possible circumstances under which the mercury had found its way into the vehicle. The Strasbourg assistant prosecutor of the case, Claude Palpaceur, stressed that the quantity of mercury found was probably not sufficient to cause serious health consequences.[29] One French police official cited possible explanations for the mercury other than attempted poisoning, including that its presence could have been an accident or could have been associated with Moskalenko's purchase of the car in August 2008.[30]

Previous Pressure Tactics

This was not the first time that Moskalenko's struggles as a Russian human rights lawyer had captured headlines. Moskalenko also found herself in the spotlight in 2007 when the International Helsinki Foundation for Human Rights urged Russia to end its "ongoing harassment" against her, saying Moscow's efforts to disbar her "were aimed at punishing her for her work on politically sensitive cases."[31] Although Moskalenko's case record in Russian courts is full of numerous losses, she has won 27 cases against Russia in the European Court of Human Rights, and has over 100 other cases pending in the court that are an apparent thorn in Moscow's side.[32]

In addition to the personal pressure exerted on Moskalenko, in 2006 the International Protection Center, which she runs in Moscow, came under scrutiny by the Russian tax police. In response, Moskalenko opened a sister office in Strasbourg, France, to take up the slack should her Moscow office be closed by Russian authorities.[33] In 2007 Moskalenko said that "across the whole world it is well known that lawyers who are carrying out their professional activities cannot be subjected to pressure. . . . But it seems to me that today's Russian authorities are not driven by logic."[34]

International Press Coverage

News of Moskalenko's illness quickly hit the wires and was carried by prominent newspapers worldwide. The reports led with the familiar themes of Russian poisoning and political pressure, and in many cases they noted the curious timing of the poisoning, just a few days before the pretrial date in the Politkovskaya case:

French police fear that Russian agents may have tried to poison top human rights lawyer Karinna Moskalenko—a well-known critic of the Kremlin. They have started an inquiry after Ms. Moskalenko complained that "a substance similar to mercury" had been placed in her car in the French city of Strasbourg on Monday. "I feel worse and worse. My children also feel bad," she told reporters yesterday. . . . If confirmed as a poisoning, the Moskalenko case would carry echoes of the 2006 murder of former security service officer Litvinenko in London.

—*The Courier Mail* (Australia)[35]

A lawyer representing the family of investigative journalist Anna Politkovskaya has apparently been targeted by poisoners as the trial of three men accused of involvement in her murder was about to begin. French police confirmed the discovery of mercury pellets in the car of Karinna Moskalenko, who suffered headaches, dizziness and nausea after getting into the vehicle. Ms. Moskalenko was taken to hospital for tests in Strasbourg on Tuesday, which prevented her from flying to Moscow for the Politkovskaya trial.

—*The Independent* (UK)[36]

French Police are investigating how toxic mercury pellets ended up in the car of a human rights lawyer who fell ill in Strasbourg on Tuesday, a day before pretrial hearings in the Moscow into the killing of one of her best-known clients, the journalist and Kremlin critic Anna Politkovskaya. . . . Kremlin critics have often been the targets of poisoners. Ms. Politkovskaya herself fell ill after drinking a cup of tea while on her way to cover the aftermath of the Beslan school siege in which more than 300 people died.

—*International Herald Tribune*[37]

Another lawyer for [jailed former Yukos oil executive] Khodorkovsky, Robert Amsterdam, said the timing was suspicious. "This type of event gives all pause to consider what it takes now in Russia to defend human rights. There are ongoing attacks on lawyers and journalists. . . . What matters is not if it's related to Yukos or Politkovskaya but that it's another human rights defender that's in this situation."[38]

The Court of Public Opinion

Within days of the Moskalenko poisoning, the international court of public opinion, including newspapers, journals, blogs, television, and radio, was looking askance at Russia. The *Washington Post* editorial page, on 22 October 2008, stated the verdict most plainly:

Perhaps this was an unfortunate accident; the police in Strasbourg say they are still investigating. But history suggests otherwise. Numerous opponents of Mr. Putin have been killed or gravely sickened by poisoning. They include Ukrainian President Viktor Yushchenko; dissident former KGB officer Litvinenko; journalist Yuri Shchekochikin; and Ms. Politkovskaya.[39]

RECOMMENDED READING

Andrew, Christopher, and Vasili Mitrokhin. *The Sword and the Shield: The Mitrokhin Archive and the Secret History of the KGB*. New York: Basic Books, 1999.

Table 1.1 ▶ Case Snapshot: Who Poisoned Karinna Moskalenko?		
Structured Analytic Technique Used	Heuer and Pherson Page Number	Analytic Family
Premortem Analysis	p. 221	Challenge Analysis
Structured Self-Critique	p. 226	Challenge Analysis
Starbursting	p. 102	Idea Generation

WHO POISONED KARINNA MOSKALENKO? STRUCTURED ANALYTIC TECHNIQUES IN ACTION

Analysts often are asked to render judgments on fast-breaking events for which there is limited information. In these situations, the Premortem Analysis, Structured Self-Critique, and Starbursting can help analysts avoid a rush to judgment and illuminate important areas for further consideration by facilitating creative thinking and simply asking the right questions.

Technique 1: The Premortem Analysis and Structured Self-Critique

The goal of these techniques[40] is to challenge—actively and explicitly—an established mental model or analytic consensus in order to broaden the range of possible explanations or estimates that are seriously considered. This process helps reduce the risk of analytic failure by identifying and analyzing the features of a potential failure before it occurs.

Task 1. Conduct a Premortem Analysis and Structured Self-Critique of the reigning view in the case study that "Karinna Moskalenko is the latest victim in a series of alleged Russian attacks on Kremlin critics."

STEP 1: Imagine that a period of time has passed since you published your analysis that contains the reigning view above. You suddenly learn from an unimpeachable source that the judgment above was wrong. Then imagine what could have caused the analysis to be wrong.

STEP 2: Use a brainstorming technique to identify alternative hypotheses for how the poisoning could have occurred. Keep track of these hypotheses.

STEP 3: Identify key assumptions underlying the consensus view. Could any of these be unsubstantiated? Do some assumptions need caveats? If some are not valid, how much could this affect the analysis?

STEP 4: Review the critical evidence that provides the foundation for the argument. Is the analysis based on any critical item of information? On a particular stream of reporting? If any of this evidence or the source of the reporting turned out to be incorrect, how much would this affect the analysis?

STEP 5: Is there any contradictory or anomalous information? Was any information overlooked that is inconsistent with the lead hypothesis?

STEP 6: Is there a potential for deception? Does anyone have motive, opportunity, and means to deceive you?

STEP 7: Is there an absence of evidence, and does it influence the key judgment?

STEP 8: Have you considered the presence of common analytic pitfalls such as analytic mindsets, confirmation bias, "satisficing," premature closure, anchoring, and historical analogy? (See Table 1.2.)

Table 1.2 ▶ Common Analytic Pitfalls

Pitfall	Definition
Analytic mindset	A fixed view or attitude that ignores new data inconsistent with that view or attitude.
Anchoring	The tendency to rely too heavily on one trait or piece of information when making decisions.
Confirmation bias	The tendency to favor information that confirms one's preconceptions or hypotheses, independently of whether they are true.
Historical analogy	Using past events as a model to explain current events or to predict future trends.
Mirror imaging	Assuming that the subject of the analysis would act in the same way as the analyst.
Premature closure	Coming to a conclusion too quickly based on initial and incomplete information.
Satisficing	Generating a quick response that satisfies all stakeholders associated with the issue.

STEP 9: Based on the answers to the themes of inquiry outlined above, list the potential deficiencies in the argument in order of potential impact on the analysis.

Analytic Value Added. As a result of your analysis, would you retain, add a caveat to, or dismiss the mainline judgment, and why?

Task 2. Rewrite the lead judgment of the case so that it reflects any changes you would incorporate as a result of the Premortem Analysis.

Figure 1.3 ▶ Starburst Template

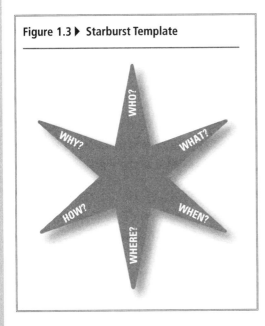

Technique 2: Starbursting

Starbursting is a form of structured brainstorming that helps to generate as many questions as possible. It is particularly useful in developing a research project, but it can also be helpful to elicit many questions and ideas about conventional wisdom. This process allows the analyst to consider the issue at hand from many different perspectives, thereby increasing the chances that the analyst may uncover a heretofore unconsidered question or new idea that will yield new analytic insights.

Task 3. Starburst the case "Who Poisoned Karinna Moskalenko?"

STEP 1: Use the template in Figure 1.3 or draw a six-pointed star and write one of the following words at each point of the star: Who? What? When? Where? How? Why?

STEP 2: Start the brainstorming session, using one of the words at a time to generate questions about the topic. Do not try to answer the questions as they are identified; just focus on generating as many questions as possible.

STEP 3: After generating questions that start with each of the six words, the group should either prioritize the questions to be answered or sort the questions into logical categories.

Analytic Value Added. As a result of your analysis, which questions or categories deserve further investigation?

NOTES

1. Miriam Elder, "Poison Stalks Trial of Murdered Putin Critic," *Independent* (London), October 16, 2008, http://www.independent.co.uk/news/world/europe/poison-stalks-trial-of-murdered-putin-critic-962727.html.

2. Steve Gutterman, "Anti-Kremlin Lawyer Fears Mercury Poisoning Plot," *Advertiser* (Adelaide, Australia), October 17, 2008.

3. Michael Schwirtz and Alan Cowell, "Toxins Found in Russian Rights Lawyer's Car," *International Herald Tribune,* October 15, 2008, http://www.nytimes.com/2008/10/16/world/europe/16russia.html.

4. "Obituary: Chechen Rebel Khattab," BBC News, April 26, 2002, http://news.bbc.co.uk/2/hi/europe/1952053.stm.

5. Ibid.

6. Scott Peterson and Fred Weir, "KGB Legacy of Poison Politics," *Christian Science Monitor,* December 13, 2004, http://www.csmonitor.com/2004/1213/p01s02-woeu.html.

7. Ibid.

8. "Russia 'Silent' on Poison Inquiry," BBC News, July 6, 2007, http://news.bbc.co.uk/2/hi/europe/6278524.stm.

9. Ibid.

10. Associated Press, "Yushchenko Poison Made in Lab, Study Says," Boston.com, August 5, 2009, http://articles.boston.com/2009-08-05/news/29266668_1_dioxin-levels-poison-ukrainian-presidential-candidate/.

11. Scott Shane, "Poison's Use as Political Tool: Ukraine Is Not Exceptional," *New York Times,* December 14, 2004, http://www.nytimes.com/2004/12/15/international/europe/15poison.html; Tony Halpin, "Viktor Yushchenko Points Finger at Russia over Poison That Scarred Him," *Times* (London), September 11, 2007, http://www.timesonline.co.uk/tol/news/world/europe/article2426190.ece; Ron Synovitz, "Ukraine: Yushchenko Convinced He Was Poisoned by 'Those in Power,' " Radio Free Europe/Radio Liberty, December 13, 2004, http://www.rferl.org/content/article/1056378.html.

12. Shane, "Poison's Use as Political Tool."

13. James Meek, "Dispatches from a Savage War," *Guardian,* October 15, 2004, http://www.guardian.co.uk/world/2004/oct/15/gender.uk.

14. Ibid.

15. "Anna Politkovskaya," *New York Times,* updated June 26, 2009, http://topics.nytimes.com/topics/reference/timestopics/people/p/anna_politkovskaya/index.html.

16. This bizarre poisoning by a radioactive substance is not the first reported incident of such tradecraft. Indeed, a postmortem investigation into the death of a former Putin bodyguard, Roman Tsepov two years before the Litvinenko poisoning in 2004 found that Tsepov had been poisoned by an unspecified radioactive material. See Jonathan Calvert, "The Putin Bodyguard Riddle," *Sunday Times* (London), December 3, 2006, http://www.timesonline.co.uk/tol/news/uk/article658488.ece. Tsepov had survived three previous assassination attempts in the 1990s. See "King of Shadows Poisoned," *St. Petersburg Times* (Russia), September 28, 2004, http://www.sptimes.ru/index.php?action_id=2&story_id=1697.

17. Jon Elsen, "Alexander V. Litvinenko," *New York Times*, May 31, 2007, http://topics .nytimes.com/topics/reference/timestopics/people/l/alexander_v_litvinenko/index.html.

18. Ibid.

19. Ibid.

20. Ibid.

21. Oleg Gordievsky, "Russia's Killing Ways," *Washington Post*, December 14, 2006, http://www.washingtonpost.com/wp-dyn/content/article/2006/12/13/AR2006121 301909.html.

22. Ibid.

23. David Wise, "Poison with a Familiar Scent," *Los Angeles Times*, November 26, 2006, http://articles.latimes.com/2006/nov/26/opinion/op-wise26.

24. Ibid.

25. Ibid.

26. Cyrille Louise and Laure Mendeville, "Une avocate russe affirme avoir été empoisonnée [Russian lawyer shown to have been poisoned]," *Le Figaro* (France), October 14, 2008, http://www.lefigaro.fr/actualite-france/2008/10/15/01016–20081015ART FIG00023-une-avocate-russe-affirme-avoir-ete-empoisonnee-.php.

27. Ibid.

28. Ibid.

29. Ibid.

30. Ibid.

31. "Russia Urged to End Harassment Against Lawyer," Radio Free Europe/Radio Liberty, May 9, 2007, http://www.rferl.org/content/article/1076361.html.

32. Yuri Zarakhovich, "Murder, Russian-Style: Political Assassination," *Time*, October 19, 2008, http://www.time.com/time/world/article/0,8599,1851854,00.html.

33. Peter Finn, "Russia's Champion of Hopeless Cases Is Targeted for Disbarment," *Washington Post*, June 3, 2007, http://www.washingtonpost.com/wp-dyn/content/article/ 2007/06/02/AR2007060201135.html.

34. Christian Lowe, "Russian Defense Lawyers in Hazardous Profession," Reuters, July 23, 2007, http://www.reuters.com/article/2007/07/23/us-russia-justice-lawyers-idUSL2171073820070723.

35. "Kremlin Foe 'Poisoned' Lawyer Says: Mercury Placed in Her Vehicle," *Courier Mail* (Brisbane, Australia), October 16, 2008, http://www.nexislexis.com/.

36. Miriam Elder, "Poison Stalks Trial of Murdered Putin Critic."

37. Michael Schwirtz and Alan Cowell, "Toxins Found in Russian Rights Lawyer's Car."

38. Miriam Elder, "Poison Stalks Trial of Murdered Putin Critic."

39. "More Poison: Another Prominent Adversary of Vladimir Putin Is Mysteriously Exposed to Toxins [editorial]," *Washington Post*, October 22, 2008, http://www.washing tonpost.com/wp-dyn/content/article/2008/10/21/AR2008102102342.html.

40. The steps as outlined in this case combine the processes for a Premortem Analysis and Structured Self-Critique. This combination is particularly helpful in cases that require analysts to think broadly, imaginatively, and exhaustively about how they might have been wrong. The Premortem Analysis taps the creative brainstorming process, and the Structured Self-Critique provides a step-by-step assessment of each analytic element. To aid students' learning process, the questions in this case have already been narrowed from the fuller set of Structured Self-Critique questions found in Richards J. Heuer Jr. and Randolph H. Pherson, *Structured Analytic Techniques for Intelligence Analysis* (Washington, DC: CQ Press, 2011).

2 Is Wen Ho Lee a Spy?

CASE NARRATIVE

In the 1990s, as the Clinton administration sought to expand diplomatic and trade relations with China, Chinese espionage against US technology targets—especially nuclear weapons data at national laboratories—received widespread publicity. As charges and countercharges surfaced, US scientists at Los Alamos National Laboratory (LANL) who were studying Chinese nuclear tests concluded that a 1992 test demonstrated a sudden advance in the miniaturization of Beijing's nuclear warheads. They argued that the Chinese warhead was very similar to the United States' most advanced weapon, the W-88 (see Figure 2.1).[1] With this advance, the Chinese had the basis of a modern, nuclear force.

Robert M. Henson, a weapons designer at Los Alamos National Laboratory, believed that the only way the Chinese could have made such advances was by stealing US secrets.[2] Henson's view was seconded by John L. Richter, a bomb designer who specialized in creating the trigger for the hydrogen bomb. He argued that the sketchy evidence available pointed to the Chinese having acquired significant data on the trigger in the W-88.[3] An investigation ensued, the results of which led investigators to believe that the theft of the W-88 data from the national laboratories occurred in the 1980s and that there was evidence of ongoing Chinese espionage at the increasingly open national laboratories in the 1990s. Given the small community of scientists with access to such data, investigators quickly focused on identifying who was responsible for the apparent leak.

The Chinese Threat

Counterintelligence officials report that China is aggressive at collecting information on US advanced technology.[4] Beijing employs both soft—and mostly

Figure 2.1 ▶ Schematic of the W-88 Nuclear Warhead

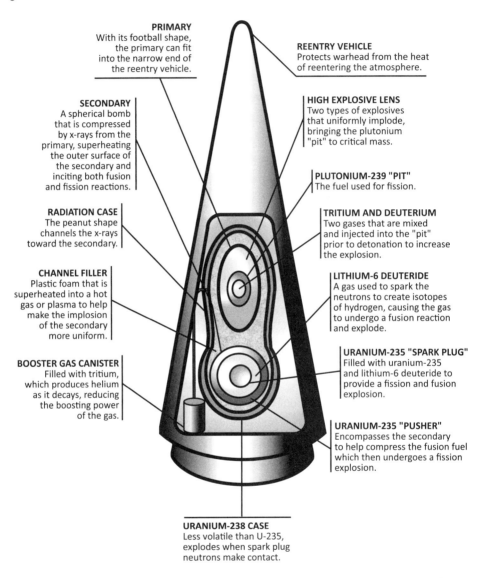

PRIMARY
With its football shape, the primary can fit into the narrow end of the reentry vehicle.

REENTRY VEHICLE
Protects warhead from the heat of reentering the atmosphere.

SECONDARY
A spherical bomb that is compressed by x-rays from the primary, superheating the outer surface of the secondary and inciting both fusion and fission reactions.

HIGH EXPLOSIVE LENS
Two types of explosives that uniformly implode, bringing the plutonium "pit" to critical mass.

PLUTONIUM-239 "PIT"
The fuel used for fission.

RADIATION CASE
The peanut shape channels the x-rays toward the secondary.

TRITIUM AND DEUTERIUM
Two gases that are mixed and injected into the "pit" prior to detonation to increase the explosion.

CHANNEL FILLER
Plastic foam that is superheated into a hot gas or plasma to help make the implosion of the secondary more uniform.

LITHIUM-6 DEUTERIDE
A gas used to spark the neutrons to create isotopes of hydrogen, causing the gas to undergo a fusion reaction and explode.

BOOSTER GAS CANISTER
Filled with tritium, which produces helium as it decays, reducing the boosting power of the gas.

URANIUM-235 "SPARK PLUG"
Filled with uranium-235 and lithium-6 deuteride to provide a fission and fusion explosion.

URANIUM-235 "PUSHER"
Encompasses the secondary to help compress the fusion fuel which then undergoes a fission explosion.

URANIUM-238 CASE
Less volatile than U-235, explodes when spark plug neutrons make contact.

Source: Figure created by Nigah Ajaj, Pherson Associates, LLC. Adapted from Dan Stober and Ian Hoffman, *A Convenient Spy: Wen Ho Lee and the Politics of Nuclear Espionage* (New York: Simon & Schuster, 2007), p. 43.

legal—as well as classic, hard spying techniques to gain access to critical information. While the Chinese approach all scientists, they focus on ethnic Chinese, both from the mainland and from Taiwan.[5] The Chinese informally collect tidbits from individuals in social settings, from Chinese visitors to US national laboratories and industrial sites, from scientific papers, and from Chinese students. In addition, Chinese intelligence officials approach scientists traveling in China or attending scientific conferences. Beijing also employs classic spying techniques, recruiting spies and running double-agent operations.[6]

The immediacy of the threat posed by Chinese espionage became apparent in 1995 after a critical piece of nuclear weapons intelligence came to the attention of Notra Trulock, Director of Intelligence at the Department of Energy (DOE).[7] Henson shared with Trulock his concerns that China might have stolen nuclear secrets from the United States in the mid-1980s, although the theft had not been discovered until 1995.[8] Henson was particularly concerned that China had managed to shrink the size of its warheads in a surprisingly short time.[9] The 1992 test had demonstrated that the Chinese could build missiles carrying multiple warheads and could now install them in submarines.[10]

The DOE Investigation: The Kindred Spirit Case

In the summer of 1995, DOE launched an assessment of China's nuclear weapons program as well as an administrative inquiry (AI) named Kindred Spirit to identify individuals within DOE who might have passed US nuclear secrets to the Chinese.[11] Trulock assembled a team, the Kindred Spirit Analytical Group (KSAG), to review the available data on Chinese bomb making.[12] The team found that the nuclear trigger ("primary") of the Chinese weapon was very similar in size and shape to that of the US W-88 warhead—one of the most sophisticated weapons in the US arsenal.

While the team was working this issue, they learned that an individual from mainland China had voluntarily provided classified Chinese documents to the CIA in June 1995.[13] One document that attracted a lot of attention was a seventy-page paper that contained crude pictures, along with weights and measurements, of a variety of US weapons, including the W-88 warhead.[14] Although much information about the W-88 was available in unclassified papers, certain details were not. The "walk-in" document described the outer measurements of the casing for the nuclear trigger.[15]

Former LANL Chief of Personnel and Information Security Robert Vrooman later recalled that the particular data referred to the engineering of the trigger, not to its design. According to Vrooman, if there had been espionage, it was not likely to have occurred at a design laboratory like LANL but in an engineering and production lab. In addition, the sketch of the W-88 in the walk-in document contained design flaws that had been added after the Los Alamos involvement.[16]

Trulock's team was unable to find a definitive link between the 1992 Chinese bomb test and the W-88. Team members were divided among three positions:

1. China had developed the new bomb on its own.[17]
2. China had benefited from a slow but steady accumulation of secrets over the years to develop its own miniaturized bomb.[18]
3. China had a master spy somewhere.[19]

Some knowledgeable scientists believed that the Chinese did not need to steal the data. They argued that as much as 99 percent of the data needed to build a weapon similar to the W-88 was available on the Internet.[20] There was also a possibility that China might have obtained the technology from another country, such as Russia. Following the demise of the Soviet Union, many Russian nuclear experts were marketing their skills around the world.[21]

KSAG eventually reached a consensus that the Chinese weapons program had been aided by espionage. Trulock was among those who were convinced that a spy at one of the National Defense laboratories had passed the design keys for the W-88 nuclear warhead to the Chinese.[22] Trulock informally asked the FBI if it would open an investigation at the end of the summer of 1995. The FBI declined, saying the case was too old and too cold and suggested that Trulock pursue the AI that he had launched in June.

Trulock assigned veteran investigators to undertake the inquiry, which began in November 1995. On the basis of the KSAG findings, the investigators were guided by three criteria for identifying suspects:

1. Individuals who had traveled to China between 1984 and 1988 (the period after final approval of the W-88 design and before the walk-in document).
2. Individuals with clearance to work with top secret nuclear weapons data.
3. Individuals who dealt with visiting delegations from China.[23]

The investigators quickly narrowed their search to LANL and the Lawrence Livermore National Laboratory (LLNL).[24] They identified some seventy individuals at LANL who met some of the criteria and subsequently narrowed the list down to twelve who met all three criteria.[25] Trulock and his team quickly homed in on one individual, Wen Ho Lee, a nuclear weapons specialist at LANL.[26]

Some officials would later question the list as inconsistent and unreliable. For example, it included only those individuals whose travel expenses were paid by DOE. The short list included three individuals who had no access to classified data and one with no clearance.[27] DOE's acting chief of counterintelligence recommended that the case be closed for lack of evidence, but it remained active.

In May 1996, DOE completed its AI and submitted its report to the FBI. The central message of the report was that espionage had occurred and the most likely source was at LANL.[28] The report named LANL scientist Wen Ho Lee and his wife, Sylvia, as the most logical suspects, noting that Lee was the only target who had opportunity, motive, and legitimate access.[29,30] Lee had traveled to China twice during the specified time frame, in 1986 and 1988.[31] Both times, he had received DOE approval to attend scientific conferences. He possessed a Q clearance, which gave him access to all classified material in his field at LANL. He and Sylvia had met visiting Chinese delegations frequently, she eagerly acted as an interpreter for the Chinese visitors, and she accompanied Lee on his two trips to China.[32]

Wen Ho Lee's Background

Wen Ho Lee was born in Nantou, Taiwan, on December 21, 1939. He received a BS degree from National Cheng Kung University in Taiwan. Lee came to the United States in 1964 and became a citizen in 1974. He earned a PhD in mechanical engineering from Texas A&M University in 1970 and was hired by LANL as a research mathematician in 1978. In 1980 he joined the X Division, where nuclear

Wen Ho Lee pictured with his daughter, Alberta Lee.

weapons are designed. His job was to create computer codes that modeled the fluidlike movement of explosions and to archive any related information developed. Scientists used these computer programs in nuclear weapons design and nuclear test simulations.[33]

Lee made professional and personal trips to China and to Taiwan.[34] During the 1980s, he traveled twice to China. In 1986 he delivered a paper at a scientific conference in Beijing.[35] Two years later, he attended another conference in Beijing.[36] During the conference, Lee met with Dr. Hu Side and another Chinese scientist in a Beijing hotel room.[37] Dr. Hu was head of the Chinese Academy of Engineering Physics—the Chinese bomb makers—and the designer of the two-point nuclear bomb trigger. At the meeting, Dr. Hu asked Lee how to make a smaller hydrogen bomb using an oval-shaped fuel case. Later Lee said that he did not answer the question.[38]

During the 1980s, Wen Ho Lee became an FBI informant.[39] He reportedly provided useful information on at least one case under investigation.[40] His wife, Sylvia Lee, was a secretary at LANL where she helped entertain visiting Chinese scientists and provided tours of local sights.[41] She also was a research contact for Chinese scientists. In 1985, Sylvia Lee was invited to speak at a Beijing conference on sophisticated computers, even though she was only a secretary. Wen Ho Lee attended the conference with his wife.[42] In 1987, she became an informant to the FBI on the Chinese delegations she met with at LANL.[43] She also served as a source for the CIA. During these years, there was no significant change in the lifestyle of Wen Ho Lee or his wife.[44]

Lee did not report all his contacts with Chinese scientists at the 1988 conference or other conferences he attended.[45] The absence of reports by Lee was noted by LANL security chief Vrooman.[46] Lee admitted to investigators that he had unauthorized contacts with Chinese scientists over the years.

Lee first came to the attention of investigators in December 1982 when he was overheard on a wiretap making a phone call to a Taiwanese-American scientist who was suspected of providing the Chinese with neutron bomb secrets from LLNL.[47,48] During the phone call, Lee offered to help find out who had "squealed on" the scientist.[49] Although no indictment of the suspect scientist was issued in what the FBI called the Tiger Trap case[50] because of insufficient evidence, the suspect was fired from LLNL.[51] Lee denied making the call until investigators looking into the Tiger Trap case confronted him with evidence of the conversation.[52] He also explained to investigators that he gave Taiwanese officials unclassified documents on nuclear-reactor safety but that he had not told US government officials at the time as required by security regulations.[53]

Lee made two trips to Taiwan in the 1990s. In 1994, he traveled to Hong Kong, a trip that he did not report to security officials as required.[54] Investigators later found that he made two credit card purchases at a Hong Kong travel agency. One purchase was for $100 and one for $700.[55,56] Investigators report that $700 would have covered the purchase of an airplane ticket to Shanghai.[57,58] Lee traveled to Taiwan in 1998, where he had been putting out feelers for jobs.[59] During March and April of that year, he spent six weeks at the Chung Shan Military Institute in Taiwan, where he received a fee of about $5,000. While in Taiwan, Lee called the LANL computer help desk to ask if could access the classified computer at the lab. He was told that he could not access the classified system from Taiwan. Investigators later learned that he had downloaded an unclassified computer code from LANL to his computer in Taiwan.[60] In December 1998, Lee traveled for three weeks to Taiwan, and the trip was paid for by a private Taiwanese company.[61]

In 1994, Wen Ho Lee attended a party at Los Alamos for visiting Chinese scientists, even though he was not on the invitation list.[62] During the party, Dr. Hu Side greeted Lee warmly. Some sources report that Dr. Hu hugged Lee.[63] According to a translator at the party, Hu thanked Lee for computer software and calculations on hydrodynamics Lee had supplied. Dr. Hu added that the information had aided China greatly.[64]

The FBI Investigation

In May 1996—two days after receiving the DOE report—the FBI agreed to open an investigation based on DOE's administrative inquiry.[65] With a full case load, the local agent had only limited time to devote to Kindred Spirit. As a result, no agent worked full-time on the case.[66]

In April 1997, Lee brought himself to the attention of the FBI by submitting a standard request to hire a postdoctoral researcher who happened to be a Chinese citizen. Lee said he needed an assistant to help with his work on codes used to model some aspects of nuclear weapons tests. This spurred the FBI to request an electronic surveillance warrant under the Foreign Intelligence Surveillance Act (FISA).[67]

The FBI wanted to monitor Lee's contacts with his graduate student. Over the summer of 1996, the FBI presented three separate drafts of its request for a FISA warrant to the Department of Justice (DOJ). DOJ took the unusual step of denying the FBI request in August 1997, citing a lack of "probable cause" that Lee was a spy.[68,69] The FISA request could not demonstrate a link between the theft of the W-88 design and Lee. DOJ was also disturbed by the failure to investigate other possible suspects.[70]

FBI director Louis J. Freeh appreciated the anxiety of DOE over Lee's continuing presence in X Division and his access to nuclear secrets. After a top-level review, the FBI concluded it did not have sufficient evidence to arrest Lee, but there was no reason to leave Lee in place.[71] Miscommunications between FBI headquarters, LANL, and DOE headquarters, however, resulted in Lee staying in his job.[72,73]

Little progress was made on the investigation in 1997 and 1998. Neither the FBI nor DOE knew that Lee had left the country during March and April 1998 to work as a consultant at a nuclear weapons research institute in Taiwan.[74] Since LANL was not paying for the trip, Lee was not required to ask for permission. The FBI initiated a "false flag" operation in August 1998 in which FBI agents posing as Chinese officials sought to recruit Lee. Lee rebuffed them, but he did not report the pitch to his superiors as required.[75]

The case did not get much attention until later in 1998, when two House Committees conducted hearings on Chinese nuclear activities. US-China relations had been politically charged for many years.[76] The Reagan administration had expanded scientific exchanges with China and declassified millions of documents relating to nuclear arms. Washington had also encouraged weapons specialists to exchange unclassified information with foreign counterparts.[77] The Clinton administration had continued to expand ties with China.[78] In 1994, National Labs were no longer required to conduct background checks on foreign[79] scientists visiting the labs for scientific exchanges.[80] Republicans charged that the Clinton White House was downplaying Chinese spying because it conflicted with the administration's drive for a greater strategic and commercial partnership with Beijing. President Clinton had already eased the sale of supercomputers and satellite technology to China.[81]

The House Permanent Select Committee on Intelligence (HPSCI) in 1998 requested an update on the W-88 Chinese espionage case from DOE.[82] Meanwhile, a special House Committee, headed by Rep. Christopher Cox (R-CA), was conducting hearings on the transfer of technology to China and had begun to focus on suspected Chinese nuclear espionage. Trulock testified before the Cox Committee in November 1998 that the Chinese had stolen the design of the W-88. In December, the FBI told the Committee that the Chinese had probably penetrated US weapons laboratories and that a suspected spy was still unexposed at LANL with his security clearances unchanged. At the time, Lee was in Taiwan on a trip approved by DOE.[83]

Polygraph Results and the Missing Computer Files

Information on Chinese nuclear espionage at the national laboratories began leaking to the press from the Cox Committee from December 1998 into early 1999. DOE decided to interview and polygraph Lee after his return from Taiwan in late December 1998.[84] During the 23 December interview, Lee admitted that he had met two Chinese scientists interested in miniaturized nuclear bombs in his hotel room during a visit to Beijing in 1988. He claimed that he told the Chinese that he didn't know the answer and refused to discuss the issue with them. When asked why he did not report the meeting at the time, Lee said he forgot.[85] Lee did not go home after this meeting but made several attempts to enter X Division after his access was suspended, including an unauthorized visit to the laboratory at 0330 on Christmas Eve. He succeeded in entering X Division on two occasions. DOE subsequently assigned Lee to another department, T Division.[86]

FBI and DOE forensic specialists discovered that Lee had transferred a large number of files from a classified to an unclassified part of LANL's computer system.[87,88] According to press reports, Lee maintained that he had been instructed to archive the bomb data.[89,90] Lee had begun the transfers as early as 1988[91] but made the bulk of them in 1993. In fact, the bulk of the downloads occurred in 1993 and 1994.[92] Lee told a fellow scientist at Los Alamos that he needed to transfer the files from a classified computer to an unclassified computer because the classified computer did not have tape drives and he could not download files from it directly. At the time of the downloads in 1993, Lee learned that he might be laid off from LANL due to budget cuts.[93] Investigators later found seven letters dated 1993 and 1994 on Lee's home computer addressed to universities and institutes and inquiring about job prospects, but there was no evidence that the letters had been mailed.[94]

The FBI believed that Lee had transferred files from a classified to an unclassified system and downloaded them onto tapes. The computer index confirmed that he had downloaded all the files he had transferred.[95] The contents of a tenth tape, copied in 1997,[96] were never transferred to the unclassified system because Lee's X Division computer had a tape drive by then. LANL experts told the FBI that the later tape contained up-to-date information that would have made the 1993–94 tapes more useful. Lee at first denied making the tapes,[97] but when confronted with the list, he admitted that there had been tapes. He denied any criminal intent in making the tapes. Wen Ho Lee last downloaded information from the classified computer system to the tape drive on his own classified computer in 1997.[98] The case had morphed from a counterintelligence investigation to a possible criminal case.

The transferred files did not include user manuals for the computer codes.[99] The 1993–94 transfers took nearly forty hours over seventy days.[100] The transfers were neither quick nor easy to do, requiring numerous deliberate steps to move data from the secure partition to the open partition of the system.[101] Lee left some files on the open system for as long as six years.[102] When LANL computer experts looked for the files, however, they found Lee had deleted them. In fact he had been busy since the polygraph of 23 December 1998, trying to gain physical access to X Division and to his X Division computer account. In all, he deleted 360 files—some 800 megabytes or 450,000 pages of data.[103] Agents found materials in his office desk that included handwritten Chinese-language notes on how to download codes used to develop various nuclear weapons, including the W-88.[104] They also found documents on Lee's desk with the classification markings removed. But there was no direct evidence that Wen Ho Lee had ever passed or tried to pass any classified national security information to China.[105]

Over the next several months, the FBI conducted an exhaustive computer-network analysis in an effort to discover the contents of the files Lee had transferred, downloaded, and deleted.[106] The FBI was able to recover three of the tapes from Lee's T Division office,[107] but seven remained missing.[108] Lee told the FBI that he had destroyed them. He gave no explanation of why he had made the tapes or why and how he had disposed of them. He denied taking them home.

After the FBI identified the deleted files, it turned to experts at DOE and LANL to determine their value. Lee apparently had downloaded almost all of LANL's nuclear weapons source codes and other files, which together provided the means for computer-simulated tests of nuclear weapons.[109] Substantial amounts of the material Lee had downloaded were classified as PARD, which stands for "Protect as Restricted Data." Such data are controlled, but at that time a determination had not been made as to whether they were classified. PARD is often applied to large volumes of data such as computer printouts, much of which are unclassified. During Lee's investigation, some of the PARD material was later reclassified as "Confidential" and "Secret."[110]

Officials at the FBI placed a new emphasis on the case in early 1999.[111] When they interviewed Lee in January, he provided previously unknown information about contacts he had made with Chinese scientists in the 1980s, including a meeting with Hu Side.[112] The FBI interviewers were satisfied with Lee's responses and were prepared to clear him, but they still wanted to see the results of the DOE polygraph. After some delay, they obtained the results of the polygraph, which cleared Lee. Later that month, FBI specialists discovered problems with the polygraph and questioned its results. In February Lee underwent an FBI polygraph interview, which he failed.[113] He returned to his office, where he told a supervisor that he had failed the polygraph and that he might have inadvertently passed classified information to a foreign country.[114]

The FBI stepped up its investigation in early March when it learned that the *New York Times* was preparing an article about an espionage investigation involving an unidentified LANL scientist.[115] The FBI interviewed Lee, who could not explain the differences between the travel report following his 1988 visit to China and the information he had given to investigators after his polygraphs.[116] Lee consented to a search of his office computers[117] but not to a search of his home.[118]

The Case Goes Public

A *New York Times* article on 6 March 1999 reported that nuclear secrets stolen from a US government laboratory had enabled China to make a leap in nuclear weapons development: the miniaturization of its bombs.[119] It said there was a suspect, a Chinese-American scientist at Los Alamos.[120] It cited comments by unidentified officials that the White House had minimized the espionage investigation for political reasons. One official said that exposing the espionage would undercut the administration's efforts to have a strategic partnership with China.[121]

Once the case against Wen Ho Lee surfaced publicly, his defenders charged that he was singled out for investigation because he was Chinese-American.[122] Charges of racial profiling became a key element in his defense. Additionally, his defense claimed that there was no definitive evidence that Wen Ho Lee actually passed data to the Chinese[123] or any proof of theft.[124] In this politically charged atmosphere, many commentators believed that politics drove the prosecution of Wen Ho Lee for espionage and produced intense pressure for prosecutors to bring home a conviction.

Lee the Spy?

On Monday, 8 March 1999, Lee was fired after nearly twenty years at LANL on orders of Secretary of Energy Bill Richardson.[125] Richardson ordered a tightening of security at all the national laboratories, including reinstating background checks for foreign scientists visiting the laboratories from sensitive countries.[126] On 10 December 1999, Lee was indicted on fifty-nine counts of illegally removing highly classified information from LANL.[127] Wen Ho Lee was jailed in January 2000 and held in solitary confinement.[128] He ultimately pled guilty to one count of mishandling a controlled document, was sentenced to time served, and was released in September 2000.[129] At the time of his release, Wen Ho Lee agreed to undergo sixty hours of debriefing, under oath, by the government. During the debriefing, Dr. Lee acknowledged making as many as a dozen trips to Taiwan during the last twenty years—more than officials previously knew about—but the purpose of the trips was not clear. Dr. Lee insisted that he threw the missing tapes into the trash; they have never been found.[130]

RECOMMENDED READINGS

Lee, Wen Ho. *My Country versus Me: The First-Hand Account by the Los Alamos Scientist Who Was Falsely Accused of Being a Spy.* With Helen Zia. New York: Hyperion, 2002.

Stober, Dan, and Ian Hoffman. *A Convenient Spy: Wen Ho Lee and the Politics of Nuclear Espionage.* New York: Simon & Schuster, 2007.

Trulock, Notra. *Code Name Kindred Spirit: Inside the Chinese Nuclear Espionage Scandal.* San Francisco: Encounter Books, 2003.

Table 2.1 ▶ Case Snapshot: Is Wen Ho Lee a Spy?		
Structured Analytic Technique Used	Heuer and Pherson Page Number	Analytic Family
Force Field Analysis	p. 281	Decision Support
Deception Detection	p. 173	Hypothesis Generation and Testing
Premortem Analysis	p. 221	Challenge Analysis
Structured Self-Critique	p. 226	Challenge Analysis

IS WEN HO LEE A SPY?
STRUCTURED ANALYTIC TECHNIQUES IN ACTION

Is Wen Ho Lee a spy? When the stakes are this high, it is important to ensure that all the data have been considered from every possible angle before rendering a judgment. The following combination of techniques—Force Field Analysis, Deception Detection, Premortem Analysis, and Structured Self-Critique—can be used in concert to examine the case of Wen Ho Lee and the possibility that he is a spy, or not.

Technique 1: Force Field Analysis

A Force Field Analysis helps analysts identify and assess all of the forces and factors for and against an outcome and avoid premature or unwarranted focus only on one side of the analysis. It is particularly helpful at the beginning of a project or investigation as a tool to sort and consider all evidence as an evidentiary base is amassed. Furthermore, the weighting mechanism allows analysts to more easily identify the strongest and weakest forces or factors and recommend strategies to reduce or strengthen the effect of forces that support or work toward a given outcome.

In this case, investigators amassed a long list of counts against Wen Ho Lee, but Lee only pled guilty to—and was convicted of—one relatively minor count of mishandling a controlled document. Many observers questioned the government's case; the government remained solid in its conviction that Wen Ho Lee was a spy. A Force Field Analysis helps to illuminate both sides of the case.

Task 1. Conduct a Force Field Analysis of the arguments for and against Wen Ho Lee being guilty of passing nuclear secrets to China.

Step 1: Define the problem, goal, or change clearly and concisely.

Step 2: Use a form of brainstorming to identify the main factors that will influence the issue.

Step 3: Make one list showing the strongest arguments supporting Wen Ho Lee's innocence and another list showing the strongest arguments showing his guilt.

Step 4: Array the lists in a table like Table 2.2.

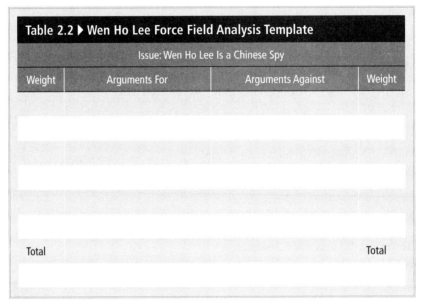

Table 2.2 ▶ Wen Ho Lee Force Field Analysis Template			
Issue: Wen Ho Lee Is a Chinese Spy			
Weight	Arguments For	Arguments Against	Weight
Total			Total

Step 5: Assign a value to each factor or argument for and against to indicate its strength. Assign the weakest-intensity scores a value of 1 and the strongest a value of 5. The same intensity score can be assigned to more than one factor if you consider the factors equal in strength.

Step 6: Calculate a total score for each list to determine whether the arguments for or against are dominant.

Step 7: Examine the two lists to determine if any of the factors balance each other out.

Step 8: Analyze the lists to determine how changes in factors might affect the overall outcome. If the technique is being used as a decision tool, devise a manageable course of action to strengthen those forces that lead to the preferred outcome and weaken the forces that would hinder the desired outcome.

Analytic Value Added. What are the strongest arguments for and against Lee's guilt in your analysis of the issue? Do any factors deserve further investigation? Have you identified any information gaps that should be further investigated?

Technique 2: Deception Detection

Analysts should routinely consider the possibility that adversaries are attempting to mislead them or to hide important information. The possibility of deception cannot be rejected simply because there is no evidence of it; if deception is well done, one should not expect to see evidence of it. There are, however, some indicators that should alert analysts that they may be the targets of deception, such as the timing of reporting or the bona fides of a source or when there are known and potentially serious consequences if the source is believed.

Task 2. Use Deception Detection to determine if deception may be occurring in the case of Wen Ho Lee.

Sᴛᴇᴘ 1: Determine if deception detection should be conducted using Table 2.3 as your guide. Assuming that the United States and the FBI would be the target, who would be the most likely perpetrators of deception? If a case can be made that someone may have a motive to deceive, state this as a hypothesis to be proved or disproved. Note which indicators best apply to this case.

Table 2.3 ▶ When to Use Deception Detection

Analysts should be concerned about the possibility of deception when:

The potential deceiver has a history of conducting deception.

Key information is received at a critical time, that is, when either the recipient or the potential deceiver has a great deal to gain or to lose.

Information is received from a source whose bona fides are questionable.

Analysis hinges on a single critical piece of information or reporting.

Accepting new information would require the analyst to alter a key assumption or key judgment.

Accepting the new information would cause the Intelligence Community, the US government, or the client to expend or divert significant resources.

The potential deceiver may have a feedback channel that illuminates whether and how the deception information is being processed and to what effect.

STEP 2:   Consider Motive, Opportunity, and Means; Past Opposition Practices; Manipulability of Sources; and Evaluation of Evidence for the potential deceiver. Use the templates and questions in Table 2.4 as your guide.

Table 2.4 ▶ Deception Detection Templates

Motive, Opportunity, and Means (MOM)

Motive: What are the goals and motives of the potential deceiver?	
Channels: What means are available to the potential deceiver to feed information to us?	
Risks: What consequences would the adversary suffer if such a deception were revealed?	
Costs: Would the potential deceiver need to sacrifice sensitive information to establish the credibility of the deception channel?	
Feedback: Does the potential deceiver have a feedback mechanism to monitor the impact of the deception operation?	

Past Opposition Practices (POP)

Does the adversary have a history of engaging in deception?	
Does the current circumstance fit the pattern of past deceptions?	
If not, are there other historical precedents?	
If not, are there changed circumstances that would explain the use of this form of deception at this time?	

Manipulability of Sources (MOSES)

Is the source vulnerable to control or manipulation by the potential deceiver?	
What is the basis for judging the source to be reliable?	

Table 2.4 ▶ *(Continued)*	
Does the source have direct access or only indirect access to the information?	
How good is the source's track record of reporting?	
Does the source have personal reasons for providing faulty information, for example, to please the collector, promote a personal agenda, or gain more revenue? Or could a well-meaning source just be naïve?	
Evaluation of Evidence (EVE)	
How accurate is the source's reporting? Has the whole chain of evidence, including translations, been checked?	
Does the critical evidence check out? Remember, the subsource can be more critical than the source.	
Does evidence from one source of reporting (e.g., human intelligence) conflict with that coming from another source (e.g., signals intelligence or open source reporting)?	
Do other sources of information provide corroborating evidence?	

Analytic Value Added. Summarize the results of all four matrices in terms of whether they tend to prove or disprove the deception hypothesis. Did the technique expose any embedded assumptions or critical gaps that need to be examined more critically?

Task 3. Assess if the overall potential for deception is an insignificant threat, a possibility but one with no significant policy or resource implications, or a serious concern that merits attention and warrants further investigation.

Technique 3: The Premortem Analysis and Structured Self-Critique
The goal of these techniques[131] is to challenge—actively and explicitly—an established mental model or analytic consensus in order to broaden the range of possible explanations or estimates that are seriously considered. This process

helps reduce the risk of analytic failure by identifying and analyzing the features of a potential failure before it occurs.

Task 4. Conduct a Premortem Analysis and Structured Self-Critique of the reigning view in the case study that Wen Ho Lee passed nuclear secrets to the People's Republic of China.

STEP 1: Imagine that a period of time has passed since you concluded that Wen Ho Lee was guilty of espionage. You suddenly learn from an unimpeachable source that the judgment was wrong. Then imagine what could have happened to cause the analysis to be wrong.

STEP 2: Use a brainstorming technique to identify alternative hypotheses that might explain Wen Ho Lee's pattern of behavior. Keep track of these hypotheses.

STEP 3: Identify key assumptions underlying the consensus view that Wen Ho Lee is guilty of passing nuclear secrets to the Chinese. Could any of these be unsubstantiated? Do some assumptions need caveats? If some are not valid, how much could this affect the analysis?

STEP 4: Review the critical evidence that provides the foundation for the argument. Is the analysis based on any critical item of information? On a particular stream of reporting? If any of this evidence or the source of the reporting turned out to be incorrect, how much would this affect the analysis?

STEP 5: Is there any contradictory or anomalous information? Was any information overlooked that is inconsistent with the lead hypothesis?

STEP 6: Is there a potential for deception? Does anyone have motive, opportunity, and means to deceive you, either intentionally or unintentionally?

STEP 7: Is there an absence of evidence, and does it influence the key judgment?

STEP 8: Have you considered the presence of common analytic pitfalls such as confirmation bias, "satisficing," and historical analogy? (Use Table 1.2 in Chapter 1 as your guide to do so.)

STEP 9: Based on the answers to the themes of inquiry outlined above, list the potential deficiencies in the argument in order of potential impact on the analysis.

Analytic Value Added. As a result of your analysis, would you retain, add a caveat to, or dismiss the mainline judgment, and why?

Task 5. Rewrite the lead judgment of the case so that it reflects any changes you would incorporate as a result of the Premortem Analysis.

NOTES

1. James Risen and Jeff Gerth, "Breach at Los Alamos: A Special Report; China Stole Nuclear Secrets for Bombs, US Aides Say," *New York Times.* March 6, 1999, http://www .nytimes.com/1999/03/06/world/breach-los-alamos-special-report-china-stole-nuclear-secrets-for-bombs-us-aides.html.
2. Matthew Purdy, "The Prosecution Unravels: The Case of Wen Ho Lee," with James Sterngold, *New York Times,* February 5, 2001, http://www.nytimes.com/2001/02/05/us/the-prosecution-unravels-the-case-of-wen-ho-lee.html.
3. Ibid.
4. Ibid.
5. Ibid.
6. Risen and Gerth, "Breach at Los Alamos."
7. Purdy, "The Prosecution Unravels."
8. Ibid.
9. Ibid.
10. Ibid.
11. Ibid.
12. Ibid.
13. Risen and Gerth, "Breach at Los Alamos."
14. Ibid.
15. Purdy, "The Prosecution Unravels."
16. Robert Scheer, "What's Left of Case Against Lee? Not Much," *Los Angeles Times,* December 14, 1999, http://articles.latimes.com/1999/dec/14/local/me-43741.
17. Purdy, "The Prosecution Unravels."
18. Ibid.
19. Ibid.
20. William J. Broad, "Ideas & Trends: Bombshells; Are There Any Nuclear Secrets Left to Steal?" *New York Times,* September 3, 2000, http://www.nytimes.com/2000/09/03/weekinreview/ideas-trends-bombshells-are-there-any-nuclear-secrets-left-to-steal.html.
21. Risen and Gerth, "Breach at Los Alamos."
22. Purdy, "The Prosecution Unravels."
23. James Risen and David Johnston, "US Will Broaden Investigation of China Nuclear Secrets Case," *New York Times,* September 23, 1999, http://www.nytimes.com/1999/09/23/us/us-will-broaden-investigation-of-china-nuclear-secrets-case.html.
24. Purdy, "The Prosecution Unravels."
25. Risen and Johnston, "US Will Broaden Investigation."
26. Risen and Gerth, "Breach at Los Alamos."

27. James Sterngold, "US to Reduce Case against Scientist to a Single Charge," *New York Times*, September 11, 2000, http://www.nytimes.com/2000/09/11/us/us-to-reduce-case-against-scientist-to-a-single-charge.html.

28. Purdy, "The Prosecution Unravels."

29. Ibid.

30. Ibid.

31. Ibid.

32. Ibid.

33. Ibid.

34. Ibid.

35. Jeff Gerth and James Risen, "1998 Report Told of Lab Breaches and China Threat," *New York Times*, May 2, 1999, http://www.nytimes.com/1999/05/02/world/1998-report-told-of-lab-breaches-and-china-threat.html.

36. Ibid.

37. David Johnston, "Suspect in Loss of Nuclear Secrets Unlikely to Face Spying Charges," *New York Times*, June 15, 1999, http://www.nytimes.com/1999/06/15/world/suspect-in-loss-of-nuclear-secrets-unlikely-to-face-spying-charges.html.

38. Purdy, "The Prosecution Unravels."

39. Gerth and Risen, "1998 Report Told of Lab Breaches."

40. James Risen and Jeff Gerth, "US Says Suspect Put Code on Bombs in Unsecure Files," *New York Times*, April 28, 1999, http://www.nytimes.com/1999/04/28/world/us-says-suspect-put-code-on-bombs-in-unsecure-files.html.

41. Risen and Gerth, "Breach at Los Alamos."

42. Ibid.

43. Risen and Gerth, "US Says Suspect Put Code on Bombs in Unsecure Files."

44. Johnston, "Suspect in Loss of Nuclear Secrets Unlikely to Face Spying Charges."

45. Ibid.

46. Purdy, "The Prosecution Unravels."

47. Jeff Gerth and James Risen, "A Visit from China: New Spy Case; Intelligence Report Points to 2nd China Nuclear Leak," *New York Times*, April 8, 1999, http://www.nytimes.com/1999/04/08/world/visit-china-new-spy-case-intelligence-report-points-2d-china-nuclear-leak.htm.

48. Gerth and Risen, "1998 Report Told of Lab Breaches and China Threat."

49. Purdy, "The Prosecution Unravels."

50. Ibid.

51. Gerth and Risen, "1998 Report Told of Lab Breaches and China Threat."

52. Purdy, "The Prosecution Unravels."

53. Ibid.

54. Risen and Gerth, "Breach at Los Alamos."

55. Ibid.

56. David Johnston, "Suspect in Loss of Nuclear Secrets Unlikely to Face Spying Charges."

57. Risen and Gerth, "Breach at Los Alamos."

58. David Johnston, "Suspect in Loss of Nuclear Secrets Unlikely to Face Spying Charges."

59. Purdy, "The Prosecution Unravels."

60. Ibid.

61. Ibid.

62. Ibid.

63. Gerth and Risen, "1998 Report Told of Lab Breaches and China Threat."

64. Purdy, "The Prosecution Unravels."

65. Ibid.

66. Risen and Gerth, "Breach at Los Alamos."

67. The Foreign Intelligence Surveillance Act (1978) sets in place procedures for the FISA court to approve requests from the FBI to conduct physical and/or electronic surveillance of US persons and on US territory.

68. James Risen and Jeff Gerth, "China Spy Suspect Reportedly Tried to Hide Evidence," New York Times, April 30, 1999, http://www.nytimes.com/1999/04/30/world/china-spy-suspect-reportedly-tried-to-hide-evidence.html.

69. Gerth and Risen, "1998 Report Told of Lab Breaches and China Threat."

70. Purdy, "The Prosecution Unravels."

71. Risen and Gerth, "Breach at Los Alamos."

72. Gerth and Risen, "1998 Report Told of Lab Breaches and China Threat."

73. Risen and Gerth, "Breach at Los Alamos."

74. Purdy, "The Prosecution Unravels."

75. Gerth and Risen, "1998 Report Told of Lab Breaches and China Threat."

76. Purdy, "The Prosecution Unravels."

77. Ibid.

78. Ibid.

79. Ibid.

80. Risen and Gerth, "Breach at Los Alamos."

81. Ibid.

82. Ibid.

83. Ibid.

84. Ibid.

85. Purdy, "The Prosecution Unravels."

86. Risen and Garth. "1998 Report Told of Lab Breaches and China Threat."

87. Ibid.

88. Risen and Gerth, "US Says Suspect Put Code on Bombs in Unsecure Files."

89. Gerth and Risen, "1998 Report Told of Lab Breaches and China Threat."

90. Purdy, "The Prosecution Unravels."

91. Ibid.

92. James Risen, "Officials Describe Loss of Nuclear Secrets at Los Alamos," New York Times, December 12, 1999, http://www.nytimes.com/1999/12/12/us/officials-describe-loss-of-nuclear-secrets-at-los-alamos.html.

93. Purdy, "The Prosecution Unravels."

94. Ibid.

95. Janet Reno and Louis J. Freeh, "Excerpts from Testimony at Hearing on the Wen Ho Lee Case," New York Times, September 27, 2000, http://www.nytimes.com/2000/09/27/us/excerpts-from-testimony-at-hearing-on-the-wen-ho-lee-case.html.

96. Risen, "Officials Describe Loss of Nuclear Secrets at Los Alamos."

97. Purdy, "The Prosecution Unravels."

98. Risen, "Officials Describe Loss of Nuclear Secrets at Los Alamos."

99. Purdy, "The Prosecution Unravels: The Case of Wen Ho Lee."

100. Reno and Freeh, "Excerpts from Testimony at Hearing on the Wen Ho Lee Case."

101. Risen, "Officials Describe Loss of Nuclear Secrets at Los Alamos."

102. Reno and Freeh, "Excerpts from Testimony at Hearing on the Wen Ho Lee Case."

103. Ibid.

104. Purdy, "The Prosecution Unravels."

105. Johnston, "Suspect in Loss of Nuclear Secrets Unlikely to Face Spying Charges."

106. Purdy, "The Prosecution Unravels: The Case of Wen Ho Lee."

107. Risen, "Officials Describe Loss of Nuclear Secrets at Los Alamos."

108. David Johnston and James Risen, "The Los Alamos Secrets Case: The Overview; Nuclear Weapons Engineer Indicted in Removal of Data," *New York Times*, December 11, 1999, http://www.nytimes.com/1999/12/11/us/los-alamos-secrets-case-overview-nuclear-weapons-engineer-indicted-removal-data.html.

109. Risen and Gerth, "US Says Suspect Put Code on Bombs in Unsecure Files."

110. William J. Broad, "Files in Question in Los Alamos Case Were Reclassified," *New York Times*, April 15, 2000, http://www.nytimes.com/2000/04/15/us/files-in-question-in-los-alamos-case-were-reclassified.html.

111. Purdy, "The Prosecution Unravels."

112. Ibid.

113. Risen and Gerth, "Breach at Los Alamos."

114. William J. Broad, "Files in Question in Los Alamos Case Were Reclassified."

115. Purdy, "The Prosecution Unravels."

116. James Risen, "Los Alamos Scientist Admits Contacts with Chinese, US Says," *New York Times*, March 16, 1999, http://www.nytimes.com/1999/03/16/world/los-alamos-scientist-admits-contacts-with-chinese-us-says.html.

117. Risen and Gerth, "US Says Suspect Put Code on Bombs in Unsecure Files."

118. Purdy, "The Prosecution Unravels."

119. Risen and Gerth, "Breach at Los Alamos."

120. Purdy, "The Prosecution Unravels."

121. Risen and Gerth, "Breach at Los Alamos"

122. Johnston and Risen, "The Los Alamos Secrets Case: Overview, Nuclear Weapons Engineer Indicted."

123. Johnston, "Suspect in Loss of Nuclear Secrets Unlikely to Face Spying Charges."

124. Ibid.

125. James Risen, "Los Alamos Scientist Admits Contacts with Chinese, US Says."

126. Ibid.

127. Johnston and Risen, "The Los Alamos Secrets Case: Overview, Nuclear Weapons Engineer Indicted."

128. Broad, "Files in Question in Los Alamos Case Were Reclassified."

129. Sterngold, "US to Reduce Case against Scientist to a Single Charge."

130. Purdy, "The Prosecution Unravels."

131. The steps as outlined in this case combine the processes for a Premortem Analysis and Structured Self-Critique. This combination is particularly helpful in cases that require analysts to think broadly, imaginatively, and exhaustively about how they might have been wrong. The Premortem Analysis taps the creative brainstorming process, and the Structured Self-Critique provides a step-by-step assessment of each analytic element. To aid students' learning process, the questions in this case have already been narrowed from the fuller set of Structured Self-Critique questions found in Richards J. Heuer Jr. and Randolph H. Pherson, *Structured Analytic Techniques for Intelligence Analysis* (Washington, DC: CQ Press, 2011).

3 The Road to Tarin Kowt

CASE NARRATIVE

The route from Kandahar to Tarin Kowt rises out of the dusty and largely uninhabited Iranian plateau south of Kandahar and continues into the rocky foothills of the Hindu Kush, the central mountain range in Afghanistan. The topography and weather are inhospitable, if not brutal, and the dry and dusty region—often obscured by sudden *khahbad* (dust-winds)—becomes gravelly and boulder strewn as the foothills grow more mountainous near Tarin Kowt.

In 2004, the 117-kilometer route between these two provincial capitals was not much more than a dusty path through a known Taliban stronghold. International donor conferences had identified building road infrastructure as a critical element in efforts to stabilize, modernize, and democratize Afghanistan, so the United States had taken on the challenge of building a modern road along this centuries-old route. By April 2005, the US Army had completed 46.5 kilometers of road over a period of nine months.[1] With the road about a third complete and Afghanistan's first parliamentary elections since the overthrow of the Taliban announced for 18 September, the Army considered embarking on a highly accelerated schedule to complete the road in time for the election. Lt. Gen. Karl Eikenberry, who assumed command of the US Combined Forces Command Afghanistan in early May 2005, assessed the stakes involved in the project succinctly: "Wherever the road ends, that's where the Taliban starts."[2,3]

Completing another 70.5 kilometers of road in a mere five months not only would be a formidable engineering and logistical challenge but also would raise serious questions about mission security and engagement with the local population. The United States faced an important decision point that had

By the spring of 2005, US Army Engineers had completed 46.5 kilometers of road between Kandahar City in Kandahar Province and Tarin Kowt in Uruzgan Province.

major strategic, operational, and tactical implications. A sound course of action would require a thorough analysis of the operating environment, anticipated enemy response, and the potential impact on broader US goals for Afghanistan.

The Pashtun Way

The road from Kandahar to Tarin Kowt traverses a region that is heavily Pashtun—a predominantly Sunni Muslim group of some 40 million people concentrated in southern and eastern Afghanistan and neighboring parts of Pakistan. The Pashtun are the world's largest ethnicity lacking an independent state. The mostly agrarian society practices a stringent code of Pashtunwali—or "way of the Pashtun"—that provides a different set of social norms than those of central government or traditional tribal rule (see Table 3.1). Abjuring hierarchal leadership and formal courts and laws, Pashtunwali is built on complex traditions of individual independence, collective conflict-resolution mechanisms, and shared honor codes that guide all aspects of Pashtun life. The main tenets of Pashtunwali stress aspects of hospitality, bravery, and justice,

Table 3.1 ▶ Tenets of Pashtunwali

A Pashtun derives honor from practicing the following tenets of Pashtunwali:

To avenge blood.

To fight to the death for a person who has taken refuge with me no matter what his lineage.

To defend to the last any property entrusted to me.

To be hospitable and provide for the safety of the person and property of guests.

To refrain from killing a woman, a Hindu, a minstrel, or a boy not yet circumcised.

To pardon an offense on the intercession of a woman of the offender's lineage, a sayyid [Islamic chief], or a mullah [Islamic cleric].

To punish all adulterers to the death.

To refrain from killing a man who has entered a mosque or the shrine of a holy man so long as he remains within its precincts; also to spare a man in battle who begs for quarter.

Source: Louis Dupree, *Afghanistan*, Princeton, NJ: Princeton University Press, 1980, p. 126.

which means that "honor and hospitality, hostility and ambush, are paired in the Afghan mind."[4]

In Pashtun society, no adult male has the authority to tell another man what to do. Unlike the neighboring Baluchi ethnic group, whose *sardars* have many of the powers of a traditional tribal chief, "any sort of external direction is not merely abhorrent to Pashtuns, but lies beyond their mental compass."[5] In the absence of traditional tribal leadership, informal patronage networks have come to determine politics in Afghanistan's provincial regions. Whereas Pashtunwali and Islam are time honored, patronage networks are temporary constructs. Local patrons—*khans* or warlords—are not elected and do not hold any formal office. A warlord's power is based on his ability "to distribute resources to make a convincing case for his leadership."[6] As a result, the dynamics are unique to the network, reflecting shifts in local power relationships.[7]

Although all Pashtuns practice Pashtunwali, there are significant differences between those farming at lower elevations, who have historically been susceptible to taxation, and those living in the hills, who pride themselves on their social equality and freedom from any authority. For rural Pashtuns in the former group, day-to-day life centers around farming and subsistence living.[8] Their homes are principally mud, and they are sparsely decorated with essential cooking implements and mats for sleeping. They must serve as their own irrigation specialists, construction experts, veterinarians, and security force. Their survival depends on their ability to farm the land successfully, and they guard their land closely. Village Pashtuns view any outsider with great skepticism, which is shaped by a shared memory of battles against infidel invaders, but Pashtunwali obligates them to extend hospitality and temporary protection to all guests who seek it, even those they regard as enemies.[9] As a result, the village defends its ways by building a metaphorical "mud curtain"—a cultural defense mechanism that Pashtuns have developed over centuries of interactions with invaders, well-meaning central governments, and foreign "modernizers."[10] They quickly agree with outsiders and accept their projects, but only because the more quickly they do, the sooner the outsiders will leave and the villagers can return to their "old, group-reinforcing patterns."[11]

Kandahar and Uruzgan provinces are largely agrarian outside the major cities. Predominantly ethnic Pashtun inhabitants of the region practice a strict code of Pashtunwali that governs all aspects of daily life. Farmers must also serve as their own irrigation specialists in a region that can see both drought and flood in a single season.

For Pashtun hill society, "central government and externally imposed order are not simply anathema but the antithesis of what is good,"[12] and it passionately resists them. Insurgency in Afghanistan has typically arisen from this hill culture, driven less by economic deprivation than by deeply held cultural and religious norms. Moreover, the Pashtunwali code makes the attrition of Pashtun insurgents nearly impossible; the death in battle of a Pashtun guerrilla invokes an obligation of revenge among all his male relatives, making the killing of a guerrilla an act of insurgent multiplication, not subtraction. The Soviets learned this lesson, as they killed nearly a million Pashtuns but only increased the number of opposition fighters by the end of the war.[13] It was from this Pashtun hill culture that the Taliban arose.

Box 3.1 SOVIET LESSONS LEARNED

From 1979 until 1989, the Soviet Union fought a grueling war in Afghanistan. The Soviets invaded the country ostensibly to support the pro-Soviet communist leadership and to "stabilize the country."[i] They expected a quick and successful military operation, but the plan backfired in the face of significant resistance from US- and Pakistani-backed mujahidin, the Kabul regime's weak capacity for governance, and Afghanistan's unforgiving geography.[ii]

Soon after the invasion, the war "devolved into a fight for the control of the limited lines of communication, [specifically] the road network which connected the cities of Afghanistan with each other and to Pakistan and the Soviet Union."[iii] Despite the Soviets' massive influx of troops, which at the height of the war topped 100,000, the mujahidin became skilled at conducting ambushes on Afghanistan's road network. These disrupted Soviet supply lines and contributed to heavy personnel and equipment losses, including "11,389 trucks, 1314 armored personnel carriers, 147 tanks, [and] 433 artillery pieces."[iv] The mujahidin's weapons of choice against the convoys included "antitank, antipersonnel, and dummy mines, as well as controlled mines and improvised explosive charges."[v]

In the face of repeated losses, the Soviets eventually learned that for a convoy escort to have a chance at success, it needed dedicated security units with a rapid reaction capability; armored vehicles, armed with sufficient firepower and forces ready for ground combat; route reconnaissance units reinforced with ground forces to secure flanks and identify ambush sites; planned air and artillery support; engineers embedded with the convoys for route clearance; and operational security underpinned by unpredictability of movement.[vi]

Despite marginal improvements in convoy security, when Mikhail Gorbachev became general secretary of the Communist Party of the Soviet Union in 1985, it was becoming increasingly clear that victory was impossible, and Gorbachev soon made ending the conflict a top priority.

Box 3.1 SOVIET LESSONS LEARNED *(Continued)*

The result of the invasion, he later said, was "the opposite of what we had intended: even greater instability, a war with thousands of victims, and dangerous consequences for our own country. . . . The greatest mistake was failing to understand Afghanistan's complexity—its patchwork of ethnic groups, clans and tribes, its unique traditions and minimal governance."[vii] By the time of the Soviet withdrawal, the war had officially claimed 15,000 Soviet and 1 million Afghan lives, although many experts believe that the conflict took many more lives than officially reported.

---

i. Mikhail Gorbachev, "Soviet Lessons From Afghanistan," *New York Times,* February 4, 2010, http://www.nytimes.com/2010/02/05/opinion/05iht-edgor bachev.html.
ii. Ibid.
iii. Lester W. Grau, "Convoy Escort in Guerrilla Country: The Soviet Experience," *Military Police,* Winter 1995, http://fmso.leavenworth.army.mil/documents/convoy/convoy.htm.
iv. Ibid., "The Road War."
v. Graham H. Turbiville Jr., "Soviet Combat Engineers in Afghanistan: Old Lessons and Future Wars," *Military Engineer* 80, no. 524 (1988), "Mine Clearing and Movement Support," http://fmso.leavenworth.army.mil/documents/sovcombat/sovcombat.HTM.
vi. Ibid.
vii. Gorbachev, "Soviet Lessons From Afghanistan."

"Land of the Unruly"

Afghanistan's Amir Abdur Rahman Khan (1840 or 1844–1901) famously called his country the "Land of the Unruly." This was certainly an apt description of the Kandahar region in 2004, when it was the hotbed of a formidable Taliban insurgency focused on destroying the central Afghan administration and driving out the US and NATO presence.[14] The Taliban had its origins in the brutal civil war among rival warlords and their militias that followed the Soviet withdrawal in 1989, which devastated the country and destroyed what was left of the traditional tribal leadership system. With funding from Saudi Arabia and support from Pakistan's Inter-Services Intelligence Directorate (ISID), the Taliban emerged from madrassas (Islamic religious schools) near Ghazni and Kandahar in Afghanistan and in Pakistan's North-West Frontier Province (NWFP) and federally administered tribal area (FATA). It arrived on the Afghan scene in 1994 with little warning and vowed to install a traditional Islamic government and end the fighting among rival militias. With massive covert assistance from Pakistan, it overthrew the largely Tajik (and northern) regime in Kabul, capturing the capital in September 1996, in part by using "stunningly effective use of the roadways . . . to move forces faster and strike quicker."[15] War-weary Afghans initially welcomed the Taliban, but Afghanistan soon became a training ground for Islamic activists and other radicals from the Middle East and around Asia. The country's optimism turned to fear as the Taliban introduced a stringent interpretation of Islamic law, banned women from work, and introduced such punishments as death by stoning and amputations.[16]

By the time the United States drove the Taliban from Kabul in late 2001, the Taliban's popularity in the country had waned considerably, but by most accounts it retained significant support in Kandahar and other parts of the Pashtun belt. This support was particularly strong among the Taliban's core of Ghilzai Pashtuns, longtime rivals of the nationalist and more moderate Durrani Pashtuns.[17] Afghan President Karzai is a Durrani Pashtun. Support for the Taliban was high among the rural Pashtun population, and ethnic Pashtuns comprised a large percentage of the Taliban ranks; to extend its control, the

Map 3.1 ▶ Pashtun Tribal Areas and Insurgent Strongholds

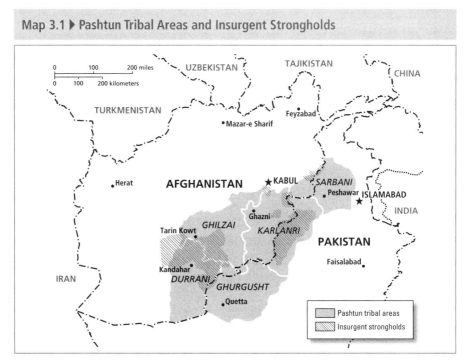

As of 2005, the area between Kandahar City and Tarin Kowt was an insurgent stronghold.

Source: Pashtun Tribal Areas and Key Insurgent Strongholds, 2006, Figure 1, p. 77 in "Understanding the Taliban and Insurgency in Afghanistan," http://www.nps.edu/programs/ccs/docs/pubs/understanding%20the%20taliban%20and%20insurgency%20in%20afghanistan.pdf. Reproduced with permission from Thomas H. Johnson and M. Chris Mason.

Taliban played on the people's distrust of the cities, frustration with government corruption that disrupts basic services, and fear of foreigners.[18,19] By 2004, the Taliban had regrouped and refocused its efforts on utilizing guerrilla warfare to rid Afghanistan of all US and NATO military forces. The Taliban's resurgence paralleled the Karzai government's struggles to establish a firm and legitimate foundation. The Kabul government was plagued by a weak capacity for governance, inexperience, corruption, and an almost complete lack of presence in rural areas outside of the provincial capitals. US and NATO forces were able to do little to provide long-term security for those communities where the Taliban contested the power of village elders and warlords through coercion, intimidation, and assassination.[20]

Inroads with the People

The Soviet Union and the United States built most of Afghanistan's asphalt road infrastructure in the late 1950s and early 1960s as part of their foreign aid initiatives. Soviet and US aid supported the first two of Afghanistan's Five-Year Plans, which emphasized the creation of transportation and telecommunications infrastructure as means of improving the central government's connections with the people and its efforts to build a nation.[21] During this period, foreign aid poured into Afghanistan and resulted in "one of the better road systems in Central Asia."[22] The aid built most of the existing portions of the Ring Road, which connects several of the provincial capitals to Kabul, and resulted in the famous Salang Tunnel that cuts directly through the Hindu Kush, a subrange of the Himalayas between central Afghanistan and northern Pakistan.

But by 2001, after decades of war and neglect, Afghanistan's roads were in disrepair, if not sharp decline. Only 16 percent of Afghanistan's roads were paved, and key communications and commerce links between many of Afghanistan's provincial capitals did not exist.[23] To address this problem, the government of Afghanistan and international donors agreed in 2003 on a building and repair program for the country's road network, including completion of the Ring Road and construction of radial spokes from the ring to Afghanistan's outer provinces, in order to "spur economic development, promote governance, and improve security."[24] The donors pledged billions of dollars to build Afghanistan's road infrastructure, and as of 2004, many international partners had begun construction on various roads. Leading the effort for the United States was the US Agency for International Development (USAID), along with the Department of Defense. In some cases, USAID paid contractors to build entire roads and, in other cases, to provide the finishing work—mostly paving—that USAID or the US Army could not complete itself.

One of the complicating factors in the road construction initiative was that Afghanistan's government, although ostensibly committed to upgrading roads, lacked clear legal delineation of roles and responsibilities among its various ministries and other organizations for managing and overseeing this work (see Table 3.2). As a result, there were redundancies in some areas—fee collecting, for example—and vacuums in others, such as maintenance.[25] Furthermore, the Afghan government faced "significant human and financial constraints" that limited its ability to develop and carry out a plan to maintain the roads.[26] Ensuring road security was another complicating factor, given the lack of effective state oversight. The roads were simultaneously an important part of the international community's efforts to stabilize the country, the central government's efforts to deliver services to and cultivate relations with the people, and the Taliban's efforts to undo government ties with the people.[27]

Table 3.2 ▶ Afghan Ministries with Responsibilities for Roads, 2004–2005	
Ministry	Road-Related Function
Public Works	Manages construction and maintenance for regional and national highways and most provincial roads.
Rural Rehabilitation and Development	Manages construction of rural infrastructure, including rural roads and some provincial roads.
Transportation and Civil Aviation	Inspects and issues commercial transit permits and collects fees from all domestic and international commercial vehicles.
Finance	Collects road tolls on major highways.
Interior	Manages registration and collection of fees for commercial and private vehicles, safety inspections, and traffic control.
Commerce	Collects transit fees and can also charge a penalty for loads in excess of authorized limits.
Foreign Affairs	Issues transit permits to foreign commercial vehicles entering and exiting Afghanistan.
Economy	Conducts baseline studies for infrastructure projects. Its donor-supported unit currently is also responsible for all government procurement of goods and services, including road maintenance over $200,000.
Afghanistan Security Force	Responsible for ensuring security of roads but often delegates this role to local police and contract militia.

Source: This chart is largely taken from the USAID information cited in the US Government Accountability Office report *Afghanistan Reconstruction Progress Made in Constructing Roads, but Assessments for Determining Impact and a Sustainable Maintenance Program Are Needed,* GAO-08-689, July 2008, 34, with the exception of the additional line on the Afghanistan National Security Force.

Task Force Pacemaker

Building a road through rough terrain is difficult enough, but building a road in a war zone presents unique and dangerous challenges. The Department of Defense funded the road project via the Commanders' Emergency Relief Fund and tasked the US Army Corp of Engineers with the project (USACE).[28] Between July 2004 and February 2005, the 528th Engineer Battalion of the Louisiana National Guard completed 46.5 km of the road from Kandahar City heading north toward Tarin Kowt. In March 2005, the 528th Engineers returned home, and the 864th Engineer Battalion from Fort Lewis, Washington, was poised to complete the road.

USACE has a long history of combat and reconstruction operations, and as a result, the 864th was equipped with an abundance of earth-moving heavy equipment, such as bulldozers, graders, and dump trucks; construction personnel, from land surveyors to construction designers and planners; additional combat engineers trained to clear minefields and find hidden improvised explosive devices (IEDs); and additional maintenance personnel and repair assets to assist with the vehicles and equipment. The 864th would be operating in the most demanding of environments: at high altitude under a desert sun and working with fine, sticky, clay-based sand. This conglomeration of Army engineer units became known as Task Force Pacemaker.[29]

Map 3.2 ▶ Route between Kandahar and Tarin Kowt

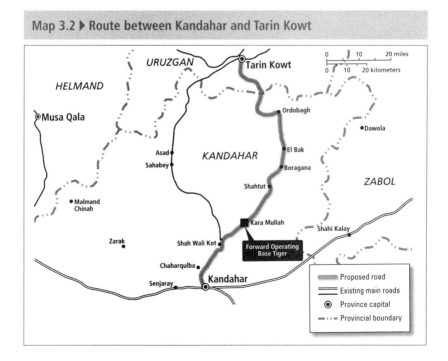

The engineers would have to step up the pace of road building if they were to complete another 70.5 kilometers in only five months. The Army usually builds roads efficiently but at a pace of a few hundred meters a day. Doing so involves a multistep, mostly sequential process of route planning, surveying, ensuring job site security, sustaining the flow of materiel and water, and maintaining the heavy engineering equipment. To ensure the final integrity of the road, the engineers begin by using dozers to clear grub and remove topsoil, including brush and small hills. Graders level the path to create a suitable foundation. The engineers scout the area to find a source of appropriate subbase material. Once this is located, they send the candidate material away for content analysis by a contracting company. If the material is suitable, dump trucks and scrapers use this "borrow pit" to harvest material that they use to build up an eight- to twelve-inch subbase on the leveled foundation. This material is so important that engineers will opt to continue use of a good borrow pit even if it is a long distance from the job site, sometimes up to five kilometers away. Graders subsequently create a crown in the center of the road to aid water runoff. A finishing crew uses water trucks to douse the road, and rollers compact the soil. Finding sources of water is just as important as finding good subbase materials, because it is this last step that molds the dust into a road.[30]

Translating these procedures to the Kandahar–Tarin Kowt corridor on an accelerated schedule would pose particular problems. In addition to issues surrounding survey, materials, maintenance, and water, job site security would be a continual challenge. Regional conditions meant that dust clouds would billow upward as the engineers worked, signaling the engineers' presence and making them a static and easily visible target. Although the units would have embedded combat engineers, the long, ninety-minute convoys to and from the job site required by an accelerated schedule would run counter to the engineers' training in operational security, which calls for the use of varied routes and times. During work, the engineers would have to halt and search all traffic along the route, which would take precious time and resources away from the construction effort and would pose cultural challenges if Afghan women had to be searched.[31] Moreover, such searches would not address the threat posed by insurgents who dotted the surrounding hills and whom the engineers themselves could not flush out.

Despite these challenges, the US Army was leaning heavily toward adopting the accelerated schedule for Taskforce Pacemaker in April 2005. Construction on the road had proceeded so far without incident amid the difficult conditions and security risks, and the road could provide an important supply link to US and NATO forces in Uruzgan. Ultimately, victory in Afghanistan depended on demonstrating to its people that the US-backed government was improving their lives in tangible ways, and few projects had greater visibility than modern road systems, where "every cut is a blow to the primary weapons of the Taliban—isolation and hardship."[32] The road would bring clear commercial benefits to a region heavily dependent on imported goods, and in turn these benefits could generate more and more support for the Afghan government. Moreover, a rapid success could deal a critical psychological blow to the insurgents, showing the region what the United States could accomplish inside the Taliban's heartland on the eve of critically important legislative elections. The potential impact of the project was not lost on anyone: it promised to be, as one US Army engineer put it, "not just an engineering feat . . . [but] a show of political force."[33]

RECOMMENDED READING

Dupree, Louis. *Afghanistan*. Princeton, NJ: Princeton University Press, 1980.

Table 3.3 ▶ Case Snapshot: The Road to Tarin Kowt		
Structured Analytic Technique Used	Heuer and Pherson Page Number	Analytic Family
Key Assumptions Check	p. 183	Assessment of Cause and Effect
Devil's Advocacy	p. 240	Challenge Analysis
Strengths-Weaknesses-Opportunities-Threats	p. 288	Decision Support

THE ROAD TO TARIN KOWT
STRUCTURED ANALYTIC TECHNIQUES IN ACTION

The goal of a Red Team analysis is to minimize surprise by encouraging divergent, open-minded thinking. This approach can be applied to "exercises, experiments, planning, and strategy."[34] A Red Team in its broadest definition challenges conventional wisdom by checking assumptions; encouraging devil's advocacy; and modeling adversaries' behaviors at the strategic, operational, and tactical levels.[35] The exact techniques used in a successful Red Team analysis can vary based on such factors as the type of decision or issue at hand, the length of time available to conduct the analysis, and the expertise of the analysts. What is most important is choosing techniques that thoroughly challenge a course of action in order to reveal and redress risks and increase the chances of success.

In this case, the 18 September 2005 Afghan National Assembly election is driving a decision about whether to accelerate construction of the road from Kandahar city to Tarin Kowt. The use of a Key Assumptions Check; Devil's Advocacy; and Strengths-Weaknesses-Opportunities-Threats (SWOT) analysis can help analysts view the elements of the decision through a variety of prisms to troubleshoot the intended course of action and thereby produce more effective policy results.

Technique 1: Key Assumptions Check

The Key Assumptions Check is a systematic effort to make explicit and question the assumptions that guide an analyst's interpretation of evidence and reasoning about any particular problem. Assumptions are usually a necessary and unavoidable means of filling gaps in the incomplete, ambiguous, and sometimes deceptive information with which the analyst must work. They are driven by the analyst's education, training, and experience, including the cultural and organizational contexts in which the analyst lives and works. It can be difficult to identify assumptions, because many are sociocultural beliefs that are unconsciously or so firmly held that they are assumed to be truth and not subject to challenge. Nonetheless, identifying key assumptions and assessing the overall impact should they be invalid are critical parts of a robust analytic process.

Task 1. Conduct a Key Assumptions Check of the following issue: The United States is leaning toward making a decision to complete the road from Kandahar to Tarin Kowt in time for the 18 September National Assembly elections as part of its broader goals to "spur economic development, promote central governance, and improve security."

STEP 1: Gather a small group of individuals who are working on the issue along with a few "outsiders." The primary analytic unit already is working from an established mental model, so the "outsiders" are needed to bring other perspectives.

STEP 2: Ideally, participants should be asked to bring a list of assumptions when they come to the meeting. If not, start the meeting with a silent brainstorming session. Ask each participant to write down several assumptions on 3-by-5-inch cards.

STEP 3: Collect the cards and list the assumptions on a whiteboard for all to see. A simple template can be used, as in Table 3.4.

Table 3.4 ▶ Key Assumptions Check Template				
Key Assumption	Commentary	Supported	With Caveat	Unsupported

STEP 4: Elicit additional assumptions. Work from the prevailing analytic line back to the key arguments that support it. Use various devices to help prod participants' thinking. Ask the standard journalistic questions: Who? What? When? Where? Why? and How?

Phrases such as "will always," "will never," or "would have to be" suggest that an idea is not being challenged and perhaps should be. Phrases such as "based on" or "generally the case" usually suggest that a challengeable assumption is being made.

STEP 5: After identifying a full set of assumptions, critically examine each assumption. Ask:

▶ Why am I confident that this assumption is correct?

▶ In what circumstances might this assumption be untrue?

▶ Could it have been true in the past but no longer be true today?

▶ How much confidence do I have that this assumption is valid?

▶ If the assumption turns out to be invalid, how much impact would this have on the analysis?

STEP 6: Using Table 3.4, place each assumption in one of three categories:

1. Basically supported.
2. Correct with some caveats.
3. Unsupported or questionable—the "key uncertainties."

STEP 7: Refine the list, deleting those assumptions that do not hold up to scrutiny and adding new assumptions that emerge from the discussion.

STEP 8: Consider whether key uncertainties should be converted into collection requirements or research topics.

Analytic Value Added. What impact could unsupported assumptions have on the decision to build the road? How confident should military decision makers be that the benefits of building the road will outweigh the risks?

Technique 2: Devil's Advocacy

Devil's Advocacy can be used to critique a proposed analytic judgment, plan, or decision. Devil's Advocacy is often used before a final decision is made, when a military commander or policy maker asks for an analysis of what could go wrong. The Devil's Advocate builds the strongest possible case against the proposed decision and its prospect for achieving its broader goals, often by examining critical assumptions and sources of uncertainty, among other issues.

Task 2. Build the strongest possible case against the United States' pending decision to build the road from Kandahar to Tarin Kowt before the election.

STEPS: Although there is no prescribed procedure for a Devil's Advocacy, begin with the strategic goals of the project, assumptions, and gaps. These can serve as a useful starting point from which to build the case against the road project. Next, build a logical argument that undermines each goal.

Analytic Value Added. Which issues could undermine the goals of the project, and why?

Technique 3: Strengths-Weaknesses-Opportunities-Threats (SWOT)
SWOT can be used to evaluate a goal or objective by providing a framework for organizing and collecting data for strategic planning. SWOT is designed to illuminate areas for further exploration and more detailed planning, and therefore it is typically an early step in a robust policy process. SWOT analysis can also be an important part of troubleshooting a policy option and identifying specific actions that may improve the chances of success.

Task 3. Conduct a SWOT analysis of the pending decision to spur economic development, promote central governance, and improve security in the region by building a road connecting Kandahar City to Tarin Kowt prior to the September election.

STEP 1: Clearly define the objective.

STEP 2: Fill in Table 3.5 by listing the Strengths, Weaknesses, Opportunities, and Threats that are expected to facilitate or hinder achievement of the objective.

Table 3.5 ▶ SWOT Template	
US Strengths	**US Weaknesses**
1.	1.
2.	2.
3.	3.
Opportunities for the US	**Threats to the US**
1.	1.
2.	2.
3.	3.

STEP 3: Identify possible strategies for achieving the objective by asking:

> ▶ How can we use each Strength?
> ▶ How can we improve each Weakness?
> ▶ How can we exploit each Opportunity?
> ▶ How can we mitigate each Threat?

Fill in Table 3.6 with your strategies.

Table 3.6 ▶ SWOT Second-Stage Analysis Template	
Use Strengths	**Improve Weaknesses**
1.	1.
2.	2.
3.	3.
Exploit Opportunities	**Mitigate Threats**
1.	1.
2.	2.
3.	3.

Analytic Value Added. What steps should the US Army take to prepare for road construction?

NOTES

1. Laura M. Walker, "Task Force Pacemaker Constructing a Road to Democracy," *Army Engineer*, September–October 2005, p. 19.

2. Vincent C. Fusco, "Eikenberry Takes Command of Coalition Forces in Afghanistan," American Forces Press Service, May 4, 2005, http://osd.dtic.mil/news/May2005/20050504_881.html.

3. Karl F. Inderfurth, "Afghanistan's Good News: Seeds of Economic Progress," *Christian Science Monitor*, September 29, 2005, http://www.csmonitor.com/2006/0929/p09s01-coop.html.

4. Louis Dupree, *Afghanistan*, Princeton, NJ: Princeton University Press, 1980, 127.

5. Thomas H. Johnson and M. Chris Mason, "No Sign of Burst Until the Fire," *International Security* 32, no. 4 (2008): 62.

6. US Army, "My Cousin's Enemy Is My Friend: A Study of Pashtun 'Tribes' in Afghanistan," Afghanistan Research Reachback Center White Paper, TRADOC G2

Human Terrain System, Fort Leavenworth, KS: US Army, 2009, 14. Available at http://smallwarsjournal.com/documents/cousinsenemy.pdf.

7. Ibid.

8. Dupree, *Afghanistan.*

9. Gilles Dorronsoro, "The Taliban's Winning Strategy in Afghanistan," Washington, DC: Carnegie Endowment for International Peace, 2009, http://www.carnegieendowment.org/files/taliban_winning_strategy.pdf.

10. Dupree, *Afghanistan,* 249.

11. Ibid.

12. Johnson and Mason, "No Sign of Burst Until the Fire," 55.

13. Thomas H. Johnson and M. Chris Mason, "Understanding the Taliban and Insurgency in Afghanistan," *Orbis* 51, no. 1 (2007): 88.

14. Dorronsoro, "The Taliban's Winning Strategy in Afghanistan."

15. Matthew Nasuti, "The Ring Road: A Gift Afghanistan Cannot Afford," *Kabul Press*, September 29, 2009, http://kabulpress.org/my/spip.php?article4093.

16. Johnson and Mason, "Understanding the Taliban and Insurgency in Afghanistan," 74.

17. Ibid., 71–89.

18. Dorronsoro, "The Taliban's Winning Strategy in Afghanistan."

19. Greg Mills, "Kandahar Through the Taliban's Eyes," *Foreign Policy*, May 27, 2010, http://www.foreignpolicy.com/articles/2010/05/27/kandahar_through_the_talibans_eyes/.

20. Johnson and Mason, "Understanding the Taliban and Insurgency in Afghanistan."

21. Dupree, *Afghanistan.*

22. Ibid., 644.

23. US Government Accountability Office, *Afghanistan Reconstruction Progress Made in Constructing Roads, but Assessments for Determining Impact and a Sustainable Maintenance Program Are Needed* (GAO-08–689), July 8, 2008, 5. Available at http://www.gao.gov/products/GAO-08–689/.

24. Ibid.

25. Ibid.

26. Ibid., 4.

27. Dorronsoro, "The Taliban's Winning Strategy in Afghanistan."

28. US Government Accountability Office, *Afghanistan Reconstruction Progress Made in Constructing Roads*, 11.

29. Walker, "Task Force Pacemaker Constructing a Road to Democracy," 20–24.

30. Ibid.

31. Ibid., 24.

32. Ibid.

33. Ibid., 24.

34. Defense Science Board, *Report of the Defense Science Board 2008 Summer Study on Capability Surprise. Volume I: Main Report*, Washington, DC: Office of the Under Secretary of Defense for Acquisition, Technology, and Logistics, 2009. Available at http://www.acq.osd.mil/dsb/reports/ADA506396.pdf.

35. Defense Science Board, *Defense Science Board Task Force on the Role and Status of DoD Red Teaming Activities*, Washington, DC: Office of the Under Secretary of Defense for Acquisition, Technology, and Logistics, 2003. Available at http://www.fas.org/irp/agency/dod/dsb/redteam.pdf.

4 Who Murdered Jonathan Luna?

CASE NARRATIVE

Jonathan Luna was an energetic and affable federal prosecutor whose death in December 2003 shocked his friends and colleagues. Luna's story is one of professional and personal success; by the time of his death in 2003, he had risen from his modest roots in New York to become an assistant US attorney in Baltimore, Maryland, near which he lived with his wife and two small children. But in the early hours of 4 December 2003, Luna's body—riddled with thirty-six stab wounds—was found facedown in a creek in rural Lancaster County, Pennsylvania, his car still idling nearby. A multiyear, multistate investigation ensued, the public details of which ignited controversy about just how and why Jonathan Luna died.

The Investigation Begins
Upon finding Luna's badly beaten and stabbed body, state and federal authorities immediately opened an investigation and fanned out across the region in the hope of tracking down clues that might lead them to the killer.

Investigators combed the area off the two-lane Dry Tavern Road near Denver, Pennsylvania, where a Sensening & Weaver employee had found Luna's car at about 0530 on 4 December 2003.[1,2] The rural area is about a mile off the Pennsylvania Turnpike and about seventy miles northeast of Baltimore.[3] Authorities arriving at the scene found Luna's 2003 Honda Accord nose down in a creek and still idling.[4] On the exterior of the car, blood was smeared on the driver's side door and left front fender.[5] Inside the vehicle,

Map 4.1 ▶ Jonathan Luna's Home, Work, and Location of Body

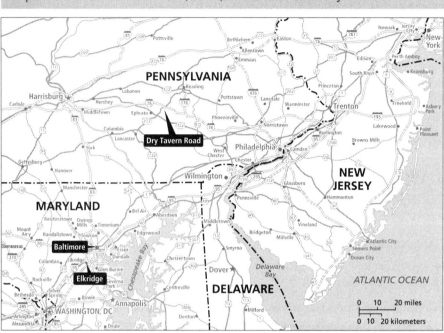

Jonathan Luna's home in Elkridge was not far from his workplace at the US District Courthouse in Baltimore. His body was found lying facedown in a creek off of Dry Tavern Road near Denver, Pennsylvania.

money and cell phone equipment were scattered throughout, and a large pool of blood had accumulated on the right rear floor.[6] Luna's body lay nearby, facedown in the creek.[7]

Within the first 48 hours, more than 100 police cadets searched the surounding area for clues, and details began to emerge about the cause of death.[8] Lancaster County coroner Dr. Barry Walp said that Luna was found fully clothed in his suit, shirt and tie, overcoat, socks, and shoes, along with his wallet, cash, and work identification badge.[9,10] A Pennsylvania State Police affadavit quoted in press reports indicated that Luna had suffered a "traumatic wound to the right side of his head," while other press reports citing a federal law enforcement source said that some of Luna's thirty-six stab wounds were defensive in nature.[11] Walp, however, said he did not observe any defensive wounds during the autopsy and that Luna's wounds were in the neck and upper chest.[12] Although investigators found no weapon at the scene, they said

that Luna's wounds were consistent with a small   FBI photo of Jonathan
blade, possibly a penknife.[13] There were also signs he   Luna's car.
had been restrained and had sustained injuries to his genitals, according to law
enforcement sources.[14] Ultimately, Walp assessed that Luna had died from
drowning.[15]

In Baltimore, federal authorities descended upon the US District Courthouse, where building records indicated Luna had been present as late as 2330
the night before.[16] They immediately began to comb through Luna's work files,
and they spoke with his colleagues and family members as they tried to piece
together his last hours.

The FBI, along with Luna's boss, US Attorney Thomas M. DiBiagio, held a
press conference in which they vowed to find and "bring those responsible for
this tragedy to justice."[17] They declined to cite possible motives or suspects, but
initial press reports noted the curious timing of his death; Luna was scheduled
to be in court as lead prosecutor in the trial of two allegedly violent drug traffickers on the morning his body was found, and he had been working on the
plea bargain at the courthouse the night of his death.[18]

An Impressive Rise

Jonathan Luna ascended from a less than privileged upbringing in the rough
Mott Haven neighborhood in the Bronx, New York, where he lived with his
parents, Paul and Rosezella Luna, and his brother David. In a 1991 letter to the
New York Times, Luna defended his neighborhood and praised his parents'
tenacity and hard work, saying, "You and your readers should know that there

FBI photo of Jonathan Luna.

are decent, hard-working people like my parents who are struggling every day to make a life for themselves and their families in Mott Haven."[19]

He went on to beat the odds by attending Fordham University and the University of North Carolina Law School, where he served as class president and graduated in 1992.[20] After law school, he worked as a staff attorney with the Federal Trade Commission in Washington, D.C., and as an assistant district attorney in Brooklyn, New York.[21] In 1999 he landed a job in the US Attorney's Office in Baltimore, Maryland. Then US Attorney Lynne Battaglia hired him for the job and shortly after his death remembered the "excitement and idealism" he brought to her office.[22]

At the time of his death, the 38-year-old prosecutor lived with his wife and two young sons in Elkridge, Maryland, about ten miles from his office at the Federal District Court Building in Baltimore. According to family members, who described the pair as "the perfect couple," they doted on their two young sons.[23] Luna's parents remember him as a loving father, husband, and son who helped support them and visited them every week with his children.[24] Immediately following his death, the family issued a statement expressing shock, deep grief, and sadness; his parents said that they believed his death was related to his work prosecuting violent criminals.[25,26]

A Likely Victim?

Luna's work for the US Attorney's office often put him in contact with the region's more unsavory characters. Over the twelve months prior to his death, Luna had prosecuted cases involving prostitution, child stalkers, bank robbers, and violent drug offenders. In one high-profile case, he prosecuted a US Navy physicist who allegedly used the Internet to seek out underage girls for sexual encounters. He also won convictions in a case involving a series of violent bank robberies across Baltimore.[27]

On the morning of 3 December, Luna was in the midst of prosecuting Baltimore-based rap musician Deon Lionnel Smith and his associate, Walter Oriley Poindexter, on conspiracy charges involving the use of their Stash House Records studio to operate a violent drug ring and distribute heroin.[28] The day had not started well. Luna was late to court for the third day of the trial, citing a late-night trip to the hospital with a sick child. Judge William Quarles admonished him and fined him $25.[29] Next, a key witness who was an FBI informant with a criminal past changed his story on the stand.[30] In the face of this setback, Luna worked with defense attorneys to reach a deal. Late in the day on 3 December, Poindexter agreed to plead guilty to three counts of the lesser crime of heroin distribution, and Smith agreed to plead guilty to one count each of heroin distribution and possessing a firearm during a drug transaction.[31] Luna agreed to drop the conspiracy charges and not to raise evidence at sentencing that linked Poindexter to a fatal shooting.[32]

Smith's attorney, Kenneth Ravenell, told reporters that he saw Luna at the courthouse at 1730 shortly after negotiating the plea agreement.[33] Ravenell dismissed the possibility of Smith's involvement in Luna's death, pointing out that Smith and Poindexter remained in jail at the time of the murder, and said it would be "just silly of these men to have been involved in this murder because they got what they wanted from their plea.[34,35] Poindexter's attorney, Arcangelo Tuminelli, said that he received a call from Luna around 2100; he said Luna told him he was returning to the office to finish paperwork for the plea agreement and would try to fax the agreements to both defendants' lawyers by morning.[36] Tuminelli said that it was "implausible" that either defendant would have wanted to harm Luna since they had "every incentive to want to see Jonathan Luna show up [at court] today" to enter the plea agreement.[37] In fact, Luna himself had urged reporters that evening to be on time the next morning.[38]

Upon hearing of Luna's death, Judge Quarles noted that "prosecutors have two sources of danger in their lives—they are subject to any random act of violence, just like the rest of us, and they are targets to people who have grudges against them. When any prosecutor dies, you can't exclude either possibility."[39]

Piecing Together Luna's Final Hours

Authorities zeroed in on Luna's work, investigating the possibility that he may have been killed in connection with the case.[40,41] FBI agents were waiting outside the courtroom on 4 December to question Poindexter's and Smith's family members.[42] But law enforcement sources quickly pointed out that they were also examining a range of non-work-related scenarios. A joint task force of state and federal authorities worked over the ensuing weeks and months to compile a clearer picture of Luna's movements during his final hours. Their work revealed the following:

Sometime after 2300 on 3 December Luna received a cell phone call and told his wife he had to return to the office.[43] He left home shortly thereafter. Police officers searched his office on the morning of 4 December found his office lights and computer on, with the half-finished plea bargain on the screen. His glasses and cell phone were on his desk.[44] Building records indicate that Luna's car left the courthouse parking garage at 2338.[45]

Luna's car, equipped with an electronic toll payment transmitter, E-ZPass, headed northbound on Interstate 95 and passed through the Fort McHenry Tunnel toll gate at 2349.[46] The car, still traveling northbound, passed through the Perryville, Maryland, toll plaza at 0028 and the Delaware Line toll plaza at 0046.[47]

Luna's debit card was used at the JFK Plaza in Newark, Delaware, at 0057[48] to make a $200 ATM withdrawal, but security cameras did not capture that transaction.[49,50] At approximately 0237 the car entered the New Jersey turnpike at Exit 6A from Route 130.[51] Tolls on that section of the turnpike are only taken westbound (New Jersey to Pennsylvania), so there is no electronic record of the car crossing from Delaware to New Jersey or from New Jersey to Pennsylvania.

At 0247, Luna's car entered the Pennsylvania Turnpike at Exit 359, the Delaware River Bridge.[52] It then exited the Pennsylvania Turnpike and reentered, picking up a paper toll ticket rather than passing through the E-ZPass lane.[53]

At 0320, Luna's credit card was used at a Sunoco gas station along the Pennsylvania Turnpike in King of Prussia, Pennsylvania, in the western suburbs of the metropolitan Philadelphia area.[54,55] Employees at the Sunoco Station said he bought gasoline for two cars, two sodas, and a bottle of water, but authorities found no sign of him on the grainy video surveillance tapes, and investigators said they were "about 99 percent sure" there was not a second car traveling with him, according to a law enforcement source.[56,57,58] Another employee said he had seen Luna at about 0300 when he purchased drinks, saying Luna did not appear to be under any duress and "was just very calm. He must have been with people, but I don't think he knew they were going to kill him."[59]

A Roy Rogers Restaurant manager at a rest stop in Elverson, Pennsylvania, thirty miles west, said she saw Luna there before 0330.[60] She said that she remembered that he looked like television host Bryant Gumbel.[61] She did not recall seeing anyone else with him.[62] The FBI would not comment on the report.[63]

Twenty miles and two exits west of Elverson, Luna's vehicle exited the Pennsylvania Turnpike at the Reading-Lancaster interchange, Exit 286, near Ephrata, Pennsylvania, at 0404.[64] The driver handed over a paper ticket rather than use the E-ZPass lane.[65]

At 0530, Luna's body was discovered off Dry Tavern Road in Lancaster County, Pennsylvania, after a Sensening and Weaver employee reported an unknown car on company property, its engine still idling.[66]

According to Dr. Walp, Luna was alive when he arrived at the scene and died of freshwater drowning. Walp classified the death a homicide.[67]

Questions Arise

As authorities combed the scene of the crime, Luna's workplace, and Luna's home; interviewed his friends, family, and coworkers; and tracked down hundreds of possible leads, they began to uncover information that raised important questions about Luna's life and work.

Luna's financial records revealed that he had financial problems, some of which he had kept from his wife. He had run up $25,000 in credit card debt on as many as sixteen credit cards, which prompted investigators to reopen an investigation into the unsolved disappearance of $36,000 used as evidence in a bank robbery that Luna had prosecuted in 2002.[68,69,70] An online loan application Luna filled out at about the time of that trial intrigued investigators.[71] They found that Luna had applied for a loan of about $30,000 but canceled the application not long after the evidence money went missing.[72]

Luna's computer data revealed another set of questions. Although Luna's caseload included the prosecution of online child pornography and child predators, a law enforcement official said federal agents found adult pornographic files on Luna's Justice Department computer that appeared unrelated to his caseload.[73] They also examined his relationships with two women and, separately, uncovered messages posted by a Jonathan Luna on an online dating Web site.[74] In one post, the individual posting as Jonathan Luna said he was a 31-year-old black male seeking a white, preferably blonde or redheaded female, for sexual encounters.[75]

Authorities also discovered that Luna had made frequent trips to the Philadelphia area, often at odd hours. A gas station employee on the Pennsylvania Turnpike said she saw Luna at the station late at night about once a month over a six-month period.[76] Luna's father told authorities that Luna had traveled to the Philadelphia area several times in the month preceding his death. Paul Luna said his son even canceled a Thanksgiving weekend trip to New York City in order to travel to Pennsylvania for work.[77] Luna's colleagues dismissed the possibility that Luna could have been engaged in indiscriminate activities on such trips, pointing out that Luna went to Philadelphia several times to interview the key witness in the case of Smith and Poindexter, who were being detained there.[78]

In addition to investigating possible financial problems and allegedly indiscriminate personal behavior, authorities pursued information that Luna's work situation was apparently suffering as well. Several friends and colleagues said that Luna had told them he felt that his job was in peril and that his relationship with his supervisors in the US Attorney's office was eroding. He told one friend that he feared he would need to look for a new job.[79] US Attorney DiBiagio, however, rejected any suggestion that Luna was at risk of being fired, saying "his job was not in jeopardy in any respect."[80] Instead, DeBiagio lauded Luna's prosecution of a rare pornography-production case and noted that Luna had not expressed concerns about his job security at an employee review meeting in June.[81]

New Information Emerges

As the investigation continued, evidence emerged that apparently led investigators to consider a range of alternative motives and suspects. Authorities refused in the initial months of the investigation to comment on possible suspects, but law enforcement sources did state that "since his death, investigators have addressed and covered over 1,000 leads, including neighborhood canvasses, physical searches, review of financial and telephone records, [E-ZPass] travel information, and the analysis of over 10 [gigabytes] of computer data."[82]

Although they refused to release the autopsy report, some law enforcement sources said that injuries to Luna's genitals suggested a "highly personal" motive behind the crime.[83] Also, the fact that he left both his cell phone and his eyeglasses in his office on the night of his murder led investigators to speculate that Luna may have known his attacker.[84] However, Dr. Walp said Luna had a number of shallow "prick" marks on his chest and neck in addition to several deeper, more serious stab wounds. Press reports suggested that the prick marks are sometimes the result of "hesitation wounds" in suicide cases that involve stab wounds.[85] Another press report raised the possibility that the prick marks could suggest that Luna was tortured.[86] According to three law enforcement sources, authorities believed that the motivation behind Luna's wounds was "personal."[87]

In February, during another search of the area where Luna's body was found, investigators found a penknife that they believed was not only the weapon used to cause the stab wounds but also the penknife that Luna regularly carried.[88] They also found blood on the paper toll-booth ticket that was turned in at the exit near Ephrata.[89] Anonymous law enforcement sources said that authorities found blood from a second person in Luna's car, but investigators never released any information about the alleged evidence of a second person.[90]

Controversy Ensues

The FBI field office in Baltimore pursued the case for more than a year but did not publicly identify any suspects or make any arrests. By December 2004, the case took a strange turn when the FBI released a statement that Luna was alone from the time he left his office on 3 December 2003 until his body was found on 4 December 2003.[91] The statement implied, without rendering a clear judgment, that the death was a suicide. Lancaster County coroner Gary Kirchner, who took over after Walp retired in January 2004 and whose office conducted Luna's autopsy, rejected the suicide theory and said he was "at least 98 percent" certain that Luna's death was a homicide.[92] Luna's mother also rejected the suicide theory, saying "he wouldn't do something like that."[93] Fellow prosecutor Jacabed Rodriguez-Coss said she could "never see Jonathan ever committing suicide."[94] Years later, Luna's friend, attorney Richard Reuland, also questioned the defensive wounds explanation, telling reporters, "Some of these wounds, he would have had to have been double- or triple-jointed to inflict on himself. Some of these wounds were in the middle of his back."[95]

The FBI pronouncement served as the capstone on a year of controversy. First there were reports of the FBI's possible mishandling of a witness in the case while investigating whether the witness, who was also an FBI agent, had engaged in an affair with Luna. Press reports cited rumors that the FBI may have investigated the alleged affair and that the two may have gone to the gym together a few times.[96] The witness balked at the treatment, and an internal FBI inquiry ensued. The FBI released a statement in February 2004 saying that "any time an FBI employee makes a serious allegation of wrongdoing against a manager or fellow employee, the matter is investigated by independent investigators."[97]

Next, reports surfaced that US Attorney DiBiagio admitted to staff members in a meeting in August 2004 that he had lied to the news media about whether Luna's job was in jeopardy to protect Luna's family, according to employees in the US Attorney's office.[98] Finally, in 2005, a source close to the investigation revealed that Luna was scheduled for a polygraph examination concerning the missing $36,000 from the bank robbery case.[99] The source said that investigators found that more than $10,000 mysteriously came into Luna's possession just after the money went missing.[100] The FBI declined to comment on the reports, but the revelations prompted speculation that Luna may have accidentally killed himself when staging his own abduction to generate sympathy and stall the polygraph examination.[101]

William Keisling fueled the controversy and provided fodder for conspiracy theorists in a 2005 book *The Midnight Ride of Jonathan Luna*. In it, Keisling argued that Luna's death was most likely associated with his profession, claiming Luna had frustrations surrounding the FBI's alleged mishandling of its informant in the Smith and Poindexter case.[102] Likewise, the Luna family's private investigator believes that Luna's professional life—including his dealings with the FBI informant—should again be the focus of the case.[103] The FBI case is still open, but authorities have not issued any public statements since 2004, the same year it offered a $100,000 reward for information leading to the "resolution of the investigation" into Luna's death.[104]

An Unsolved Mystery

Jonathan Luna's mysterious death in December 2003 has been widely reported, but attempts to reignite the investigation have stalled. It has been the subject of national attention and two nonfiction books. And yet, the mystery has never been solved. Vigils in his honor have become increasingly rare. His family has fallen silent after unsuccessfully attempting in 2007 to persuade the state of Pennsylvania to open an inquiry into his death. The US Attorney's Office for the Eastern District of Pennsylvania in 2008 was unsure if it was still overseeing the case.[105] The question remains: How did Jonathan Luna die?

Recommended Readings

Brown, Ethan. *Snitch: Informants, Cooperators, and the Corruption of Justice.* New York: PublicAffairs, 2007. See chapter 7.
Keisling, William. *The Midnight Ride of Jonathan Luna.* Harrisburg, PA: Yardbird, 2006.

Table 4.1 ▶ Case Snapshot: Who Murdered Jonathan Luna?		
Structured Analytic Technique Used	Heuer and Pherson Page Number	Analytic Family
Chronologies and Timelines	p. 52	Decomposition and Visualization
Simple Hypotheses	p. 151	Hypothesis Generation and Testing
Multiple Hypotheses Generator	p. 153	Hypothesis Generation and Testing
Analysis of Competing Hypotheses	p. 160	Hypothesis Generation and Testing

WHO MURDERED JONATHAN LUNA?
STRUCTURED ANALYTIC TECHNIQUES IN ACTION

When confronting a case in which so much significant information is unknown, Timelines, Chronologies, Hypothesis Generation, and Analysis of Competing Hypotheses can be used to devise and execute a solid analytic process that frames the problem and brings order to the jumble of data points, assumptions, and gaps that form the case. The following exercises use these techniques to sort, array, and analyze the data set in a way that can bring this complex set of events into better focus.

Technique 1: Chronologies and Timelines

Chronologies and Timelines are simple but useful tools that help order events sequentially; display the information graphically; and identify possible gaps, anomalies, and correlations. In addition, these techniques pull the analyst out of the evidentiary weeds to view a data set from a more strategic vantage point. Chronologies and Timelines can be paired with mapping software to create geospatial products that display multiple layers of information such as time, location, terrain, weather, and other travel conditions.

The details of this case make an annotated timeline and map particularly useful in identifying key pieces of evidence, confidence levels in the reporting, and gaps in the information.

Task 1. Create a Timeline of Luna's last hours.

Step 1: Identify the relevant information from the case narrative with the date and order in which it occurred. Consider how best to array the data along the Timeline. Can any of the information be categorized?

Step 2: Review the Timeline by asking the following questions:

▶ Are there any missing pieces of data?

▶ Do any of the events appear to occur too rapidly or slowly to have reasonably occurred in the order or timing suggested by the data?

▶ Could any events outside the Timeline have influenced the activities?

▶ Are there any underlying assumptions about the evidence that should be taken into consideration?

Task 2. Create annotated map of events based on your Timeline.

Step 1: Use publicly available software of your choosing to create a map of the area.

Step 2: Overlay the route.

Step 3: Annotate the map with appropriate times and locations presented in the case.

Analytic Value Added. What does the sequence of events tell you? Are there any gaps in the information that should be addressed? What additional information should you seek? How confident are you in the sources of information?

Technique 2: Multiple Hypothesis Generation—Simple Hypotheses
Multiple Hypothesis Generation is part of any rigorous analytic process because it helps the analyst avoid common pitfalls such as coming to premature closure or being overly influenced by first impressions. Instead, it helps the analyst think broadly and creatively about a range of possibilities. The goal is to develop an exhaustive list of hypotheses that can be scrutinized and tested over time against both existing evidence and new data that may become available in the future.

This case is well suited to Simple Hypotheses, which employs a group process that can be used to think creatively about a range of possible explanations that go beyond those raised by authorities in the case. Using a group helps to generate a large list of possible hypotheses; group the lists; and refine the groupings to arrive at a set of plausible, clearly stated hypotheses for further investigation.

Task 3. Use Simple Hypotheses to create a list of alternative hypotheses that explain Jonathan Luna's death.

STEP 1: Ask each member of the group to write down on separate 3-by-5-inch cards or sticky notes up to three plausible alternative hypotheses or explanations. Think broadly and creatively but strive to incorporate the elements of a good hypothesis:

- ▸ It is written as a definite statement.
- ▸ It is based on observations and knowledge.
- ▸ It is testable and falsifiable.
- ▸ It contains a dependent and an independent variable.

STEP 2: Collect the cards and display the results. Consolidate the hypotheses to avoid duplication.

STEP 3: Aggregate the hypotheses into affinity groups and label each group.

STEP 4: Use problem restatement and consideration of the opposite to develop new ideas.

STEP 5: Update the list of alternative hypotheses.

STEP 6: Clarify each hypothesis by asking, Who? What? When? Where? How? and Why?

STEP 7: Select the most promising hypotheses for further exploration.

Technique 3: Multiple Hypothesis Generation—Multiple Hypotheses Generator

The Multiple Hypotheses Generator is a useful tool for broadening the spectrum of plausible hypotheses. It is particularly helpful when there is a reigning lead hypothesis—in this case, the hypothesis that Luna was alone the night he died and therefore must have committed suicide.

Task 4. Use the Multiple Hypotheses Generator to create and assess alternative hypotheses that explain Jonathan Luna's death. Contact Pherson Associates at ThinkSuite@pherson.org or go to www.pherson.org to obtain access to the Multiple Hypotheses Generator software if it is not available on your system.

STEP 1: Identify the lead hypothesis and its component parts using Who? What? When? Where? How? and Why?

Steps 2 & 3: Identify plausible alternatives for each key component and strive to keep them mutually exclusive. Discard any "given" factors.

Steps 4, 5, & 6: Generate a list of possible permutations, discard any permutations that simply make no sense, and evaluate the credibility of the remaining hypotheses on a scale of 1–5, where 1 is low credibility and 5 is high credibility.

Step 7: Re-sort the remaining hypotheses, listing them from most to least credible.

Step 8: Restate the permutations as hypotheses.

Step 9: Select from the top of the list those alternative hypotheses most deserving of attention and note why these hypotheses are most interesting.

Analytic Value Added. Which hypotheses should be explored further? What motives should be considered, and why? Which hypotheses from the original list were set aside, and why?

Technique 4: Analysis of Competing Hypotheses
Analysts face a perennial challenge of working with incomplete, ambiguous, anomalous, and sometimes deceptive data. In addition, strict time constraints on analysis and the need to "make a call" often conspire with a number of natural human cognitive tendencies to zero in on a single hypothesis too early in the analytic process. The result is often inaccurate or incomplete judgments. Analysis of Competing Hypotheses (ACH) improves the analyst's chances of overcoming these challenges by requiring the analyst to identify and refute possible hypotheses using the full range of data, assumptions, and gaps that are pertinent to the problem at hand.

Task 5. Use the top hypotheses compiled with the Multiple Hypotheses Generator to conduct an Analysis of Competing Hypotheses of the Luna case. Contact Pherson Associates at ThinkSuite@pherson.org or go to www.pherson.org to obtain access to the basic software, or the collaborative version called Te@mACH, if it is not available on your system.

Step 1: List the hypotheses to be considered, striving for mutual exclusivity.

Step 2: Make a list of all relevant information, including significant evidence, arguments, gaps, and assumptions.

STEP 3: Assess the relevant information against each hypothesis by asking, "Is this information highly inconsistent, inconsistent, neutral, not applicable, consistent, or highly consistent vis-à-vis the hypothesis?" (The Te@mACH software does not include the "neutral" category.)

STEP 4: Rate the credibility of each item of relevant information.

STEP 5: Refine the matrix by reconsidering the hypotheses. Does it make sense to combine two hypotheses, add a new hypothesis, or disaggregate an existing one?

STEP 6: Draw tentative conclusions about the relative likelihood of each hypothesis. An inconsistency score will be calculated by the software; the hypothesis with the lowest inconsistency score is tentatively the most likely hypothesis. The one with the most inconsistencies is the least likely.

STEP 7: Analyze the sensitivity of your tentative conclusion to a change in the interpretation of a few critical items of evidence by using the software to sort the evidence by diagnosticity.

STEP 8: Report the conclusions by considering the relative likelihood of all the hypotheses.

STEP 9: Identify indicators or milestones for future observation.

Analytic Value Added. As a result of your analysis, what are the most and least likely hypotheses? What are the most diagnostic pieces of information? What, if any, assumptions underlie the data? Are there any gaps in the relevant information that could affect your confidence? How confident are you in your assessment of the most likely hypothesis? Why do you think that the case remains unsolved?

NOTES

1. Gail Gibson, "Prosecutor of Drug Case Found Killed," *Baltimore Sun,* December 5, 2003, http://www.baltimoresun.com/news/maryland/crime/bal-luna1205,0,2335211. story.

2. "Jonathan Luna's Last Hours," *Washington Post,* March 14, 2004, http://www .washingtonpost.com/.

3. Gibson, "Prosecutor of Drug Case Found Killed."

4. Gail Gibson, "Personal Motive Suspected in Killing of US Prosecutor," *Baltimore Sun,* December 6, 2003, http://www.baltimoresun.com/news/maryland/crime/ bal-luna1206,0,2400748.story.

5. Ibid.

6. Ibid.

7. Gibson, "Prosecutor of Drug Case Found Killed."

8. Ibid.

9. Gibson, "Personal Motive Suspected in Killing of US Prosecutor."

10. Lauren Johnston, "Prosecutor May Have Been Tortured," *CBS News*, December 6, 2003, http://www.cbsnews.com/stories/2003/12/08/national/main587250.shtml.

11. Gibson, "Personal Motive Suspected in Killing of US Prosecutor."

12. Lauren Johnston, "New Puzzle in Prosecutor's Death," *CBS News*, December 12, 2003, http://www.cbsnews.com/stories/2003/12/04/national/main586958.shtml.

13. Gail Gibson, "Blood of Second Person in Car," *Baltimore Sun,* December 12, 2003, http://www.baltimoresun.com/news/maryland/bal-md.luna12dec12,0,1042873 .story.

14. Gail Gibson and Lynn Anderson, "Missing Money Noted in Probe," *Baltimore Sun,* December 10, 2003, http://www.baltimoresun.com/news/maryland/bal-md .luna10dec10,0,125365.story.

15. Gibson, "Personal Motive Suspected in Killing of US Prosecutor."

16. Gibson, "Prosecutor of Drug Case Found Killed."

17. Ibid.

18. Ibid.

19. Ibid.

20. Ibid.

21. Gibson, "Prosecutor of Drug Case Found Killed."

22. Ibid.

23. Gail Gibson and Gus G. Sentementes, "Decision in Slaying Probe Set for Today," *Baltimore Sun,* December 8, 2003, http://articles.baltimoresun.com/2003–12–08/ news/0312080348_1_luna-body-law-enforcement/.

24. Gus G. Sentementes, "Luna Parents Wait, Hope for Word on Son's Killer," *Baltimore Sun,* December 11, 2003, http://www.baltimoresun.com/.

25. Gibson, "Blood of Second Person in Car."

26. Gail Gibson, "Slain Prosecutor's Relationships with Women Examined," *Baltimore Sun,* December 9, 2003, http://articles.baltimoresun.com/2003–12–09/ news/0312090426_1_luna-law-enforcement-lancaster-county/.

27. Ibid.

28. Faye Fiore, "Missing Federal Attorney Found Slain," *Los Angeles Times,* December 5, 2003, http://articles.latimes.com/2003/dec/05/nation/na-luna5/.

29. Gibson, "Personal Motive Suspected in Killing of US Prosecutor."

30. Tricia Bishop, "Five Years Later, Prosecutor's Death Still a Mystery," *Baltimore Sun,* November 30, 2008, http://www.baltimoresun.com/news/maryland/bal-md .luna30nov30,0,2938855.story.

31. Gibson, "Prosecutor of Drug Case Found Killed."

32. Ibid.

33. Kenneth Ravenell, interviewed by Wolf Blitzer, *PM Edition*, CNN, December 5, 2003, http://edition.cnn.com/TRANSCRIPTS/0312/05/wbr.00.html.

34. Ibid.

35. Eric Lichtblau, "Federal Prosecutor Found Dead with Stab Wounds," *New York Times,* December 5, 2003, http://www.nytimes.com/2003/12/05/national/05PROS.html.

36. Gibson, "Prosecutor of Drug Case Found Killed."

37. Ibid.

38. Gibson, "Personal Motive Suspected in Killing of US Prosecutor."

39. Gibson, "Prosecutor of Drug Case Found Killed."

40. Eric Rich and Allan Lengel, "FBI Finds No Culprit in Death of Prosecutor; Probe Suggests Luna Was Alone," *Washington Post,* December 3, 2004, http://www.wash ingtonpost.com/.

41. Gibson, "Prosecutor of Drug Case Found Killed."

42. Ibid.

43. Gibson, "Personal Motive Suspected in Killing of US Prosecutor."

44. Brooklyn Eagle, May 25, 2011.

45. "Jonathan Luna's Last Hours," *Washington Post.*

46. Ibid.

47. Ibid.

48. Ibid.

49. Gail Gibson, "Blood Found on Slain Prosecutor's PA Toll Ticket," *Baltimore Sun,* December 17, 2003, http://www.baltimoresun.com/news/maryland/bal-md.luna 17dec17,0,3336643.story.

50. Gail Gibson and Lynn Anderson, "Probe in Killing of Prosecutor Luna Stalls," *Baltimore Sun,* January 9, 2004, http://www.baltimoresun.com/news/maryland/crime/ bal-probe0109,0,5329212.story.

51. "Jonathan Luna's Last Hours," *Washington Post.*

52. Ibid.

53. Gibson, "Blood of Second Person in Car."

54. "Jonathan Luna's Last Hours," *Washington Post.*

55. Gibson, "Blood Found on Slain Prosecutor's PA Toll Ticket."

56. Gibson, "Blood of Second Person in Car."

57. Gibson, "Blood Found on Slain Prosecutor's PA Toll Ticket."

58. Matt Apuzzo, "Slain Prosecutor's Route Home Adds to Mystery," *Red Orbit,* December 14, 2003, http://www.redorbit.com/news/oddities/35770/slain_prosecutors_ route_home_adds_to_mystery/index.html.

59. Gibson, "Blood of Second Person in Car."

60. Apuzzo, "Slain Prosecutor's Route Home Adds to Mystery."

61. Ibid.

62. Ibid.

63. Ibid.

64. "Jonathan Luna's Last Hours," *Washington Post.*

65. Gibson, "Blood Found on Slain Prosecutor's PA Toll Ticket."

66. "Jonathan Luna's Last Hours," *Washington Post.*

67. Bishop, "Five Years Later, Prosecutor's Death Still a Mystery."

68. Rich and Lengel, "FBI Finds No Culprit in Death of Prosecutor; Probe Suggests Luna Was Alone."

69. Eric Rich and Allan Lengel, "Polygraph Loomed for MD Lawyer," *Washington Post,* December 20, 2005, http://www.washingtonpost.com/wp-dyn/content/article/ 2005/12/19/AR2005121901827.html.

70. Stephanie Hanes, "Luna Reportedly Feared Losing Job, Hired Lawyer," *Baltimore Sun,* August 18, 2004, http://www.baltimoresun.com/news/maryland/bal-md .luna18aug18,0,7793110.story.

71. Rich and Lengel, "Polygraph Loomed for MD Lawyer."

72. Ibid.

73. Gibson, "Slain Prosecutor's Relationships with Women Examined."

74. Ibid.

75. Ibid.

76. Rich and Lengel, "FBI Finds No Culprit in Death of Prosecutor; Probe Suggests Luna Was Alone."

77. Gibson and Sentementes, "Decision in Slaying Probe Set for Today."

78. Gibson, "Blood of Second Person in Car."

79. Gibson, "Slain Prosecutor's Relationships with Women Examined."

80. Rich and Allan, "FBI Finds No Culprit in Death of Prosecutor; Probe Suggests Luna Was Alone."

81. Gibson, "Slain Prosecutor's Relationships with Women Examined."

82. Rich and Lengel, "FBI Finds No Culprit in Death of Prosecutor; Probe Suggests Luna Was Alone."

83. Gibson and Sentementes, "Decision in Slaying Probe Set for Today."

84. Gibson, "Personal Motive Suspected in Killing of US Prosecutor."

85. Gail Gibson, "Search Uncovers Luna's Penknife," *Baltimore Sun,* February 13, 2003, http://www.baltimoresun.com/news/maryland/bal-md.luna13feb13,0,1960380 .story.

86. Johnston. "Prosecutor May Have Been Tortured."

87. Gibson, "Personal Motive Suspected in Killing of US Prosecutor."

88. Gibson, "Search Uncovers Luna's Penknife."

89. Gibson, "Blood Found on Slain Prosecutor's PA Toll Ticket."

90. Gibson, "Blood of Second Person in Car."

91. Rich and Lengel, "FBI Finds No Culprit in Death of Prosecutor; Probe Suggests Luna Was Alone."

92. Ibid.

93. Ibid.

94. Rich and Lengel, "Polygraph Loomed for MD Lawyer."

95. Brooklyn Eagle, May 25, 2011.

96. Brooklyn Eagle, May 25, 2011.

97. "Statement of FBI Assistant Director Cassandra M. Chandler," February 12, 2004, http://www.fbi.gov/news/pressrel/press-releases/statement-of-fbi-assistant-director-cassandra-m.-chandler/.

98. Hanes, "Luna Reportedly Feared Losing Job, Hired Lawyer."

99. Rich and Lengel, "Polygraph Loomed for MD Lawyer."

100. Ibid.

101. Rich and Lengel, "Polygraph Loomed for MD Lawyer."

102. William Kiesling, *The Midnight Ride of Jonathan Luna*, Harrisburg, PA: Yardbird Press, 2005.

103. Bishop, "Five Years Later, Prosecutor's Death Still a Mystery."

104. Ibid.

105. Ibid.

5 The Assassination of Benazir Bhutto

CASE NARRATIVE

Only two months after Benazir Bhutto returned from exile to Pakistan to take up the family's political banner, she was assassinated on 27 December 2007 as her caravan departed a political rally in Rawalpindi, just south of New Delhi. Bhutto had been warned not to return to Pakistan to run for the presidency and, after she returned, had earlier been denied permission to hold a rally in Rawalpindi because of the tenuous security situation. Bhutto, however, refused to be intimidated by the numerous threats on her life and saw such political rallies as key to demonstrating popular support for her candidacy in upcoming presidential elections. The suicide-bomber assassin was later identified as a fifteen-and-a-half-year-old teenager, but questions remained about who had ordered the killing. The list of potential masterminds was not short. It included Islamic militant extremists, political rivals, senior officials in the Pakistani government, and even family members. The event and subsequent investigations captured the attention of the world, as both experts and amateurs sought to determine who ultimately was responsible for her death.

Intertwining Politics and Family

Pakistan has suffered a history of political turbulence since its genesis in 1947. No elected government has survived until the end of its term since the nation was created as a homeland for Muslims during the British partition of South Asia. The main fault lines, then and now, run between secular and fundamentalist Muslims and between civilian leaders and the military.[1]

Benazir Bhutto personified this political turmoil. The military ousted her father as prime minister in 1979, convicted him of complicity in the death of a political opponent, and hanged him.[2] The family was forced into exile. In 1986, Bhutto returned from exile in England to head the secular Pakistan People's Party (PPP), founded by her father. She led the party to victory in 1988, becoming the first female prime minister of a Muslim country. The Pakistani president dismissed her in 1990 for alleged corruption and her failure to curb ethnic violence. She regained office in 1993.

Violence continued to plague members of the Bhutto family even during Bhutto's years in office. Her brother, Murtaza, who challenged her for control of the PPP, was gunned down near his home by police in 1996.[3] His daughter, Fatima, has since called the attack a carefully planned assassination in which Murtaza was allowed to bleed to death after being shot at close range. Fatima, now a newspaper columnist and pro-democracy activist in Karachi, holds Benazir morally responsible for Murtaza's death. In 1996, Bhutto was once again dismissed from office for alleged corruption.[4] She was later convicted in 1999 for failing to appear in court, but that judgment was subsequently overturned. Facing corruption charges in five separate cases, she fled the country that same year.

Violent Homecoming

Bhutto returned from exile once again on 18 October 2007 after President and Army Chief of Staff Pervez Musharraf, signed a "corruption amnesty."[5] The declaration, drafted under pressure from the White House and the US Congress, not only paved the way for Bhutto's homecoming but also held out at least a vague promise of power sharing.[6] Another prominent regime opponent, twice-deposed Prime Minister Nawaz Sharif, returned to Pakistan in the fall of 2007; he and Bhutto were longtime political rivals and had no plans to make common cause.[7]

The country was tense after months of protests against the Musharraf government.[8] Much of the tumult was driven by political bickering surrounding the upcoming presidential elections and a possible return to democracy after more than eight years of military rule. While individual politicians, political parties, and the military all jockeyed with one another for power in advance of the upcoming vote, Islamic militants increased their attacks, seeking to stall the country's sudden move toward democracy. At the same time, the United States and the international community increased pressure on Pakistan to take a more active role in suppressing the Taliban and

Map 5.1 ▶ Pakistan

Al-Qaeda. Some observers claimed that the turmoil was driving Pakistan to "the brink" and left it "the main contender for the title of most dangerous country on earth."[9]

About 200,000 supporters greeted Bhutto at the Karachi airport.[10] The government deployed over 20,000 security personnel to maintain order. Despite her personal security worries, Bhutto refused a request by Pakistani authorities to use a helicopter.[11] When leaving the airport en route to the tomb of Muhammad Ali Jinnah, the founder of Pakistan, she also decided not to use the bulletproof glass cubicle mounted on her open-air truck (see photo, page 82). She stood at the front railing surrounded by other party officials.

Benazir Bhutto returns to Pakistan on 18 October 2007 atop an open-air truck. (Bhutto pictured center, with scarf.)

The procession crept forward, with supporters dancing in the streets. Suddenly, there was a small explosion ahead of the truck. It was followed by a large blast near the truck itself, which set an escorting police van on fire and broke windows in Bhutto's vehicle.[12] Bhutto was shaken but not injured in the attack. In all, 179 people were left dead, including several police officers, and more than 600 were injured.[13] Police officer Raja Khitab later said evidence at the scene (see photo, facing page) pointed to a suicide bombing.[14]

Bhutto was well aware of the dangers. Two days before her return to Pakistan, she wrote a letter to Musharraf in which she named four people she believed were plotting to kill her: Ijaz Shah, current chief of the Intelligence Bureau, which answers to the Interior Ministry; Chaudhry Pervaiz Elahi, former chief minister of the Punjab region; Arbab Ghulam, former chief minister of Sindh; and Hamid Gul, former chief of the Pakistani intelligence service, ISID.[15]

After the bombing, Bhutto rephrased her warning and made it public:

> On Oct 16, before returning home, I wrote a letter to Gen Musharraf in which I informed him that if anything happens to me as a result of these attacks, then I will neither nominate the Afghan Taliban, nor Al Qaeda, not even Pakistani Taliban or the fourth group. I will nominate those people

who, I believe, mislead the people. I have spelt out names of such people in the letter. . . . I have named three people, and more, in that letter to Gen Musharraf. I have named certain people with a view to the attack that took place yesterday so that if I was assassinated, who should be investigated.[16]

Probable suicide bombing near Bhutto's bus on 18 October 2007.

According to Mark Siegel, her US representative, Bhutto tried to obtain security personnel from the US firm Blackwater and the UK-based Armor-Group, but the Pakistani government refused to grant visas.[17]

Strident Messages Inflame Opponents

Upon her return to Pakistan, Bhutto used the media to crusade against Islamic militants.[18] She denounced jihadi terrorists with statements that few local politicians had dared to utter. During campaign appearances, she argued that suicide bombing was against the teachings of Islam.[19]

Bhutto attacked conservatives in the government, including officials close to Musharraf.[20] She accused them of aiding extremists and supporting the bombers who attacked her. Specifically, she warned against ISID and the residual power of those who had been responsible for her father's death. She assailed the military dictatorship in general but stopped short of attacking Musharraf directly, leaving the door open to the proposed power-sharing deal.[21]

Her opponents matched her rhetoric with countercharges. The chief minister of Sindh, Bhutto's home province, called the rule of a woman a curse for Pakistan. The leader of the Pakistani Muslim League, Chaudhry Hussein—a Musharraf supporter who strongly disapproved of compromise with Bhutto—suggested that the new arrival had arranged the blasts herself as a ploy for sympathy. Ejaj ul-Haq, the minister of religious affairs, blamed Bhutto for playing with people's lives by returning when she was aware of threats against her.[22]

Musharraf grudgingly approved her return under US pressure to restore civilian rule, but many Pakistani democrats were skeptical of the image in the Western press of Bhutto as a savior who would rescue the country from autocratic rule and terrorism. Critics on TV talk shows and in newspapers complained that Musharraf had offered amnesty in return for Bhutto's support for an extension of his term in office. Many portrayed the amnesty offer as implicit approval of political corruption. A popular cricketer turned politician, Imran Khan, and his ex-wife, the wealthy British socialite Jemima Khan, lambasted Bhutto in the British press, calling her "a kleptocrat in an Hermès scarf." In a London editorial, Khan highlighted Bhutto's husband's moniker, "Mr. 10 Percent," and accused the two of having stolen more than $1 billion from the Pakistani treasury during Benazir's second time as prime minister.[23] Opponents also pointed out that she was appealing a money-laundering conviction in the Swiss courts and that corruption investigations were ongoing in Britain and Spain.[24]

Bhutto's estranged niece Fatima said in an interview after Bhutto's return: "I do believe Benazir is the most dangerous thing to happen to this country."[25] She argued that Bhutto's pro-American agenda was giving democracy a bad name and was jeopardizing hard-won progress in grassroots political development. "She has put us all in danger of an Islamic backlash," Fatima declared in the interview. Fatima threatened to ally with other opposition leaders.[26]

Musharraf, meanwhile, continued his efforts to curtail Bhutto's political campaigning. On 9 November, police erected barbed wire around the Bhutto compound to prevent her from speaking at a rally protesting Musharraf's emergency rule.[27] They also rounded up thousands of her supporters. On 13 November, authorities put Bhutto under house arrest, citing concerns for her safety. She responded by calling for Musharraf's resignation and threatening to have her party boycott the elections scheduled for January 2008.

Bhutto's niece considered the complaints about a house arrest to be hollow. She pointed out that Bhutto's political planning was not stifled and, indeed, more than fifty members of her party were allowed to meet with her during the purported detention.[28] Moreover, Bhutto addressed the media twice from her garden, protected by the police, and was not reprimanded for holding a news conference. Bhutto's niece contended that other activists who even mentioned the idea of holding a press conference were jailed.

Bhutto's opponents matched her strident tone. In mid-November 2007, a leaked letter suggested that in 1990 Bhutto had sought to conspire with Pakistan's enemy, India, for political gain. It was common knowledge that Bhutto and then-US Ambassador to Croatia Peter Galbraith had been close friends since college days. In the purported letter, Bhutto was alleged to have asked Galbraith to convince the Indian prime minister to create a military incident on the border to put pressure on the Pakistani government and keep it from disqualifying her in upcoming elections. Officials in Bhutto's party denounced the letter as a forgery, citing gross grammatical errors as proof.[29]

The Final Days

By late December, nerves on all sides were frayed. Bhutto's detention had been lifted, and she had resumed her political campaign.[30] After the bombings on the day of her return to Pakistan, she had briefly considered abandoning public rallies and delivering taped messages by TV or radio instead, but she had concluded that mass rallies were crucial to her chances of electoral success. On 26 December, authorities detained a man carrying explosives near one of her rallies in Peshawar, close to the Afghan border.[31] The man claimed it was celebratory dynamite from a wedding he had attended. Bhutto's husband phoned from Dubai to say he was nervous and wanted to attend the rally planned for the next day in Rawalpindi in her place, but she dissuaded him.[32]

The controversial candidate planned to use her 27 December speech to charge that Musharraf intended to rig the elections set for 8 January.[33] She was scheduled to meet during the day with election observers from the European Union, US Senator Arlen Specter, and US Representative Patrick Kennedy. Her plan was to give them evidence that the elections would be fixed through fake polling stations and voter intimidation. Despite her busy day, she met early that morning with Afghan president Hamid Karzai to confer on the growing danger of extremism.[34]

Bhutto was apprehensive about her trip to Rawalpindi, just south of the capital. Considered the home of the military, it was where her father had been hanged in 1979 and where Pakistan's first prime minister had been assassinated in 1951.[35] Things were already going badly in Rawalpindi. In the early afternoon, a sniper on a rooftop killed four Sharif supporters and injured five others.[36] Sharif's party blamed Musharraf's group, claiming the attack was an attempt to intimidate potential voters. Despite the danger, at 1545, Bhutto and her top party officials drove the ten miles from Islamabad to Rawalpindi.

Bhutto held the rally as planned. Near dusk, as she drove away from the site in her bulletproof SUV, she raised her head through the sun roof to acknowledge the frenzied crowds chanting "Long Live Bhutto!"[37] Police constable Mohammed Qayyam, who was trying to clear a path for the vehicle, failed to see the man in sunglasses standing just behind Bhutto. Eyewitnesses later reported he raised a gun and fired three shots at close range. Nor did the constable notice the man a few paces back whose head was covered in a white scarf (see photos, facing page). Witnesses said he blew himself up moments later, killing himself, the likely gunman, and others all around. Bhutto was among those who died.

Bhutto was rushed to Rawalpindi General Hospital, where she was pronounced dead just after 1800.[38] The next day her remains were transferred to her husband and flown to Larkana. She was buried in the family's mausoleum that afternoon.

Multiple Accounts in the Aftermath

Controversy immediately swirled, beginning with disagreements over the cause of death.[39] Initial reports were that Bhutto had been shot in the head or neck before the bomb went off and had died from the gunshot wounds. The next day, Ministry of Interior officials said she had been killed by shrapnel from the bomb. Two days after the attack, the Interior Ministry issued a more definitive statement, claiming that the shooter had missed but the bomb had caused her to fall; her head had struck a protruding lever on the sun roof, and she died from a skull fracture.[40] The Interior Ministry official showed X-rays to support this claim. Witnesses and close friends who rushed her to the hospital, however, said she clearly had been shot.[41]

Doctors who had attended Bhutto initially reported that she had died of gunshot wounds. They later released findings consistent with the Interior Ministry's position. One Pakistani doctor said the government had seized Bhutto's medical records and ordered the doctors to stop talking.[42] A subsequent report issued by a UN team investigating the assassination noted that this doctor was not an attending physician, which caused some to question his credibility.[43]

There was no autopsy, despite a legal requirement for one in such cases. The government claimed this was in deference to Islamic traditions and Bhutto's husband's wishes.[44] In response to a government offer to disinter her if her

The top video image shows a man (wearing sunglasses) pointing a gun at Benazir Bhutto on 29 December 2007. The bottom image shows this suspected gunman and the suspected suicide bomber (wearing white scarf).

husband so requested, Bhutto's husband declined, saying an autopsy would be useless because the results would be rigged.[45]

An hour and a half after the attack, the senior police officer on the scene ordered police officers to wash down the street with fire hoses. Pools of blood, bullet casings, and DNA samples were all washed away.[46] Even Hamid Gul, a detractor of Bhutto with connections to both the Afghan and Pakistani Taliban, publicly questioned why the government had washed away evidence at the scene of the crime.[47] All that remained was amateur footage showing a man in a black vest brandishing what appeared to be a gun and, behind him, a man in a white head scarf believed by some to be the suicide bomber. The government established a joint investigation team headed by local Singh authorities, which later examined the vehicle and reported that it could find no blood or tissue on the hatch where Bhutto was alleged to have struck her head.[48]

Musharraf immediately took steps to distance the government from the assassination. He later acknowledged that Bhutto might have been shot, but he blamed her for poor judgment in ignoring her advisors by standing up in the vehicle, noting that no one else in the car was hurt.[49] He pointed out that most of the nineteen suicide bombings that had occurred in Pakistan in recent months were directed against the military and the intelligence service.[50] Discounting stories blaming ISID for the assassination, he stated: "No intelligence organization in Pakistan, I think, is capable of indoctrinating a man to blow himself up."[51] The government had warned Bhutto of the danger of staging a rally in Rawalpindi, he said, and, in fact, had stopped an earlier rally planned for that location by putting her briefly under house arrest. Musharraf claimed security had been as tight as possible on the day of the assassination, with 1,000 police officers on duty, including snipers on roofs and mobile squads around Bhutto's vehicle.[52]

Soon after the attack, the Interior Ministry claimed it had a communications intercept that proved that Baitullah Mehsud, a leader of the Pakistani Taliban thought to be an Al-Qaeda affiliate, had instigated the attack (see Figure 5.1).[53] Mehsud's forces had been attacking Pakistani military units that were trying, at Washington's behest, to assert control over quasi-autonomous tribal areas where diverse anti-US militants had found sanctuary. The alleged intercept purports to record Mehsud congratulating a follower on a job well done. The US Central Intelligence Agency director, General Michael Hayden, said in late January 2008 that he believed Mehsud was behind Bhutto's assassination. Hayden did not lay out his evidence and made no comment on whether the alleged intercept figured in his calculation. Some wondered

Figure 5.1 ▶ Communications Intercept Released by the Pakistani Government

Mullah: Peace be with you.

Baitullah Mehsud: And also with you.

Mullah: Chief, how are you?

Baitullah Mehsud: I am fine.

Mullah: Congratulations, I just got back during the night.

Baitullah Mehsud: Congratulations to you, were they our men?

Mullah: Yes, they were ours.

Baitullah Mehsud: Who were they?

Mullah: There was Saeed, there was Bilal from Badar and Ikramullah.

Baitullah Mehsud: The three of them did it?

Mullah: Ikramullah and Bilal did it.

Baitullah Mehsud: Then congratulations.

Mullah: Where are you? I want to meet you.

Baitullah Mehsud: I am at Makeen [town in South Warziristan], come over, I am at Anwar Shah's house.

Mullah: OK I'll come.

Baitullah Mehsud: Don't inform their house for the time being.

Mullah: OK.

Baitullah Mehsud: It was a tremendous effort. They were really brave boys who killed her.

Mullah: Mashallah. When I come I will give you all the details.

Baitullah Mehsud: I will wait for you. Congratulations, once again congratulations.

Mullah: Congratulations to you.

Baitullah Mehsud: Anything I can do for you?

Mullah: Thank you very much.

Baitullah Mehsud: Asalaam Aleikum.

Mullah: Waaleikum Asalaam.

Source: World Net Daily, "Pakistan in Crisis: 'Intercept' of al-Qaida Points to Bhutto Plot," http://www.worldnetdaily.com/index.php?pageId=45282, December 28, 2007.

whether Hayden's public statement was intended to exonerate Musharraf, a counterterrorism ally.[54]

Other US officials agreed that Mehsud was a likely candidate.[55] The Taliban leader had been critical of both Afghan president Karzai and Pakistani president Musharraf for their close alliance with the United States. He was Pashtun and, like many in the remote tribal area straddling Afghanistan and Pakistan, wanted to see his kinsmen rule a country of their own that followed strict Islamic law and tribal traditions. In 2005, Musharraf had struck a deal with Mehsud, suggesting the two could coexist. Mehsud agreed to halt cross-border attacks into Afghanistan and stop sheltering Al-Qaeda and other foreign fighters in return for the withdrawal of Pakistani military forces from Waziristan, his tribal area. He denied that he had been given large bags of cash as a sweetener. Mehsud eventually broke the agreement, allowed foreign fighters back into the safe haven, and resumed operations against the Pakistan Army.[56]

Some observers questioned the intercept's authenticity as too convenient and termed the government's accusation of Mehsud just another case of Pakistan rounding up the "usual suspects" when the police are stumped—the government had named him in previous investigations when it had no leads.[57] Mehsud quickly and publicly denied any involvement in Bhutto's assassination, just as he had rejected any role in the October bombing when Bhutto first returned. His spokesperson emphasized that striking a woman violated tribal customs and asserted that the crime was a plot by the government and the intelligence services.

Pakistani security officials arrested a fifteen-year-old, Aitezaz Shah, in the northwest tribal region on the suspicion he was involved in the assassination.[58] The Al Jazeera news network quoted security sources as saying the teenager had confessed that he was one of five suicide bombers sent to kill Bhutto.[59] During interrogation, Shah said that two of the attackers, Akram and Bilal, were to target Bhutto first. If they failed, the other three were charged with completing the operation. Bilal killed Bhutto by shooting her and detonating an explosive vest, Shah told officials. He was unable to provide details about the locations of other members of the assassination team.[60] Members of Bhutto's political party dismissed Shah's arrest, stating it was not the breakthrough the Pakistani government claimed. "Frankly, the arrest of a 15-year-old and his handler is neither here nor there," Abida Hussain, senior politician in the party, said.[61]

In her posthumously published book, Bhutto mentioned another possible assassin: Islamic radical Qari Saifullah Akhtar.[62] Bhutto claimed he had helped procure the bombs that went off in Karachi on 18 October 2007. Akhtar had been arrested previously for participating in an attempted "Islamic coup" against Bhutto's second government and had subsequently forged a relationship with the Taliban and Mullah Omar. Akhtar heads the Harkat-ul-Jihad-al-Islami (HUJI), a group with ties to terrorists in Tajikistan, Chechnya, Burma, Uzbekistan, and Bangladesh.

Scotland Yard Weighs In

As the initial international outcry over the assassination and bungled investigation quieted down, Musharraf asked Scotland Yard on 2 January to send a small team to investigate Bhutto's death.[63] The team visited the scene of the crime on 8 January. Musharraf established strict parameters for the Yard's involvement. Investigators were limited to looking into the cause of death, with Pakistani authorities retaining responsibility for identifying the culprit(s). Scotland Yard was denied permission to question some of the people Bhutto's husband accused of plotting to kill her, including several politicians and the intelligence chief.[64] Scotland Yard examined the gun purportedly used in the attack for fingerprints and linked the prints to the identity card of a man living in Swat, a town in the area controlled by Mehsud. It is unclear whether the Yard was able to match the prints to any of the victims at the scene.

Based on X-rays that were independently verified as Bhutto's (by comparison with dental records) and on reports from the doctors and family members who had washed her body before burial, the Scotland Yard team concluded that Bhutto died from a head injury when a powerful blast made her body hit the roof hatch of her SUV.[65] The only apparent injury was a major trauma to the right side of the head, which experts said was not an entry or exit wound from a gunshot. A British Home Office pathologist said "the only tenable cause for the rapidly fatal head injury is that it occurred as the result of impact due to the bomb blast. Given the severity of the injury, it is impossible that she inadvertently struck her head while ducking."[66] Scotland Yard noted the escape hatch had a solid lip of four inches and Bhutto did not completely disappear from view until 0.6 seconds before the blast. However, the limited X-ray material and the absence of a full autopsy and CAT scan meant that the pathologist could not rule out the possibility of a gunshot wound to the upper trunk or neck.

Scotland Yard concluded that only one person had been involved in the attack. The team noted that security officials found body parts from only one unidentified individual—the probable suicide bomber, according to expert opinion. Media footage placed the gunman at the rear of the vehicle and look-ing down immediately before the explosion. No suspicious movements by oth-ers in the crowd appeared on the footage. Forensic evidence indicated that the bomber was one to two meters from the vehicle with no obstruction in front of him, strongly suggesting that the gunman and bomber were at the same loca-tion. It is virtually impossible that anyone who was standing near the gunman who could be clearly seen on the video could have survived the blast and escaped. Scotland Yard's final report did not discuss the possibility that vital forensic evidence could have been removed inadvertently or willingly in the postbomb cleanup.[67]

The Scotland Yard report focused primarily on the events leading up to and just after Bhutto's assassination. Left unaddressed was the key question: Who ultimately was responsible for Bhutto's death? Bhutto's death had captured the world's attention, spawning many theories about who had ordered it. The chal-lenge is to generate a comprehensive list of suspects, identify the most diagnos-tic information and key information gaps, identify a robust and comprehensive set of suspects, and provide a compelling case for who were the most culpable players behind the scenes.

RECOMMENDED READINGS

Jones, Owen Bennett. *Pakistan: Eye of the Storm*. New Haven, CT: Yale Univer-sity Press, 2009.

Rashid, Ahmed. *Descent into Chaos: The US and the Disaster in Pakistan, Afghanistan, and Central Asia*, paperback ed. New York: Penguin Books, 2009.

Table 5.1 ▶ Case Snapshot: The Assassination of Benazir Bhutto		
Structured Analytic Technique Used	Heuer and Pherson Page Number	Analytic Family
Chronologies and Timelines	p. 52	Decomposition and Visualization
Mind Maps	p. 76	Decomposition and Visualization
Analysis of Competing Hypotheses	p. 160	Hypothesis Generation and Testing

THE ASSASSINATION OF BENAZIR BHUTTO
STRUCTURED ANALYTIC TECHNIQUES IN ACTION

In this case, law enforcement and national security analysts were faced with a similar challenge: combing through large amounts of information of varying reliability to determine who ultimately was responsible for Benazir Bhutto's death. The answer to the question could have serious consequences both within Pakistan and for Pakistani relations with other countries, particularly if any Pakistani government officials were implicated in the assassination. The challenge is to sort through the data, select the most salient and defensible items of evidence, and construct a compelling story identifying the most likely culprits. The use of techniques such as Chronologies and Timelines, Mind Maps, and Analysis of Competing Hypotheses can help analysts accomplish each of these tasks.

Technique 1: Chronologies and Timelines

Chronologies and Timelines are simple but useful tools that help order events sequentially; display the information graphically; and identify possible gaps, anomalies, or correlations. In addition, these techniques pull the analyst out of the evidentiary weeds to view a data set from a more strategic vantage point. The complex and contradictory data regarding this case make an annotated timeline particularly useful in identifying key pieces of evidence, confidence levels in the reporting, and gaps in the information.

Task 1. Create a Timeline of events surrounding Benazir Bhutto's death.

STEP 1: Label the relevant information from the case narrative with the date and order in which it reportedly occurred. Consider how best to array the data along the Timeline. Can the information be organized by category?

STEP 2: Review the Timeline by asking the following questions: Are there data gaps? Do the duration and sequence of events suggested by the data make sense? Could any events outside the Timeline have influenced the activities? Should any underlying assumptions about the evidence be taken into consideration?

Analytic Value Added. What does the sequence of events tell you? Are there any gaps in the information that should be addressed? What additional information should you seek? How confident are you in the sources of information?

Technique 2: Mind Maps
Mind Maps are visual representations of how an individual or a group thinks about a topic of interest. A Mind Map diagram has two basic elements: the ideas that are judged relevant to whatever topic one is thinking about and the lines that show and briefly describe the connections between these ideas. Whenever you try to put a series of thoughts together, that series of thoughts can be represented visually with words or images connected by lines that represent the nature of the relationships between them. Any thinking for any purpose, whether about a personal decision or analysis of an intelligence issue, can be diagrammed in this manner. In fact, Mind Mapping was originally developed as a fast and efficient way for students to take notes during briefings and lectures.

Task 2. Generate a Mind Map to explore who could have been behind Benazir Bhutto's assassination.

STEP 1: Identify the focal question or the logical starting point for an investigation. Write the focal question down in the center of the page and draw a circle around it.

STEP 2: Brainstorm a list of possible explanations that might answer the focal question.

STEP 3: Sort these ideas into groupings. These groups may be based on things they have in common or on their status as either direct or indirect causes of the matter being analyzed.

STEP 4: Give each grouping a label and distribute these labels around the focal question. Draw lines from the focal question to each label.

STEP 5: For each label, draw a line to an issue or concept related to that label. A single label could have several spokes radiating from it, and each issue related to the label could have multiple spokes radiating from it as well.

STEP 6: Continue to expand the diagram until all aspects of the issue or case have been captured.

STEP 7: While building the Mind Map, consider the possibility of cross links from one issue to another. Show directionality with arrows pointing in one or both directions.

STEP 8: While building the Mind Map, consider the possibility of conflicting evidence or conflicting concepts. If they appear, label them differently either by color, written name, or shape or by putting an asterisk or other icon inside the circle or box.

STEP 9: Reposition, refine, and expand the Mind Map structure as appropriate.

STEP 10: List all the individuals or entities who may be behind the assassination as well as their most likely motivations.

STEP 11: Identify the most likely people or entities that would have wanted to kill Benzir Bhutto.

Analytic Value Added. Does the creation of the Mind Map prompt you to consider a much broader array of potential explanations or hypotheses? Does it help you "drill down" for each hypothesis to consider second- and third-level questions? Does it help you identify potential gaps in knowledge?

Technique 3: Analysis of Competing Hypotheses

Analysts face a perennial challenge of working with incomplete, ambiguous, anomalous, and sometimes deceptive data. In addition, strict time constraints and the need to "make a call" often conspire with a number of natural human cognitive tendencies to result in inaccurate or incomplete judgments. Analysis of Competing Hypotheses (ACH) improves the analyst's chances of overcoming these challenges by requiring the analyst to identify and refute possible hypotheses using the full range of data, assumptions, and gaps that are pertinent to the problem at hand.

Task 3. Use the most credible hypotheses compiled with the Mind Map or other hypothesis-generation techniques to conduct an Analysis of Competing Hypotheses of the Bhutto case. Contact Pherson Associates at ThinkSuite@ pherson.org or go to www.pherson.org to obtain access to the basic software, or the collaborative version called Te@mACH, if it is not available on your system.

STEP 1: List the hypotheses to be considered, striving for mutual exclusivity.

STEP 2: Make a list of all relevant information, including significant evidence, arguments, gaps, and assumptions.

STEP 3: Assess the relevant information against each hypothesis by asking, "Is this information highly inconsistent, inconsistent, neutral, not applicable, consistent, or highly consistent vis-à-vis the hypothesis?" The Te@mACH software does not include the "neutral" category.

STEP 4: Rate the credibility of each item of relevant information.

STEP 5: Refine the matrix by reconsidering the hypotheses. Does it make sense to combine two hypotheses, add a new hypothesis, or disaggregate an existing one?

STEP 6: Draw tentative conclusions about the relative likelihood of each hypothesis. An inconsistency score will be calculated by the software; the hypothesis with the lowest inconsistency score is tentatively the most likely hypothesis. The one with the most inconsistencies is the least likely.

STEP 7: Analyze the sensitivity of your tentative conclusion to a change in the interpretation of a few critical items of evidence by using the software to sort the evidence by diagnosticity.

STEP 8: Report the conclusions by considering the relative likelihood of all the hypotheses.

STEP 9: Identify indicators or milestones for future observation.

Analytic Value Added. As a result of your analysis, what are the most and least likely hypotheses? What are the most diagnostic pieces of information? What, if any, assumptions underlie the data? Are there any gaps in the relevant information that could affect your confidence? How confident are you in your assessment of the most likely hypothesis?

NOTES

1. Benazir Bhutto, "When I Return to Pakistan," *Washington Post,* September 20, 2007, http://www.washingtonpost.com/wp-dyn/content/article/2007/09/19/AR2007091901705.html.

2. Rubab Saleem, "Biography of PPP Chairperson Benazir Bhutto," *Pakistan Times,* December 27, 2007, http://www.pak-times.com/2007/12/27/biography-of-ppp-chairperson-benazir-bhutto/.

3. Fatima Bhutto, "Aunt Benazir's False Promises," *Los Angeles Times,* November 14, 2007, http://www.latimes.com/news/printedition/asection/la-oe-bhutto14nov14,0,2985133.story.

4. BBC News, "Obituary: Benazir Bhutto," December 27, 2007, http://news.bbc.co.uk/2/hi/south_asia/2228796.stm.

5. Owen Bennett Jones, *Pakistan: Eye of the Storm,* New Haven, CT: Yale University Press, 2009, 301–02.

6. Declan Walsh, "Musharraf and Bhutto Close to Sharing Power," *Guardian* (UK), October 5, 2007, http://www.guardian.co.uk/world/2007/oct/05/pakistan.benazirbhutto/.

7. BBC News, "Sharif's Party 'to Contest Polls,' " December 9, 2007, http://news.bbc.co.uk/2/hi/south_asia/7135535.stm.

8. United Nations, *Report of the United Nations Commission of Inquiry into the Facts and Circumstances of the Assassination of Former Pakistani Prime Minister Mohtarma Benazir Bhutto,* March 30, 2010, http://www.un.org/News/dh/infocus/Pakistan/UN_Bhutto_Report_15April2010.pdf.

9. Garhi Khuda Bakhsh, "A Country on the Brink," *Economist,* January 3, 2008, http://www.economist.com/node/10430324/.

10. BBC News, "Huge Crowds Greet Bhutto Return," October 18, 2007, http://news.bbc.co.uk/2/hi/7050274.stm.

11. MSNBC, "2 Blasts Strike Crowd Celebrating Bhutto's Return," October 19, 2007, http://www.msnbc.msn.com/id/21344367/.

12. Carlotta Gall and Salman Masood, "Bomb Attack Kills Scores in Pakistan as Bhutto Arrives," *New York Times,* October 18, 2007, http://www.nytimes.com/2007/10/19/world/asia/19iht-19pakistan.7956073.html.

13. Ahmad Rashid, *Descent into Chaos: The US and the Disaster in Pakistan, Afghanistan, and Central Asia,* New York: Penguin Books, 2009, 379.

14. MSNBC, "2 Blasts Strike Crowd Celebrating Bhutto's Return."

15. Jones, *Pakistan: Eye of the Storm,* 4.

16. Pakistan People's Party, "Bhutto Names Suspects in Letter to Musharraf," October 24, 2007, http://www.ppp.org.pk/mbb/articles/article121.html.

17. Philip Sherwell, "Bhutto 'Blocked from Hiring US Bodyguards,'" *Sunday Daily Telegraph,* December 30, 2007, http://www.telegraph.co.uk/news/worldnews/1574054/Bhutto-blocked-from-hiring-US-bodyguards.html.

18. Gail Sheehy, "A Wrong Must Be Righted: An Interview with Benazir Bhutto," *Parade,* January 6, 2008, http://www.parade.com/articles/editions/2008/edition_01–06–2008/Benazir_bhuttoTest/.

19. Fatima Bhutto, "Aunt Benazir's False Promises."

20. Carlotta Gall and Salman Masood, "After Bombing, Bhutto Assails Officials' Ties," *New York Times,* October 20, 2007, http://www.nytimes.com/2007/10/20/world/asia/20Pakistan.html.

21. Zahid Hussain, "Musharraf and Bhutto in Power-Sharing Talks," *Times* (London), July 28, 2007, http://www.timesonline.co.uk/tol/news/world/asia/article2155462.ece.

22. Carlotta Gall, "Bhutto's Return Brings Pakistani Politics to a Boil," *New York Times,* October 30, 2007, http://www.nytimes.com/2007/10/30/world/asia/30pakistan.html.

23. Jemina Klan, "A Kletpcrat in a Hermes Scarf," *Daily Telegraph,* October 21, 2007, http://www.telegraph.co.uk/comment/3643479/Benazir-Bhutto-a-kleptocrat-in-a-Hermes-scarf.html.

24. Imran Khan, "Benazir Bhutto Has Only Herself to Blame," *Telegraph* (UK), October 21, 2007, http://www.telegraph.co.uk/comment/3643478/Benazir-Bhutto-has-only-herself-to-blame.html.

25. Gall, "Bhutto's Return Brings Pakistani Politics to a Boil."

26. Ibid.

27. BBC News, "Ex-PM Bhutto under House Arrest," November 9, 2007, http://news.bbc.co.uk/2/hi/7086272.stm.

28. Fatima Bhutto, "Aunt Benazir's False Promises."

29. Benazir Bhutto, "Benazir Bhutto's Letter to Peter Galbraith," CHOWK, November 14, 2007, http://www.chowk.com/ayesha5/iLogs/life/Benazir-Bhutto-s-letter-to-Peter Galbraith/.

30. Griff Witte and Emily Wax, "Bhutto's Last Day, in Keeping with Her Driven Life," *Washington Post,* January 16, 2008, http://www.washingtonpost.com/wp-dyn/content/article/2008/01/15/AR2008011503304.html.

31. Ali Hazrat Bacha, "Youth with Dynamite Held Near Rally Venue," *Dawn,* December 27, 2007, http://www.dawn.com/2007/12/27/top8.htm.

32. Witte and Wax, "Bhutto's Last Day, in Keeping with Her Driven Life."

33. Saeed Shah and Andrew Buncombe, "Bhutto Had 'Proof' of Plan to Rig Election," *Independent* (UK), January 1, 2008, http://www.independent.co.uk/news/world/asia/bhutto-had-proof-of-plan-to-rig-election-767540.html.

34. Associated Press, "In Meeting with Karzai, Bhutto Wanted Peace, Democracy for Afghanistan and Pakistan," December 27, 2007, http://www.afghanistannewscenter.com/news/2007/december/dec282007.html#3.

35. Witte and Wax, "Bhutto's Last Day, in Keeping with Her Driven Life."

36. Kamran Haider, "Four Dead in Pakistan Election Shooting," Reuters, December 27, 2007, http://in.reuters.com/article/article/2007/12/27/idININdia-31134720071227/.

37. Witte and Wax, "Bhutto's Last Day, in Keeping with Her Driven Life."

38. United Nations, *Report of the United Nations Commission of Inquiry into the Facts and Circumstances of the Assassination of Former Pakistani Prime Minister Mohtarma Benazir Bhutto.*

39. Ibid.

40. CNN, "Pakistan: Fractured Skull Killed Bhutto," December 28, 2007, http://www.cnn.com/2007/WORLD/asiapcf/12/28/pakistan.friday/index.html.

41. CNN, "Ministry Backtracks on Bhutto Sunroof Claims," January 1, 2008, http://www.cnn.com/2008/WORLD/asiapcf/01/01/pakistan.autopsy/index.html.

42. Ibid.

43. United Nations, *Report of the United Nations Commission of Inquiry into the Facts and Circumstances of the Assassination of Former Pakistani Prime Minister Mohtarma Benazir Bhutto.*

44. Ibid.

45. CNN, "Ministry Backtracks on Bhutto Sunroof Claims."

46. Aryn Baker and Simon Robinson, "Missing Evidence from Bhutto's Murder," *Time,* December 31, 2007, http://www.time.com/time/world/article/0,8599,1699138,00.html.

47. Simon Robinson, "Bhutto Conspiracy Theories Fill the Air," *Time,* December 28, 2007, http://www.time.com/time/world/article/0,8599,1698828,00.html.

48. United Nations, *Report of the United Nations Commission of Inquiry into the Facts and Circumstances of the Assassination of Former Pakistani Prime Minister Mohtarma Benazir Bhutto.*

49. Carlotta Gall, "Musharraf Denies Link to Attack on Bhutto," *New York Times,* January 3, 2008, http://www.nytimes.com/2008/01/03/world/asia/03iht-pakistan.4.9012655.html.

50. Ibid.

51. Ibid.

52. CNN, "Musharraf Denies Bhutto Death Role," January 4, 2008, http://www.cnn.com/2008/WORLD/asiapcf/01/03/pakistan.elections/index.html.

53. Jones, *Pakistan: Eye of the Storm,* 5–6.

54. Joby Warrick, "CIA Places Blame for Bhutto Assassination," *Washington Post,* January 18, 2008, http://www.washingtonpost.com/wp-dyn/content/article/2008/01/17/AR2008011703252.html.

55. Paul Cruickshank, "Hunting Bhutto's Killer," *Guardian* (UK), January 1, 2008, http://www.guardian.co.uk/commentisfree/2008/jan/01/huntingbhuttoskiller/.

56. *The Nation* (Pakistan), February 8, 2005, cited in Sohail Abdul Nasir, "Baitullah Mehsud: South Waziristan's Unofficial Amir," *Terrorism Focus* 3, no. 26 (2006), http://www.jamestown.org/single/?no_cache=1&tx_ttnews%5Btt_news%5D=829.

57. Afzal Khan, "Baitullah Mehsud: Scapegoat or Perpetrator in Benazir Bhutto's Assassination?" *Terrorism Monitor* 6, no. 5 (2008), http://www.jamestown.org/programs/gta/single/?tx_ttnews[tt_news]=4775&tx_ttnews[backPid]=167&no_cache=1.

58. *The Nation,* n.d., cited in "Who Is Aitezaz Shah?" *Pakistani Spectator,* February 2, 2008, http://www.pkhope.com/who-is-aitezaz-shah/.

59. " 'Bhutto Murder Suspect' Arrested," Al Jazeera, January 19, 2008, http://english.aljazeera.net/news/asia/2008/01/2008525125158691764.html.

60. "Teenager Suspect Arrested in Bhutto Assassination," *Economic Times* (India), January 20, 2008, http://economictimes.indiatimes.com/teenager-suspect-arrested-in-bhutto-assassination/articleshow/2714625.cms.

61. Farhan Bokhari, "PPP Pushes for Independent Bhutto Probe," *Financial Times* (London), January 20, 2008, http://www.ft.com/cms/s/0/333552c6-c774–11dc-a0b4–0000779fd2ac.html#axzz1PAbSOkoN.

62. Jones, *Pakistan: Eye of the Storm,* 4.

63. Scotland Yard, "Scotland Yard Report on Assassination of Benazir Bhutto," *Hindu* (India), February 9, 2008, http://www.hindu.com/2008/02/09/stories/2008020960750101.htm.

64. Alizeh Haider, "Scotland Yard Investigation Is Useless," *Washington Post*, February 14, 2008, http://onfaith.washingtonpost.com/postglobal/needtoknow/2008/02/scotland_yard_investigation_pu.html.

65. Scotland Yard, "Scotland Yard Report on Assassination of Benazir Bhutto."

66. Ibid.

67. Ibid.

Key Questions

▶ What caused a presumably healthy young Navajo couple to die suddenly?

▶ What initial assumptions were made about the cause of death?

▶ What alternative explanations should be considered?

▶ What information would best help identify the actual cause of death?

6 Death in the Southwest

CASE NARRATIVE

On 14 May 1993 in the Four Corners area of New Mexico, a young former track star collapsed on the way to his fiancée's funeral and was rushed to the Gallup Medical Center emergency room. He died a few hours later. State medical investigators performed autopsies on both the man and his fiancée, who had died five days earlier. They noted similarities in their cases: flulike symptoms of fever, coughing, and chills with quick progression to acute respiratory distress and death as their lungs filled with fluid. Their infant daughter also exhibited the same symptoms but was not as severely affected.[1] None of the medical personnel involved in treating the patients were believed to have become infected.

Three days later, Gallup Medical Center officials linked the deaths of the young couple to three other respiratory fatalities in the region and sent a warning to the New Mexico Department of Health. Doctors were concerned that they were dealing with a particularly potent flu virus that could spread quickly across the broader population. The next day the Department of Health contacted the federal Centers for Disease Control in Atlanta, Georgia, and asked it to investigate.[2]

By 31 May 1993, the disease had claimed ten victims, eight of them Navajos. Young, healthy adults were dying of an infectious disease that appeared to have a surprisingly high case-fatality rate.[3] An epidemiologist from the New Mexico Department of Health reported that all died shortly after developing symptoms similar to the flu, including a cough that quickly progressed to a severe respiratory ailment. The official said that the department did not know what the illness was or how to prevent it; initial laboratory polymerase chain reaction (PCR) tests for common viral and bacterial agents had come back negative.[4]

Medical officials realized they were facing a major challenge: people were dying, and no one knew why. Were all these deaths related? If so, what common symptoms could be identified? Doctors were concerned that if they could not determine the underlying cause of death, they could not treat those who were becoming ill and they could not prevent even more people from dying.

The Four Corners Region

Four Corners is a region of the United States that encompasses southwest Colorado, northwest New Mexico, northeast Arizona, and southeast Utah. The name comes from a monument that marks the only spot in the United States where the boundaries of four states intersect. The monument also denotes the boundary between two semi-autonomous Native American governments, the Navajo Nation, which maintains the monument as a tourist attraction, and the Ute Mountain Ute Indian Reservation.[5,6]

Many residents of the Four Corners region depend on tourism and agriculture for their livelihoods. The area hosts thousands of visitors yearly who come to the region to visit Canyon de Chelly National Monument and Mesa Verde National Park, which contain ruins of early indigenous tribes, and Monument Valley, which is notable for its large sandstone buttes. Other residents earn their livelihoods from livestock farming, seasonal migratory agricultural work, and employment off the Navajo reservation.[7,8,9]

The Four Corners Region is a high plateau: Weather systems stabilize here and then head eastward to create snow and rain in the central portion of the United States. The area itself has low humidity, sparse precipitation, and lots of sun. The winters are mild during the day with temperatures falling to or below freezing at nightfall. When El Niño occurs, usually every three to seven years, the winters and early springs tend to be wetter than usual. Stronger than usual El Niños bring significantly more rainy days and more rain per day. Summers are hot. Forty percent of the region's precipitation comes from late afternoon summer thunderstorms. Water rights and access to water are important issues in the area.[10,11,12]

The Navajo Nation constitutes the bulk of the population in the Four Corners region. The Nation's reservation encompasses more than 27,000 square miles, with three satellite locations in central New Mexico. The Navajo

Map 6.1 ▶ Four Corners Area

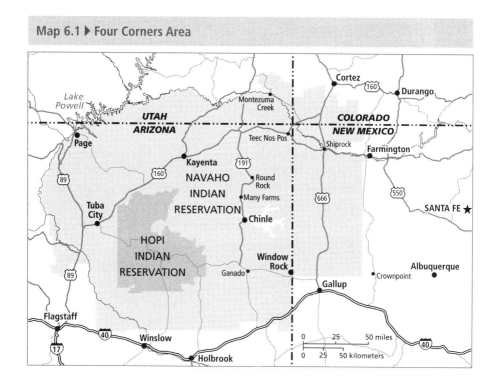

are inheritors of a cultural legacy centered on oral traditions and customs passed down for hundreds of years. The tribe's spiritual beliefs, collectively known as the Navajo Way, emphasize the importance of preserving and restoring balance and harmony with nature. According to cultural specialists at the Navajo Nation Museum in Window Rock, Arizona, sacred ceremonies performed by tribal healers are essential in perpetuating the Navajo Way. The Navajo medicine people (*hataa'lii* in the Navajo language) serve not only as healers but as historians with extensive knowledge of tribal traditions and mythology.[13,14]

The Navajo Area Indian Health Service (NAIHS), a subagency of the Department of Health and Human Services, is responsible for health care for American Indians in the Four Corners area; its primary patients are members of the Navajo Nation and the Southern Band of San Juan Paiutes, but NAIHS also provides care to other Native Americans. All NAIHS physicians must be board eligible or, preferably, board certified in a Western medical specialty. The NAIHS sensitizes its medical professionals to the intertwining of Navajo religion with the concepts of being, health, disease, and the environment. The

Navajo Nation Council's Division of Health Improvement Services—later renamed the Navajo Division of Health—also plays a role in promoting and maintaining the overall health and well-being of the Navajo population. It employs hundreds of health professionals, paraprofessionals, and technical professionals scattered throughout the Navajo Nation.[15,16]

Fear Takes Over

By the end of May, at least twenty-three patients—predominantly Navajos—with symptoms of the illness were being treated at hospitals in the Four Corners area and Albuquerque, New Mexico. Communicable disease specialists from the Indian Health Service in Albuquerque said that they had not yet been able to determine why people who were closely related to each other (family cluster cases) developed adult respiratory distress syndrome in roughly the same time period. In all cases, the disease—which some labeled the "Navajo flu"—progressed quickly, though it did not always lead to death. Press reports stated that four people appeared to have recovered, but doctors said they did not know whether treatment, primarily with antibiotics, was responsible.[17]

As news of the illness spread across the country, tourism to the Four Corners area declined. Twenty-seven young Navajos who corresponded with students at a private school in the Los Angeles area were discouraged from visiting their pen pals. Special telephone lines set up by the New Mexico Department of Health to handle inquiries about the illness were overwhelmed with calls. Hospitals in Santa Fe began seeing panicky patients who had visited the Navajo reservation within the past several weeks. Following the discovery of "new" and "unknown" diseases, it is typical behavior for a sensitized population within the presumably affected community to respond by inundating the available medical infrastructure.[18,19,20]

In Atlanta, three young investigators in the Centers for Disease Control's (CDC's) Epidemic Intelligence Service (EIS) were called on a Friday afternoon in late May and told to come to the office.[21] They were handed airline tickets and gas masks, the latter suggesting the possibility they could be exposed to a toxic substance. The EIS, the "special pathogens" branch of the CDC, is primarily deployed when a new pathogen is discovered or if there is an allegation or suspicion of bioterrorism. The service was created in 1951 during the Korean War, when the United States became worried about biological warfare. A preliminary survey of the Internet, however, revealed no postings containing extreme anti-Navajo rhetoric or any suggestions that terrorists might be targeting the Four Corners area.

The connection with bioterrorism was not far-fetched in the case of the "Navajo flu." Some residents of the reservation speculated that victims had been exposed to a toxin stored at Fort Wingate Army Depot, a munitions storage and demolition facility close to both the Navajo Nation and the Zuni Pueblo Tribe. Others asked whether there were any reports of toxic spills on or near Navajo Nation lands.[22]

Collecting the Pieces of the Puzzle

The EIS epidemiologists were skeptical that they were dealing with a flu virus. They were working against the clock to determine not only the type of illness but its root cause. EIS personnel began working with a small group of investigators assembled from the state health departments, the University of New Mexico School of Medicine, and the Navajo Area Indian Health Service. They began combing through patient logs made available by area hospitals and clinics.

Their research revealed that most patients lived in the Four Corners area, but the available data did not show the victims all visiting the same location or any obvious patterns. Most patients reported influenza-like symptoms of abrupt fever, nausea, vomiting, headache, malaise, and body aches—particularly abdominal and back pain. This was often followed by a cough, gastrointestinal manifestations, and labored breathing for four or more days before hospitalization with pulmonary edema or fluid in the lungs along with severe hypertension and oxygen deficit in body tissues. Blood tests, when conducted, also showed abnormally low blood platelet counts, which are often associated with diseases such as rickets, the plague, rabbit fever, and deer fly fever.[23] Initially, moderate cases of the illness were diagnosed as acute respiratory distress syndrome, juvenile diabetes, and even gastroenteritis. Those treating the patients did not seem to be contracting the illness.[24,25,26]

The investigators cast a wide investigatory net. Many of the pieces or clues were consistent with exposure to toxic material—either accidental or purposeful: presence of an unexplained disease in a discrete population, many cases of death from an unexplained disease, a disease that is unusual for an age group, a disease that is much more severe than expected, the failure to respond to standard therapy, and the presence of munitions or advanced weapons delivery systems.[27] A few patients reported dizziness, confusion, or impaired concentration, all of which are symptoms of exposure to toxic material. If a biological agent was being used deliberately to cause the deaths, one sign would be a high number of recent, unexplained animal deaths or crop failures, but research did not turn up any such evidence.

EIS personnel also sought out Navajo tribal healers, who were the closest thing to a historical medical registry available. The healers told EIS personnel that the cause of the disease was disharmony in the Navajo world. They recounted that many people had died of sudden, powerful diseases two other times during the twentieth century, in 1918 and 1933. Tribal elders recalled that there were particularly abundant piñon, or pine nut, crops those years because of unusually wet winters and springs. According to tribal lore, rodent populations were also very high during those times.[28]

Rodents are well-known as potential carriers of disease. Investigators asked: Was the outbreak of a similar virus and the increase in rodent populations on two other occasions earlier in the century a coincidence, or did the correlation suggest the source of the disease? Investigators needed to know as soon as possible what kinds of illnesses rodents are known to spread and whether such illnesses were endemic to the Four Corners region. Preliminary research suggested some answers, as shown in Table 6.1.

Table 6.1 ▶ Diseases Transmitted by Rodents	
Diseases Directly Transmitted by Rodents	Geographic Region Where Disease Occurs
Rat-Bite Fever	Worldwide; endemic to Four Corners area
Leptospirosis	Worldwide; endemic to Four Corners area
Salmonellosis	Worldwide; endemic to Four Corners area
Lymphocytic Choriomeningitis Virus	Worldwide
Rabies	Rodent-spread case in Florida in 1980
Plague	Western United States, South America, Africa, and Asia

The investigators reached out to climatologists as well. The climatologists confirmed that precipitation levels had increased dramatically in 1992 and 1993 in association with El Niño. The rainfall resulted in an abundance of vegetation and ample food supplies for rodent populations. When precipitation levels returned to normal, however, rodent populations became stressed due to the lack of food supply, forcing them to seek new sources of food. The National Science Foundation and the US Fish and Wildlife Service recommended that medical investigators consult scientists associated with the Sevilleta Long-Term Ecological Research Program at the Sevilleta National Wildlife Refuge in central New Mexico. Ecological researchers provided a detailed analysis of twenty-two rodent species in the area. In reviewing the reports, the investigators were struck by the fact that there had been a tenfold increase in the rodent population between 1992 and 1993.[29]

People were getting sick, and many were dying, as investigators continued to collect the various pieces of the puzzle. Doctors felt a growing sense of urgency to discover the underlying cause of death. Public concern was mounting, and people deserved an explanation. More important, the public was demanding guidance on what to do to avoid getting sick, and public health officials didn't know what to say.

RECOMMENDED READINGS

Dworkin, Mark S. *Outbreak Investigations Around the World: Case Studies in Infectious Disease Field Epidemiology.* Sudbury, MA: Jones and Bartlett, 2009.
Locke, Raymond Friday. *The Book of the Navajo.* Los Angeles: Holloway House, 1991.
McKenna, Maryn. *Beating Back the Devil.* New York: Free Press, 2008.

Table 6.2 ▶ Case Snapshot: Death in the Southwest		
Structured Analytic Technique Used	Heuer and Pherson Page Number	Analytic Family
Structured Brainstorming	p. 92	Idea Generation
Starbursting	p. 102	Idea Generation
Key Assumptions Check	p. 183	Assessment of Cause and Effect
Multiple Hypotheses Generator	p. 153	Hypothesis Generation and Testing
Analysis of Competing Hypotheses	p. 160	Hypothesis Generation and Testing

DEATH IN THE SOUTHWEST
STRUCTURED ANALYTIC TECHNIQUES IN ACTION

In a crisis situation, analysts are often forced to make difficult judgments with little solid data in hand. The following techniques and exercises can be used to tackle these types of situations by using Structured Brainstorming to think creatively and exhaustively, Starbursting to organize that thinking around key questions, the Multiple Hypotheses Generator to generate a full range of alternative hypotheses, and a Key Assumptions Check and Analysis of Competing Hypotheses (ACH) to scrutinize the evidence.

Technique 1: Structured Brainstorming

Brainstorming is a group process that follows specific rules and procedures designed to generate new ideas and concepts. The stimulus for creativity comes from two or more analysts bouncing ideas off each other. A brainstorming session usually exposes an analyst to a greater range of ideas and perspectives than the analyst could generate alone, and this broadening of views typically results in a better analytic product.

Structured Brainstorming is a systematic twelve-step process (described below) for conducting group brainstorming. It requires a facilitator, in part because participants are not allowed to talk during the brainstorming session. Structured Brainstorming is most often used to identify key drivers or all the forces and factors that may come into play in a given situation.

Box 6.1 SEVEN RULES FOR SUCCESSFUL BRAINSTORMING

1. Be specific about the purpose and the topic of the brainstorming session.

2. Never criticize an idea, no matter how weird, unconventional, or improbable it might sound. Instead, try to figure out how the idea might be applied to the task at hand.

3. Allow only one conversation at a time and ensure that everyone has an opportunity to speak.

4. Allocate enough time to complete the brainstorming session.

5. Try to include one or more "outsiders" in the group, usually someone who does not share the same body of knowledge or perspective as other group members but has some familiarity with the topic.

6. Write it down! Track the discussion by using a whiteboard, an easel, or sticky notes.

7. Summarize key findings at the end of the session. Ask the participants to write down the most important thing they learned on a 3-by-5-inch card as they depart the session. Then, prepare a short summary and distribute the list to the participants (who may add items to the list) and to others interested in the topic (including those who could not attend).

Task 1. Conduct a Structured Brainstorming exercise to explore why a healthy young Navajo couple died suddenly.

STEP 1: Gather a group of analysts with some knowledge of medicine and the Four Corners region.

STEP 2: Pass out sticky notes and Sharpie-type pens or markers to all participants. Inform the team that there is no talking during the sticky-notes portion of the brainstorming exercise.

STEP 3: Present the team with the following question: What are all the forces and factors that might explain why a young Navajo couple died suddenly?

STEP 4:   Ask the group to write down responses to the question with a few key words that will fit on a sticky note. After a response is written down, the participant gives it to the facilitator who then reads it aloud. Sharpie-type or felt-tip pens are used so that people can easily see what is written on the sticky notes later in the exercise.

STEP 5:   Place all the sticky notes on a wall randomly as they are called out. Treat all ideas the same. Encourage participants to build on one another's ideas.

STEP 6:   Usually an initial spurt of ideas is followed by pauses as participants contemplate the question. After five or ten minutes there is often a long pause of a minute or so. This slowing down suggests that the group has "emptied the barrel of the obvious" and is now on the verge of coming up with some fresh insights and ideas. Do not talk during this pause even if the silence is uncomfortable.

STEP 7:   After two or three long pauses, conclude this divergent-thinking phase of the brainstorming session.

STEP 8:   Ask all participants (or a small group) to go up to the wall and rearrange the sticky notes by affinity groups (groups that have some common characteristics). Some sticky notes may be moved several times, and some may be copied if the idea applies to more than one affinity group.

STEP 9:   When all sticky notes have been arranged, ask the group to select a word or phrase that best describes each grouping.

STEP 10: Look for sticky notes that do not fit neatly into any of the groups. Consider whether such an outlier is useless noise or the germ of an idea that deserves further attention.

STEP 11: Assess what the group has accomplished. Can you identify four or five key factors or forces that might explain why the young Navajo couple died?

STEP 12: Present the results, describing the key themes or dimensions of the problem that deserve investigation.

Analytic Value Added. Did we explore all the possible forces and factors that could explain why the young Navajo couple died? Did our ideas group themselves into coherent affinity groups? How did we treat outliers, that is, the sticky notes that seemed to belong in a group all by themselves? Did the outliers spark new lines of enquiry? Did the labels we generated for each group accurately capture the essence of that set of sticky notes?

Technique 2: Starbursting

Starbursting is a form of structured brainstorming that helps analysts generate as many questions as possible. It is particularly useful in developing a research project, but it can also help to elicit many questions and ideas to challenge conventional wisdom. This process allows the analyst to consider the issue at hand from many different perspectives, thereby increasing the chances that the analyst will uncover a heretofore unconsidered question or idea that will yield new analytic insights.

Task 2. Construct a Starbursting diagram to explore the Who? What? When? Where? Why? and How? questions relating to the untimely death of a healthy young Navajo couple.

STEP 1: Use the template in Figure 6.1 or draw a six-pointed star and write one of the following words at each point of the star: Who? What? When? Where? Why? and How?

STEP 2: Start the brainstorming session, using one of the words at a time to generate questions about the topic.
Do not try to answer the questions during the brainstorming session; just focus on generating as many questions as possible.

STEP 3: After generating questions that start with each of the six words, the group should either prioritize the questions to be answered or sort the questions into logical categories.

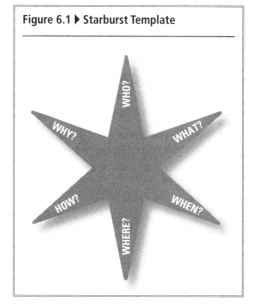

Figure 6.1 ▶ Starburst Template

Analytic Value Added. As a result of your analysis, which questions or categories deserve further investigation?

Technique 3: Key Assumptions Check

The Key Assumptions Check is a systematic effort to make explicit and question the assumptions that guide an analyst's interpretation of evidence and reasoning about any particular problem. Such assumptions are usually necessary and unavoidable as a means of filling gaps in the incomplete, ambiguous, and sometimes deceptive information with which the analyst must work. They are driven by the analyst's education, training, and experience, including the organizational context in which the analyst works. It can be difficult to identify assumptions, because many are sociocultural beliefs that are held unconsciously or so firmly that they are assumed to be truth and not subject to challenge. Nonetheless, identifying key assumptions and assessing the overall impact should conditions change are critical parts of a robust analytic process.

Task 3. Conduct a Key Assumptions Check of the initial theory that the young Navajo couple died from a particularly virulent common flu virus.

STEP 1: Gather a small group of individuals who are working the issue along with a few "outsiders." The primary analytic unit already is working from an established mental model, so the "outsiders" are needed to bring other perspectives.

STEP 2: Ideally, participants should be asked to bring their list of assumptions when they come to the meeting. If not, start the meeting with a silent brainstorming session. Ask each participant to write down several assumptions on 3-by-5-inch cards.

STEP 3: Collect the cards and list the assumptions on a whiteboard for all to see. A simple template can be used, as in Table 6.3.

Table 6.3 ▶ Key Assumptions Check Template				
Key Assumption	Commentary	Supported	With Caveat	Unsupported
1.				
2.				
3.				
4.				

STEP 4: Elicit additional assumptions. Work from the prevailing analytic line back to the key arguments that support it. Use various devices to prod participants' thinking. Ask the standard journalist questions: Who? What? When? Where? Why? and How? Phrases such as "will always," "will never," or "would have to be" suggest that an idea is not being challenged and perhaps should be. Phrases such as "based on" or "generally the case" usually suggest that a challengeable assumption is being made.

STEP 5: After identifying a full set of assumptions, critically examine each assumption. Ask:

▶ Why am I confident that this assumption is correct?

▶ In what circumstances might this assumption be untrue?

▶ Could this assumption have been true in the past but no longer be true today?

▶ How much confidence do I have that this assumption is valid?

▶ If this assumption turns out to be invalid, how much impact would it have on the analysis?

STEP 6: Using Table 6.3, place each assumption in one of three categories:

▶ Basically supported.

▶ Correct with some caveats.

▶ Unsupported or questionable—the "key uncertainties."

STEP 7: Refine the list, deleting those assumptions that do not hold up to scrutiny and adding new assumptions that emerge from the discussion.

STEP 8: Consider whether key uncertainties should be converted into collection requirements or research topics.

Analytic Value Added. When CDC investigators arrived on the scene and interviewed doctors, did they inherit any key assumptions that would have had an impact on how effectively they organized their investigation?

Technique 4: Multiple Hypothesis Generation—Multiple Hypotheses Generator

Multiple Hypothesis Generation is part of any rigorous analytic process because it helps the analyst avoid common pitfalls, such as coming to premature closure or being overly influenced by first impressions. Instead, it helps the analyst think broadly and creatively about a range of possibilities. The goal is to develop an exhaustive list of hypotheses, which can be scrutinized and tested over time against existing evidence and new data that may become available in the future.

The Multiple Hypotheses Generator is a useful tool for broadening the spectrum of plausible hypotheses. It is particularly helpful when there is a prevailing, but increasingly unconvincing, lead hypothesis—in this case, that healthy, young Navajos are dying from exposure to a virulent form of the common flu virus.

Task 4. Use the Multiple Hypotheses Generator to create and assess alternative hypotheses that explain why the young Navajo couple died. Contact Pherson Associates at ThinkSuite@pherson.org or go to www.pherson.org to obtain access to the Multiple Hypotheses Generator software if it is not available on your system.

STEP 1: Identify the lead hypothesis and its component parts using Who? What? When? Where? Why? and How?

STEPS 2 & 3: Identify plausible alternatives for the two or three most relevant key component parts and strive to keep them mutually exclusive. Discard any key component questions that one would consider to be "given" factors.

STEPS 4 & 5: Generate a list of possible permutations. Discard any permutations that simply make no sense.

STEP 6: Evaluate the credibility of the remaining permutations on a scale of 1 to 5, where 1 is low credibility and 5 is high credibility.

STEP 7: Re-sort the remaining permutations, listing them from most to least credible.

STEP 8: Restate the permutations as hypotheses.

STEP 9: Select from the top of the list those alternative hypotheses most deserving of attention and note why these hypotheses are most interesting.

Analytic Value Added. Which hypotheses should be explored further? Which of the six key components (Who? What? When? Where? Why? and How?) can be set aside because they are "givens," and why? Which hypotheses from the original list were discarded, and why?

Technique 5: Analysis of Competing Hypotheses

Analysts face a perennial challenge of working with incomplete, ambiguous, anomalous, and sometimes deceptive data. In addition, strict time constraints on analysis and the need to "make a call" often conspire with a number of natural human cognitive tendencies to result in inaccurate or incomplete judgments. Analysis of Competing Hypotheses (ACH) improves the analyst's chances of overcoming these challenges by requiring the analyst to identify and refute possible hypotheses using the full range of data, assumptions, and gaps that are pertinent to the problem at hand.

Task 5. Develop a set of hypotheses and use the Analysis of Competing Hypotheses software to identify which hypotheses provide the most credible explanation for the deaths in this case. Contact Pherson Associates at Think Suite@pherson.org or go to www.pherson.org to obtain access to the basic software, or the collaborative version called Te@mACH, if it is not available on your system.

STEP 1: Generate a set of hypotheses to be considered based on what was learned from the Structured Brainstorming exercise, the Starbursting exercise, or the Multiple Hypotheses Generator exercise, striving for mutual exclusivity.

STEP 2: Make a list of all relevant information, including significant evidence, arguments, gaps, and assumptions.

STEP 3: Assess the relevant information against each hypothesis by asking, "Is this information highly consistent, consistent, highly inconsistent, inconsistent, neutral, or not applicable vis-à-vis the hypothesis?" (The Te@mACH software does not include the "neutral" category.)

STEP 4: Rate the credibility of each item of relevant information.

STEP 5: Refine the matrix by reconsidering the hypotheses. Does it make sense to combine two hypotheses, add a new hypothesis, or disaggregate an existing one?

STEP 6: Draw tentative conclusions about the relative likelihood of each hypothesis. An inconsistency score will be calculated by the software; the hypothesis with the lowest inconsistency score is tentatively the most likely hypothesis. The one with the most inconsistencies is the least likely. The hypotheses with the lowest inconsistency scores appear on the left of the matrix, and those with the highest inconsistency scores appear on the right.

STEP 7: Analyze the sensitivity of your tentative conclusion to a change in the interpretation of a few critical items of information. If using the basic ACH software, sort the evidence by diagnosticity, and the most diagnostic information will appear at the top of the matrix. The Te@mACH software will automatically display the most diagnostic information at the top of the matrix.

STEP 8: Report the conclusions by considering the relative likelihood of all the hypotheses.

STEP 9: Identify indicators or milestones for future observation.

Analytic Value Added. As a result of your analysis, what are the most and least likely hypotheses? What are the most diagnostic pieces of information? What, if any, assumptions underlie the data? Are there any gaps in the relevant information that could affect your confidence? How confident are you in your assessment of the most likely hypotheses?

NOTES

1. *New York Times*, "Mystery Illness Takes 10th Life in the Southwest," May 31, 1993, http://www.nytimes.com/1993/05/31/us/mystery-illness-takes-10th-life-in-the-southwest.html.

2. Ecological Society of America, *Ecological Research Benefits: The Hantavirus Case Study,* August 25, 2009, http://www.esa.org/education_diversity/pdfDocs/hantavirus.pdf.

3. C. J. Peters and Ali S. Khan, "Hantavirus Pulmonary Syndrome: The New American Hemorrhagic Fever," *Clinical Infectious Diseases* 34 (2002): 1224–31, http://www2.medicine.wisc.edu/home/files/domfiles/infectiousdisease/Hantavirus.pdf.

4. *New York Times*, "Mystery Illness Takes 10th Life in the Southwest."

5. Rick Abasta, "Four Corners Monument Still the Legally Recognized Landmark Despite Reports," Navajo Nation Parks & Recreation Department, http://navajonationparks.org/pr/pr_4Cmarker.htm.

6. US Department of Energy, "Ute Mountain Ute Indian Reservation—General Setting," http://www1.eere.energy.gov/tribalenergy/guide/pdfs/ute_mountain_ute.pdf.

7. Robert S. McPherson, "Navajo Indians," http://www.historytogo.utah.gov/utah_chapters/american_indians/navajoindians.html.

8. US Department of Energy, "Ute Mountain Indian Reservation—General Setting."

9. Indian Country Extension, "Navajo Nation—Shiprock."

10. Tripcart.com, "Weather in Four Corners of New Mexico, Arizona, Utah, and Colorado," http://www.tripcart.com/usa-regions/Four-Corners,Weather.aspx.

11. Kathleen Ward, "Rainmaker Go North—Nebraska Needs Help, Too," October 10, 2002, http://www.ksre.ksu.edu/news/sty/2002/weather_winter101002.htm.

12. Western Regional Climate Center, "El Niño, La Niña, and the Western US, Alaska, and Hawaii," compiled by Kelly Redmond, updated June 26, 1998, http://www.wrcc.dri.edu/enso/ensofaq.html.

13. Lauren Monsen, "Navajo Healers, Sand Paintings Keep Tribal Traditions Alive," NewsBlaze.com, n.d., http://newsblaze.com/story/20080920133834tsop.nb/topstory.html.

14. Navajo Nation Government, "History," http://www.navajo.org/history.htm.

15. Indian Health Service, "Navajo Area Office: Navajo Area Jobs and Recruitment," http://www.ihs.gov/navajo/index.cfm?module=najr_main.

16. Indian Health Service, "Cross Culture Medicine," http://www.ihs.gov/Navajo/index.cfm?module=nao_cross_culture_medicine.

17. *New York Times*, "Mystery Illness Takes 10th Life in the Southwest."

18. "Four Corners," Wikipedia, accessed August 25, 2009, http://en.wikipedia.org/wiki/Four_Corners_region.

19. Jill Leovy and Jack Cheevers, "Visiting Navajo Children Barred from L.A. School," *Los Angeles Times*, June 2, 1993, http://articles.latimes.com/1993–06–02/news/mn-42529_1_navajo-children/.

20. Maureen Trudelle Schwarz, *Navajo Lifeways: Contemporary Issues, Ancient Knowledge*, Norman: University of Oklahoma Press, 2001, 23.

21. Tom Paulson, "Doctor on Trail of Another Deadly Virus," *Seattle Post-Intelligencer*, April 10, 2003, http://www.seattlepi.com/local/116784_outbreak10.html.

22. Ibid.

23. Peters and Khan, "Hantavirus Pulmonary Syndrome."

24. Lone Simonsen, Mary J. Dalton, Robert F. Brieman, Thomas Hennessy, Edith T. Umland, C. Mack Sewell, Pierre E. Rollin, Thomas G. Ksiazek, and Clarence J. Peters, "Evaluation of the Magnitude of the 1993 Hantavirus Outbreak in the Southwestern United States," *Journal of Infectious Diseases* 172, no. 3 (1995): 729–33.

25. John H. Grendon and Marcia J. Goldoft, "Discovery of Hantavirus Syndrome in Washington State," *Washington Public Health* 14 (1996), http://www.nwpublichealth.org/docs/wph/hanta.html.

26. Peters and Khan, "Hanta Pulmonary Syndrome."

27. Robert G. Darling and Jon B. Woods, eds., *USAMRIID's Medical Management of Biological Casualties Handbook*, 5th ed, Frederick, MD: US Army Medical Research Institute of Infectious Diseases, 2004, http://www.usamriid.army.mil/education/bluebookpdf/USAMRIID%20Blue%20Book%205th%20Edition.pdf.

28. Linda Moon Stumpff, "Hantavirus and the Navajo Nation—A Double Jeopardy Disease," Evergreen State College, 2010, http://nativecases.evergreen.edu/collection/cases/hantavirus-navajo.html.

29. Public Affairs Office, Ecological Society of America, "Ecological Research Benefits: The Hantavirus Case Study."

7 The Atlanta Olympics Bombing

CASE NARRATIVE

Carnage in Centennial Park

In the summer of 1996, world attention focused on Atlanta, Georgia, as the city proudly hosted the Centennial Olympic Games. With some 15,000 athletes from 197 countries competing and millions of spectators in attendance, state, local, and federal authorities invested a great deal of resources on site security. In all, officials spent an estimated $227 million on security to deploy about 30,000 police, military, and private guards, as well as an array of high-technology equipment.[1,2] Authorities described the effort as the largest peacetime security operation for a public event in American history.[3]

Beginning three months before the Olympics opening ceremony, the Atlanta Olympic Committee transformed a 21-acre site from an unused area of slums and old warehouses into Centennial Park—a popular entertainment venue for those attending the Games.[4] The Park attracted some 100,000 people a day to relax and party on the outskirts of the Olympics. On 26 July 1996, the ninth day of the Olympics, authorities estimated that 40,000 to 50,000 people gathered in the park to attend a Friday night concert.[5] At 0120, Jack Mack and the Heart Attack were performing on stage at the AT&T Pavillion when a bomb exploded, spreading nails and shrapnel through a portion of the crowd. The blast killed Alice Hawthorne, who had brought her daughter to the Olympics as an early birthday present, and injured 111 others.[6,7] A Turkish cameraman, Melih Uzunyol, died of a heart attack responding to the blast.[8] Hopes for holding an Olympics without a terrorist incident were shattered.

119

Eyewitnesses described a scene of horror and carnage at the Park with wounded people everywhere.[9] Police officers reported people on the ground screaming. When the smoke cleared, six state troopers and one Georgia State Bureau of Investigation agent were among those injured in the blast.[10] One 33-year-old officer reported: "I saw the flash. I saw the puff of smoke. I saw the orange flame. Then something grabbed me and threw me across the ground."[11] A nearby press center was closed immediately because guards feared another explosion. Richard Jewell, a security guard, was proclaimed a hero for spotting a suspicious knapsack, alerting authorities, and helping them clear the area prior to the explosion. Nine police officers were also involved in trying to clear the area before the bomb went off, and all were credited with having substantially reduced the number of casualties from the explosion.

Atlanta Chief of Police Beverly Harvard noted that they had been receiving bomb threats on a regular basis prior to the incident and were concerned about the potential for copycat bombings in the wake of the Centennial Park

Map 7.1 ▶ Centennial Park

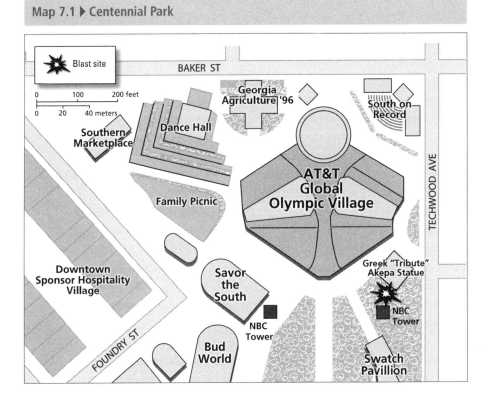

bombing. Bomb threats continued over the weekend. Law enforcement officials ordered the evacuation of a shopping center, two subway stations, a bank, and a church because of bomb threats as they worked quickly to identify those responsible for the bombing.[12]

The Broader Context

Local law enforcement officials as well as the FBI had been concerned for some time about the possibility of a terrorist attack against the Olympic Games. Just days before the opening ceremonies on 17 July 1996, TWA Flight 800 had taken off from New York's Kennedy Airport and exploded in midair over Long Island Sound, killing 228 passengers.[13] The reason for the crash was still being investigated, but a terrorist attack was a distinct possibility. Security concerns in Atlanta were underscored when a man carrying a loaded handgun sneaked into Olympic Stadium before the opening ceremony. The man was dressed as a security guard and was arrested; police later released him after deciding that he did not pose a threat.[14] Just three months earlier in April 1996, members of a militia group had been arrested in central Georgia and accused of conspiring to stockpile bombs for a "war" with the government.[15]

Law enforcement officials also remembered that the Palestinian terrorist organization known as Black September had struck at the 1972 Olympics in Munich. In that attack, the Palestinians took 11 Israeli athletes hostage for 23 hours in the hope of attracting attention to the Palestinian cause and forcing the Israeli government to free 242 political prisoners from jail. The crisis culminated in a deadly shootout on an airport tarmac that ended with the deaths of one German police officer and all 11 Israeli hostages.[16]

Since then, governments hosting the Olympic Games have devoted considerable resources to ensuring that the Games would not be stained by another terrorist attack. Billions had been spent by governments around the world since 1972 to keep the Games safe, and Atlanta authorities had taken the threat of a terrorist attack seriously.[17]

The Investigation

Just prior to the explosion, Tom Davis, a Georgia Bureau of Investigation agent, went to Centennial Park on a routine call to handle a few overexcited revelers attending a concert.[18] When he arrived at the Park, the rowdies apparently had already departed, but a stage security guard, Richard Jewell, caught his attention. Jewell was one of a handful of contract guards retained by AT&T after it had canceled a previous contract with another security company two weeks earlier.[19]

FBI photo of green bench in front of NBC's sound tower.

Jewell showed Davis a suspicious package—a green knapsack that had been left unattended under a bench at the foot of a huge NBC media sound and light tower, which had been built to support the stage shows. Davis immediately called a bomb diagnostic team and, as other officers joined him, started ushering people away from the site of the abandoned knapsack.

Jewell later said that he routinely made security sweeps around the tower, checking under benches and making sure nothing was amiss. He said he was certain the knapsack was not in the area at 2130 but he did notice it on his next check around 0050 after the rowdy group had departed.[20] He suspected the rowdy group had left the knapsack behind. Davis checked with some revelers in the area, and they said it was not their knapsack. Davis and Jewell asked several others if they knew whose knapsack it was, but no one claimed ownership.[21]

Jewell told investigators he was 40 feet away when the bomb exploded, but the impact still knocked him off his feet. When he looked up, he saw two Georgia state troopers sailing through the air.[22]

The FBI Takes Command
The FBI took the lead in the investigation.[23] At a press conference held on 29 July, FBI spokesperson David Tubbs noted that numerous law enforcement

agencies were involved and that they had received a substantial number of leads that they were tracking down. He cautioned the press that it was important not to draw any conclusions from questions that were being asked and said the Bureau had not identified a suspect. He indicated that the Bureau was focusing on domestic rather than international terrorism.

Law enforcement officials said the list of possible bombers ranged from antigovernment militia members to disgruntled employees.[24] Investigators speculated early in the investigation that an extremist militia-type group or an organization that was antigovernment could be behind the bombing.[25] Based on one of the composite sketches made after the bombing, FBI agents interviewed an Alabama militia member, but then ruled him out as a possible suspect. Other potentially violent domestic extremist groups such as white supremacists, sovereign citizens, and anti-abortion groups also merited attention. The Bureau expanded its search to consider disgruntled AT&T employees because the bomb site was next to an AT&T facility where people recently had been dismissed. FBI Director Louis Freeh would later say that the Bureau had identified "several suspects" early on in the case, but all suspects "washed out" after law enforcement discovered evidence that was exculpatory or inconsistent with investigating the individuals further.[26]

Tubbs told the press that a 911 call was made at approximately 0100 from a pay phone outside the downtown Days Inn. The next day, the FBI released the exact wording of the warning call: "There is a bomb in Centennial Park. You have 30 minutes." The FBI spokesperson said the Bureau believed the voice was that of a "white American made with an indistinguishable accent."[27]

The 911 police log obtained by the Associated Press (AP) lists three entries logged into the Atlanta police 911 computer early in the morning of 27 July.[28]

▶ 00:55:35, apparently the time the call was received. According to the dispatcher's notes, the caller was "very calm and even" and sounded like a white man.

▶ 01:08:35, followed by an abbreviation "DIS," apparently referring to the dispatch of one or more officers.

▶ 01:12:52, followed by "ARV," apparently referring to an officer arriving at an unspecified location.

Terrorism experts and Fulton County Sheriff Jacquelyn H. Babbett said the 911 warning may have been an attempt to lure police and security officers to the site of the bombing to injure them.[29] According to one terrorism expert, the phone warning was a classic ambush technique designed to clear an area of civilians but draw police to the scene to kill them. The placement of nails around the bomb showed that the intent was not just to have a big bang but to kill people.[30] A retired Bureau of Alcohol, Tobacco, and Firearms official, Robert Holland, said in an interview that when a bomber says people have 30 minutes and the bomb goes off 18 minutes later, there is a good possibility the bomber intended to take out the security forces.[31]

The bomb itself was crudely made (see Figure 7.1). Law enforcement officials described it as a pipe bomb that used a simple clock and low-grade, easily available explosive powder. The shrapnel that wounded so many people included masonry nails placed in a plastic food container around the explosives.[32] Investigators found several remnants of the bomb, including residue from a portion of the bomb that failed to explode, and shrapnel. An intact end cap from one of the three pipe bombs that were tied together to cause the blast was found by a tourist, who later turned it over to the FBI. The masonry nails had a round top, slight spiral ribs, and a very slight thread. Sources told AP that this was an odd choice of nails for a person to buy—suggesting to them that the bomber had used whatever was lying around at the time.[33]

Investigators had the telephone from which the 911 call was made and videotapes and other materials from the scene, which they hoped would lead them to a quick arrest.[34] The knapsack was identified as an olive-green, military-style backpack commonly known as a medium-size ALICE pack. It had an improvised handle made by inserting a round wooden rod at the top of the pack. Investigators said that military personnel are known to have modified packs in this way and to have taught the same technique.[35]

FBI investigators began interviewing large numbers of people who were present at the time of the explosion in search of more leads. They also screened videotape shot by sophisticated night-vision surveillance cameras, called SpeedDomes, which were mounted in Centennial Park and camouflaged to look like light poles.[36] The cameras rotate 360 degrees and have the ability to zoom in on an object of interest and magnify the image ten times. There were hundreds of SpeedDomes across the Olympic venue.

Jewell was interviewed by the Secret Service, the Georgia Bureau of Investigation, and the FBI on 27 July and again on 28 July. In these interviews, interrogators considered him a witness, not a suspect.[37] The views of investigators began to change, however, in the afternoon of 28 July following the second interview. The president of Piedmont College, Ray Cleere, called the FBI Field Office in Atlanta that afternoon after seeing Jewell on television to suggest that the FBI consider the possibility that Jewell planted the bomb. Cleere noted that

Figure 7.1 ▶ Bomb Specifications and ALICE Pack

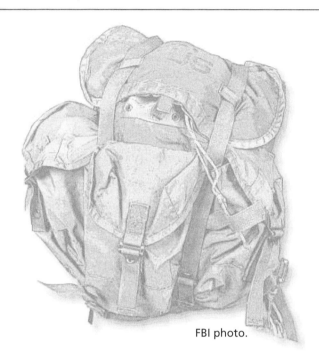

FBI photo.

The bomb in the ALICE pack consisted of three metal pipes 2 inches in diameter and 12 inches long, threaded on each end with 2-inch metal endcaps on each pipe. The bomb used three to four pounds of Accurate Arms brand #7 or #9 smokeless gunpowder. It contained about six pounds of 8d, 2 1/2-inch-long masonry nails. It used a blue, Eveready 12-volt battery; a Westclox brand "Big Ben" wind-up alarm clock; gray duct tape; and black plastic electrical tape.

Sources: FBI National Press Office, "Statement of FBI SAC Jack A. Doulton and Inspector Woody R. Enderson [press release]," November 18, 1997, http://web.archive.org/web/20000303015458/www.fbi.gov/majcases/rudolph/presrel1.htm; Federal Bureau of Investigation, Counterterrorism Division, Counterterrorism Threat Assessment and Warning Unit, National Security Division, "Terrorism in the United States: 1996," 1996, http://www.fbi.gov/stats-services/publications/terror_96.pdf.

Jewell had had problems earlier working as a police officer at Piedmont College, and Cleere's theory was that Jewell had intentionally placed the bomb because he wanted credit for having mitigated the amount of damage done by the bomb. After doing some preliminary research, FBI agents found a case in southern California not long before the Atlanta bombing when a volunteer firefighter had apparently set a series of fires so that he could extinguish them and become a hero.[38]

Later in the afternoon on 28 July, when the tip was passed to FBI officials in Washington during a conference call, someone on the call mentioned that a security guard at the 1984 Olympic Games in Los Angeles had planted a bomb on a bus so that he could discover it later and be a hero. FBI Headquarters agreed that it was logical to conduct a preliminary investigation of Jewell's background, but the investigators focused most of their attention on other suspects.[39]

The FBI's background investigation uncovered some interesting information. For starters, Jewell had been arrested in 1990 for impersonating a police officer. He also had work-related problems while serving as a deputy sheriff in Habersham County, Georgia.

The next day, the FBI's profiling unit said that Jewell "fit the profile of a person who might create an incident so he could emerge as a hero."[40] After reviewing videotape of interviews with Jewell, the profiling team said that Jewell's "account of the bombing seemed vague on important points and that he seemed uncomfortable discussing the victims."[41] An analyst on the profiling team observed that Jewell's statement that he was hoping to get a position in the Atlanta Police Department after the Games ended was highly inappropriate in the context of a lethal bombing and could indicate a motive for planting the explosives.

By the end of the day, Jewell had been transformed from a helpful witness to the FBI's principal suspect in the investigation, according to an FBI summary report prepared by its Office of Professional Integrity. In the late afternoon of 29 July, two FBI agents drove to Jewell's mother's apartment where Jewell was staying—and where TV crews were already staked out. Jewell agreed to drive down to the FBI offices in Atlanta voluntarily to be interviewed.

The pace of the investigation—and Jewell's life—changed dramatically the next day, when the *Atlanta Journal-Constitution* stated in its 30 July edition that "the security guard who first alerted police to the pipe bomb that exploded in Centennial Olympic Park is the focus of the federal investigation into the incident."[42] The story noted that Jewell's profile fit the profile of a lone bomber and that Jewell had been approaching news organizations trying to make himself into a celebrity. Jewell had in fact appeared on several programs, including CNN's *Talk Back Live*, NBC's *Today Show*, and *NBC News*, and had been cited in several newspapers, including the *Boston Globe*, the *Washington Post*, and *USA Today*. In these interviews, he discussed the sufficiency of training for security guards, the adequacy of the preparations for a possible bombing, whether authorities had responded properly to the event, and whether it was safe for people to return to Centennial Park.[43] Jewell's attorney later claimed, however, that the media relations coordinator for AT&T had "arranged for Mr. Jewell to participate in a limited number of media interviews" and that Jewell did so "to accommodate" his employer.[44]

Subsequent press stories reported that Jewell possessed a knapsack similar to the one that contained the bomb, had been dismissed earlier from two law enforcement positions, and had received bomb training at the Habersham County Sheriff's Department. Questions were also raised in the press as to whether his voice matched that of the 911 caller.[45] Such press revelations put intense pressure on local, state, and federal investigators to solve the crime.

On 10 August, the *Atlanta Journal-Constitution* reported that Jewell's defense lawyer claimed that it was physically impossible for Jewell to have made the 911 call given his known whereabouts at the time of the blast. The telephoned bomb threat came about one minute after Jewell had alerted Tom

Richard Jewell testifies about the Atlanta Olympics bombing before a House subcommittee on 30 July 1997.

Davis to the suspicious package. Investigators estimated that it would have taken about 4 minutes and 45 seconds to walk from Centennial Park to the Days Inn where the phone call was placed, which meant that Jewell could not have placed the call.[46] More likely, Jewell was helping clear the park when the phone call was made. Some retorted, however, that the timing suggested Jewell had an accomplice in the crime.

As authorities built the case against Jewell, conflicting evidence began to surface suggesting that Jewell might not have been the perpetrator of the crime. On 20 August, the *Atlanta Journal-Constitution* reported that Jewell had passed a polygraph in which he denied any involvement in the bombing. A retired FBI polygraph expert conducted the examination. A week later, Jewell's mother attended a news conference called by her son's attorneys and asked President Clinton to intervene and exonerate Jewell. Attorney General Janet Reno refused to exonerate Jewell but did say "I understand how she must feel."[47] The authorities, however, pressed on with their investigation.

RECOMMENDED READINGS

Federal Bureau of Investigation, Counterterrorism Division, Counterterrorism Threat Assessment and Warning Unit, National Security Division. "Terrorism in the United States: 1996." 1996. http://www.fbi.gov/stats-services/publications/terror_96.pdf.

Ostrow, Ron. "Richard Jewell and the Olympic Bombing: Case Study," Pew Research Center's Project for Excellence in Journalism. February 15, 2003. http://www.journalism.org/node/1791.

Table 7.1 ▶ Case Snapshot: The Atlanta Olympics Bombing		
Structured Analytic Technique Used	Heuer and Pherson Page Number	Analytic Family
Key Assumptions Check	p. 183	Assessment of Cause and Effect
Pros-Cons-Faults-and-Fixes	p. 284	Decision Support
Multiple Hypotheses Generator	p. 153	Hypothesis Generation and Testing

THE ATLANTA OLYMPICS BOMBING
STRUCTURED ANALYTIC TECHNIQUES IN ACTION

Police investigators were under severe pressure to bring the investigation to closure quickly and to identify a prime suspect. Such dynamics make analysts and investigators vulnerable to groupthink; often they respond by adopting satisficing strategies that will please all key stakeholders. The best way to cope with such pressure is to employ structured techniques that require investigators and analysts to stop and think for a few minutes or hours before plunging in to resolve the case. This case study explores how three structured analytic techniques—the Key Assumption Check, Pros-Cons-Faults-and-Fixes, and the Multiple Hypotheses Generator—can be employed to better frame the problem and avoid pursuing investigative blind alleys.

Technique 1: Key Assumptions Check

The Key Assumptions Check is a systematic effort to make explicit and question the assumptions that guide an analyst's interpretation of evidence and reasoning about any particular problem. Such assumptions are usually necessary and unavoidable as a means of filling gaps in the incomplete, ambiguous, and sometimes deceptive information with which the analyst must work. They are driven by the analyst's education, training, and experience, including the organizational context in which the analyst works. It can be difficult to identify assumptions because many are sociocultural beliefs that are held unconsciously or so firmly that they are assumed to be true and not subject to challenge. Nonetheless, identifying key assumptions and assessing the overall impact should conditions change are critical parts of a robust analytic process.

Task 1. Assume you are a member of the FBI team investigating the bombing. President Cleere has called the FBI office in Atlanta to present his rationale for making Richard Jewell a prime suspect in the case. Following consultations with Washington, D.C., your team has decided to do just that. To help kick off the investigation, you have been asked to conduct a Key Assumptions Check with your teammates to go over what assumptions the team is making about Jewell and the bombing in Centennial Park. Your task is to guide the team through the following eight steps for conducting a Key Assumptions Check.

STEP 1: Gather a small group of individuals who are working the issue along with a few "outsiders." The primary analytic unit already is working from an established mental model, so the "outsiders" are needed to bring other perspectives.

STEP 2: Ideally, participants should be asked to bring their list of assumptions when they come to the meeting. If not, start the meeting with a silent brainstorming session. Ask each participant to write down several assumptions on a 3-by-5-inch card.

STEP 3: Collect the cards and list the assumptions on a whiteboard for all to see. A simple template can be used, like the one shown in Table 7.2.

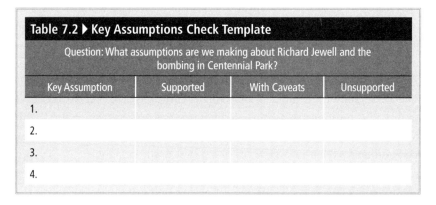

Table 7.2 ▶ Key Assumptions Check Template			
Question: What assumptions are we making about Richard Jewell and the bombing in Centennial Park?			
Key Assumption	Supported	With Caveats	Unsupported
1.			
2.			
3.			
4.			

STEP 4: Elicit additional assumptions. Work from the prevailing analytic line back to the key arguments that support it. Use various devices to prod participants' thinking. Ask the standard journalist questions: Who? What? When? Where? Why? and How? Phrases such as "will always," "will never," or "would have to be" suggest that an idea is not being

challenged and perhaps should be. Phrases such as "based on" or "generally the case" usually suggest that a challengeable assumption is being made.

STEP 5: After identifying a full set of assumptions, critically examine each assumption. Ask:

▶ Why am I confident that this assumption is correct?

▶ In what circumstances might this assumption be untrue?

▶ Could this assumption have been true in the past but no longer be true today?

▶ How much confidence do I have that this assumption is valid?

▶ If this assumption turns out to be invalid, how much impact would it have on the analysis?

STEP 6: Using Table 7.2, place each assumption in one of three categories:

▶ Basically supported.

▶ Correct with some caveats.

▶ Unsupported or questionable—the "key uncertainties."

One technique you can employ to decide which category to assign to an assumption is to ask the question: Can I make decisions about moving resources or people based on this assumption? If the answer is "yes," then the assumption can be rated as "supported." If the answer is "it depends," then the assumption merits a rating of "with caveats," and the caveat(s) needs to be recorded. If it would be inappropriate or hard to justify the movement of people or resources on the basis of this assumption, then the assumption is "unsupported."

STEP 7: Refine the list, deleting those assumptions that do not hold up to scrutiny and adding new assumptions that emerge from the discussion.

STEP 8: Consider whether key uncertainties should be converted into investigative leads, collection requirements, or research topics.

Analytic Value Added. What assumptions, if any, did law enforcement analysts and officials make as they began the investigation? Were they influenced by key assumptions of others, including the press and the experts they interviewed, who wanted to assist their work? Did the investigators fall into the trap of groupthink, or did they have sufficient cause to focus on Jewell as a suspect?

What impact did key assumptions have on how effectively the FBI organized its investigation?

Technique 2: Pros-Cons-Faults-and-Fixes

Pros-Cons-Faults-and-Fixes (PCFF) is a simple strategy for evaluating many types of decisions, including the decision to launch a police investigation. In this case, law enforcement officials are under substantial pressure to decide whether Richard Jewell was responsible for planting the bomb. PCFF is particularly well suited to situations in which decision makers must act quickly, because the technique helps to explicate and troubleshoot a decision in a quick and organized manner so that the decision can be shared and discussed by all decision-making participants.

Task 2. Use PCFF to help you decide whether Richard Jewell was responsible for planting the bomb in Centennial Park.

STEP 1: Clearly define the proposed action or choice.

STEP 2: List all the Pros in favor of the decision. Think broadly and creatively and list as many benefits, advantages, or other positives as possible. Merge any overlapping Pros.

STEP 3: List all the Cons or arguments against what is proposed. Review and consolidate the Cons. If two Cons are similar or overlapping, merge them to eliminate redundancy.

STEP 4: Determine Fixes to neutralize as many Cons as possible. To do so, propose a modification of the Con that would significantly lower the risk of the Con being a problem, identify a preventive measure that would significantly reduce the chances of the Con being a problem, conduct contingency planning that includes a change of course if certain indicators are observed, or identify a need for further research or to collect information to confirm or refute the assumption that the Con is a problem.

STEP 5: Fault the Pros. Identify a reason the Pro would not work or the benefit would not be received, pinpoint an undesirable side effect that might accompany the benefit, or note a need for further research to confirm or refute the assumption that the Pro will work or be beneficial.

STEP 6: Compare the Pros, including any Faults, against the Cons and Fixes (see Table 7.3).

Table 7.3 ▶ Pros-Cons-Faults-and-Fixes Template			
Faults	Pros	Cons	Fixes
Describe any Faults for Pro 1.	Pro 1	Con 1	Describe any fixes for Con 1.
Describe any Faults for Pro 2.	Pro 2	Con 2	Describe any Fixes for Con 2.
Describe any Faults for Pro 3.	Pro 3	Con 3	Describe any Fixes for Con 3.

Analytic Value Added. Based upon your assessment of the Pros and Cons, can you make a strong case that Richard Jewell planted the bomb in Centennial Park?

Technique 3: Multiple Hypotheses Generator
Multiple Hypothesis Generation is part of any rigorous analytic process because it helps the analyst avoid common pitfalls such as coming to premature closure or being overly influenced by first impressions. Instead, it helps the analyst think broadly and creatively about a range of possibilities. The goal is to develop an exhaustive list of hypotheses that can be scrutinized and tested over time against existing evidence and new data that may become available in the future.

The Multiple Hypotheses Generator is one of several tools that can be used to broaden the spectrum of plausible hypotheses. It is particularly helpful when there is a reigning lead hypothesis—in this case, the lead hypothesis that Richard Jewell planted the bomb in Centennial Park as part of a scheme to make himself a hero and obtain a position in law enforcement after the Olympic Games concluded.

Task 3. Use the Multiple Hypotheses Generator to create and assess alternative hypotheses for the bombing in Centennial Park. Contact Pherson Associates at ThinkSuite@pherson.org or go to www.pherson.org to obtain access to the Multiple Hypotheses Generator software if it is not available on your system.

STEP 1: Identify the lead hypothesis and its component parts using Who? What? When? Where? How? and Why? (see Table 7.4).

STEPS 2 & 3: Identify plausible alternatives for each key component and strive to keep them mutually exclusive. Discard any "given" factors.

Table 7.4 ▶ Multiple Hypotheses Generator Template		
Lead Hypothesis:		
Components	Lead Hypothesis	Alternative/Brainstormed
Who?		
What?		
When?		
Why?		
Where?		
How?		

STEP 4: Generate a list of possible permutations.

STEP 5: Discard any permutations that simply make no sense.

STEP 6: Evaluate the credibility of the remaining hypotheses on a scale of 1 to 5 where 1 is low credibility and 5 is high credibility.

STEP 7: Re-sort the remaining hypotheses, listing them from most to least credible.

STEP 8: Restate the permutations as hypotheses.

STEP 9: Select from the top of the list those alternative hypotheses most deserving of attention and note why these hypotheses are most interesting.

Analytic Value Added. Which hypotheses should be explored further? What motives should be considered, and why? Which hypotheses from the original list were set aside, and why?

NOTES

1. Federal Bureau of Investigation, Counterterrorism Division, Counterterrorism Threat Assessment and Warning Unit, National Security Division, "Terrorism in the United States: 1996," 1996, http://www.fbi.gov/stats-services/publications/terror_96.pdf.

2. Stephen Wilson, "Olympics Security Challenged," *Washington Post,* July 27, 1996, http://www.washingtonpost.com/wp-srv/national/longterm/bombing/stories/security.htm.

3. BBC, "1996: Bomb Rocks Atlanta Olympics," http://news.bbc.co.uk/onthisday/hi/dates/stories/july/27/newsid_3920000/3920865.stm.

4. Ibid.

5. FBI National Press Office, "Statement by Woody R. Enderson, Inspector in Charge Southeast Bomb Task Force" [press release], July 20, 1999.

6. Mike Lopresti, "A Decade Later, Atlanta Olympic Bombing Overshadowed," *USA Today,* July 23, 2006, http://www.usatoday.com/sports/columnist/lopresti/2006–07–23-lopresti-atl-10-years_x.htm.

7. William Booth and Thomas Heath, "Bomb Tip May Have Set Up Police in Atlanta for 'Ambush,'" July 30, 1996, *Washington Post,* http://www.washingtonpost.com/wp-srv/national/longterm/bombing/stories/ambush.htm.

8. Department of Justice, "Eric Rudolph Charged in Centennial Olympic Park Bombing" [press release], October 14, 1998, http://www.fas.org/irp/news/1998/10/477crm.htm.

9. BBC, "1996: Bomb Rocks Atlanta Olympics."

10. Booth and Heath, "Bomb Tip May Have Set Up Police in Atlanta for 'Ambush.'"

11. Joan Kirchner, "How Olympic Bomb Was Found," Associated Press, in *Washington Post,* July 27, 1996, http://www.washingtonpost.com/wp-srv/national/longterm/bombing/stories/found.htm.

12. Tom Beardon, "Security Matters [transcript]," PBS, July 29, 1996, http://www.pbs.org/newshour/bb/sports/july96/olympics_7–29.html.

13. Federal Bureau of Investigation, "Terrorism in the United States: 1996."

14. Wilson, "Olympics Security Challenged."

15. Ibid.

16. Lisa Beyer, "The Myths and Realities of Munich," *Time,* December 4, 2005, http://www.time.com/time/magazine/article/0,9171,1137646–1,00.html.

17. Lopresti, "A Decade Later, Atlanta Olympic Bombing Overshadowed."

18. Kirchner, "How Olympic Bomb Was Found."

19. Booth and Heath, "Bomb Tip May Have Set Up Police in Atlanta for 'Ambush.'"

20. Ibid.

21. Ibid.

22. Ibid.

23. Beardon, "Security Matters."

24. Booth and Heath, "Bomb Tip May Have Set Up Police in Atlanta for 'Ambush.'"

25. CNN, "Investigators Have Handful of Suspects," July 29, 1996, http://edition.cnn.com/US/9607/29/bombing.clues/index.html.

26. Kevin Sack, "No Arrests Imminent in Atlanta Bombing, F.B.I. Chief Says," *New York Times,* August 2, 1996, http://www.nytimes.com/1996/08/02/us/no-arrests-imminent-in-atlanta-bombing-fbi-chief-says.html.

27. Booth and Heath, "Bomb Tip May Have Set Up Police in Atlanta for 'Ambush.'"

28. Dick Pettys, "Source: Atlanta Cops Waited," Associated Press, *Washington Post,* July 30, 1996, http://www.washingtonpost.com/wp-srv/national/longterm/bombing/stories/10min.htm.

29. Booth and Heath, "Bomb Tip May Have Set Up Police in Atlanta for 'Ambush.'"

30. Ibid.

31. Ibid.

32. Ibid.

33. CNN, "Investigators Have 'Handful' of Suspects."

34. Booth and Heath, "Bomb Tip May Have Set Up Police in Atlanta for 'Ambush.'"

35. FBI National Press Office, "Statement of FBI SAC Jack A. Daulton and Inspector Woody R. Enderson" [press release], November 18, 1997, http://web.archive.org/web/20000303015458/www.fbi.gov/majcases/rudolph/presrel1.htm.

36. Booth and Heath, "Bomb Tip May Have Set Up Police in Atlanta for 'Ambush.'"

37. Ron Ostrow, "Richard Jewell and the Olympic Bombing: Case Study," Pew Research Center's Project for Excellence in Journalism, February 15, 2003, http://www.journalism.org/node/1791.

38. Ibid.

39. Ibid.

40. Ibid.

41. Ibid.

42. Kathy Scruggs and Ron Martz, "FBI Suspects 'Hero' Guard May Have Planted Bomb," *Atlanta Journal-Constitution,* July 30, 1996, http://www.journalism.org/print/1793.

43. Ostrow, "Richard Jewell and the Olympic Bombing: Case Study."

44. Clay Calvert and Robert D. Richards, "A Pyrrhic Press Victory: Why Holding Richard Jewell Is a Public Figure Is Wrong and Harms Journalism," *Loyola of Los Angeles Entertainment Law Review* 22, no. 2 (2002): 293–326, http://elr.lls.edu/issues/v22-issue2/calvert.pdf.

45. Ostrow, "Richard Jewell and the Olympic Bombing: Case Study."

46. Ibid.

47. Tribune News Service, "Sympathy, No Apology, for Jewell's Mom," *Chicago Tribune,* August 30, 1996, http://articles.chicagotribune.com/1996–08–30/news/9608300140_1_security-guard-richard-jewell-centennial-olympic-park-bombing-barbara-jewell.

8 The DC Sniper

CASE NARRATIVE

On Wednesday, 2 October 2002, three weeks to the day after the first anniversary of the 9/11 attacks, the American psyche was still focused on the seemingly ever-present threat of a terrorist attack on the homeland. However, it was business as usual in the suburbs of the nation's capital until a strange event occurred at Michael's Arts and Crafts store in Montgomery County, Maryland. At 1702, someone shot a single bullet into the store, located at 13850 Georgia Avenue in the Aspen Hill neighborhood.[1] No one was injured. The bullet entered the store and struck a checkout aisle register number, just a few feet above the head of a cashier. The investigators who responded to the incident found no evidence, no motive, and no suspect. The only witness report, a tentative description of two African-American men in a Thunderbird-like blue car, was dismissed as being in an improbable location relative to the shooting.[2] Investigators did not know at the time that events were about to evolve from bizarre to nightmarish.

The Killings Begin

Approximately an hour after the Michael's shooting at 1802, James Martin, a 55-year-old white father of an 18-year-old son, was shot and killed as he walked from his car to a Shoppers Food Warehouse located at 2201 Randolph Road, Wheaton, a neighborhood of Montgomery County, Maryland.[3,4] The shopping center, only a few miles from Aspen Hill, was across the street from a police station.

At first, investigators handled the case as a normal homicide. The only solid information that witnesses—including the responding officer, who had been in his parked vehicle across the street—provided was hearing a loud boom. No one saw the shooter. One witness report identified a white sedan, possibly a Toyota, but that too was discounted as improbable due to its reported position relative to the victim.[5] In addition, there was no immediately apparent motive; the victim was not robbed, and his work identification badge was still on his chest.

An examination of the wound in Martin's body was indicative of a high-powered rifle. Investigators initially suspected a .223 caliber or similar size round.[6,7] They hoped the autopsy would confirm this suspicion and provide additional information. Besides there being no apparent motive, there was no suspect or suspect vehicle and little to no real evidence. It did not take long for investigators to consider the possibility that the two cases were somehow linked, which caused a chilling thought: "Who is out there just shooting someone for no apparent reason right across from the police station in broad daylight at rush hour?"[8]

At 0741 the next day, James L. "Sonny" Buchanan, a 39-year-old white male, suffered a major chest wound and died while mowing the grass at the Colonial Dodge in the Fitzgerald Auto Mall, located at 11411 Rockville Pike, Kensington, Maryland.[9,10] It was initially reported that some kind of mower malfunction had killed him. However, it was soon clear that he had been shot. As with the other two shootings, there was no witness, no evidence, no suspect or suspect vehicle, and still no motive. And while it too was incredibly strange, nothing immediately linked this shooting to the other two shootings the day before.

As the Montgomery County Police Department (MCPD) began to handle the Buchanan homicide, Premkumar A. Walekar, a 54-year-old Indian-born male, lay dying at a Mobil gas station located at Aspen Hill Road and Connecticut Avenue in Aspen Hill.[11] He had been putting gas in his taxi when he was fatally shot at 0802 in the same manner as Buchanan and Martin. In this case, an officer was sitting in a patrol car in heavy traffic at an intersection about fifty yards away.[12]

As with the other shootings, Walekar was not robbed, and there were no witnesses or evidence. Investigators worked to account for the sudden increase in homicides. Montgomery County only averages about twenty homicides a year.[13] Now there had been three in a matter of hours. The investigators considered and immediately dismissed the shootings as either the result of a domestic crime or robbery, the most common explanations for a homicide.

About forty minutes later, at 0837, Sarah Ramos, a 34-year-old Hispanic mother of a 7-year-old son, was sitting at a bus stop in front of a post office located at 3701 Rossmoor Boulevard, Silver Spring, Maryland.[14,15] Witnesses later reported hearing a popping sound. A Spanish-speaking witness reported seeing a white box truck with black lettering drive away from the area after Ramos was shot.[16] The police later that day revealed the white box truck lead in a press conference. The media reported it extensively, and investigators considered it a significant lead in the case.

At 0958, Lori Lewis-Rivera, a 25-year-old white woman, was fatally shot while purchasing gas at a Shell station located at Knowles and Connecticut Avenue in Kensington, Maryland, only about a mile from the parking lot of the Mobil station where the investigation of Ramos's death was still ongoing.[17,18] This was the sixth shooting in seventeen hours, the fifth death overall, and the fourth death in a little over two hours.

At this point, the police set up a command post at a church near the Mobil gas station. Since the shootings all appeared to be centered on the Aspen Hill area, law enforcement devoted all resources to that area. Police began to consider additional reasons for the killing spree, such as a racial crime, a hate crime, or a terrorist act. They ultimately discounted these theories, particularly terrorism, and instead focused on finding a link among the victims in the hope of gaining insight into the murderer. The investigators thought that some common thread must connect the victims.[19]

On Thursday afternoon, the police asked citizens to call in suspicious activity to 911, especially information about white vans. They also moved the command post back to the station in Rockville, Maryland. Forensics began working on the bullet fragments from the victims, and the coroner conducted autopsies on the victims.

At 2120 on Thursday, Pascal Charlot, a 72-year-old black male carpenter originally from Haiti, was shot and killed as he was about to cross a street at the intersection of Georgia Avenue and Kalmia Road.[20,21] This shooting was like all the rest, with one major exception: it occurred in the District of Columbia, not in Montgomery County. Still, the shooting was just over the county line. The police thought they might have captured the shooter when a car ran a red light at the same time as the shooting, but this turned out to be a false lead.[22] One witness also reported that a burgundy Caprice left the area, but the vehicle was later found abandoned and burned[23] and was discounted as a suspect vehicle.[24]

Also different in the Charlot shooting was that for the first time, the police were able to use dogs to trace the gunpowder residue of the shot. The police now knew exactly the type of gun used, and although this did not help identify the shooter, the police could identify and confirm the type of weapon used: a high-powered rifle.

Investigators Join Forces

On Friday, investigators from the ever growing investigation team met to discuss what, if anything, they had determined. MCPD; the Bureau of Alcohol, Tobacco, Firearms, and Explosives (ATF); the Federal Bureau of Investigation (FBI); and the Washington Metropolitan Police Department (WMPD) joined in the investigation, although an official Joint Command was not yet formed. The investigators knew the same caliber shot was used in each shooting, most likely a .223 round. They also knew the shots were fired from approximately 100–150 yards away from each victim. For the most part, they were able to determine the general area the shots were taken from by studying the trajectory path of each shot.[25] But that was it: no motive, no suspects, and no known links between victims. There was nothing solid to act upon, although tips came in through 911. Investigators still could not confirm a connection between the shooting at Michael's and other shootings because there were no shell fragments or victims from the Michael's shooting.

At 1430 on Friday, about the time the investigators were meeting, Caroline Seawell, a 43-year-old white woman, was in the parking lot of the Spotsylvania Mall in front of a Michael's located at 3000 Plank Road, Fredericksburg, Virginia, when she was shot.[26] This time a witness reported having seen a dark-colored car with tinted windows and New Jersey tags in the area, and another witness reported seeing a black teenager inside it, but it is unclear whether the investigators in Maryland knew about the report at the time or, if they did, whether they discounted it.[27,28] The shooting was much like the others, but Seawell survived. Investigators thought the shooter was moving south and began warning police agencies in that direction.

Saturday and Sunday came and went without incident. Police on Saturday announced that ballistics tests on the bullet fragments indicated that four of the victims had been shot by the same weapon and that they were pursuing a serial killer. MCPD reconfirmed that it was looking for a white box truck, possibly with black lettering on the side.[29]

On Monday, 7 October, at 0809, Iran Brown, a 13-year-old male, was shot as he was walking into Tasker Middle School located at 490 Collington Road,

Bowie, Maryland, in Prince Georges County.[30] Prior to this, the commonly held belief was that the schools were safe, and officers had even been stationed at some schools to ensure the students' safety. Brown barely survived the attack, but as with previous shootings, there were no witnesses and no suspect. The police extensively searched the area and even used police academy recruits to assist. Their efforts resulted in finding a shell casing and, more important, a tarot card, the Death card (see Figure 8.1), with the words "For you Mr. Police. Code: 'Call me God.' Do not release to the press."[31,32] It was regarded by all to be a message from the shooter. The police decided to honor the request of the sniper, but the message was leaked to the press. However, the press incorrectly reported the phrase that appeared on the card. One variation commonly reported was "I am God."[33]

Figure 8.1 ▶ Tarot Card Found at Site of Iran Brown Shooting

After the Brown shooting but before the police knew of the tarot card, the Chief of MCPD submitted a formal request for assistance to the federal government. The US Attorney General responded immediately and personally.[34] Within a short time the Secret Service, US Marshals, and even the Department of Defense made new resources available. In addition, FBI resources dramatically increased, and the Bureau formalized its contribution to the investigation. Police created a Joint Operations Center (JOC) to coordinate the investigation, and they officially named the task force SNIPEMUR.

Source: http://www.fbi.gov/page2/oct07/ snipers102407.html.

In an attempt to identify the shooter, investigators tried to identify all owners of rifles capable of firing a .223 round in Virginia and Maryland. They cross-referenced their findings to owners of white vans.[35] Tips on such owners even came through the tip line. The leads, however, never resulted in a link to the shooter.

A Profile Emerges

The FBI stepped in to create a profile of the killer for the investigation (see Figure 8.2). While this profile was not released to the public, a similar profile was extensively discussed by the media. The FBI profile described the attacks as

> probably the work of a single shooter. . . . The sniper was likely angry, self-centered, and fascinated with weapons and violence. Probably the sniper had recently suffered a domestic or job related setback. He would stay in the Washington area, keep the same method of operation, and scout his shooting locations. The sniper was almost certainly male, was probably not a juvenile, and was not likely to display any sign of mental illness.[36]

Figure 8.2 ▶ FBI Profile of DC Sniper

- Single Shooter
- Adult White Male
- Washington Area
- Military Exposure
- Non-Confrontational
- Angry, Self-Centered
- Competent w/ Firearms
- Little to No Criminal History
- Uninvolved Romantically

The profile described an individual who frequented gun shows, was interested in books and movies about the military, and took pride in his prowess with firearms. He would most likely take calculated risks, not be confrontational, and not be involved in a long-term relationship. He would come and go as he pleased. He would be hypersensitive and suspicious and pay close attention to media coverage.[37]

The profilers pointed out that although race could not be identified, "historically similar cases have been perpetrated by white males."[38] The FBI profilers could not find a link or common trait among the victims. They also commented that the shooter would most likely be "competent with firearms . . . not likely have a lengthy criminal history . . . an angry person . . . of average or above average intelligence."[39]

The investigators had many leads consistent with the FBI profile but ruled them all out. This pattern continued for days. Police tracked dozens of leads and suspects who fit the profile, but all ultimately resulted in dead ends. The police, however, never released any suspect information to the press.

On Wednesday, 9 October, at 2010, Dean Harold Meyers, a 53-year-old disabled Vietnam veteran, was pumping gas at a Sunoco gas station located at 7203 Sudley Road near Manassas, Virginia, off of I-66 when he was fatally shot.[40,41] This shooting followed the same pattern as all the others. Witnesses heard a loud noise as Meyers went down. A white van was reported fleeing the area, but it was identified and found to be unrelated to the incident. Investigators found a map of Baltimore and Baltimore County across the street, but they neither processed it nor gave it to the task force. Instead, investigators sent it to an evidence locker.[42]

By Thursday morning, the new JOC was fully operational in a rented building across from the MCPD station. A new tip line was also created just to handle calls regarding the sniper. The tips received ranged from helpful to bizarre to useless. Investigators tried to track down every lead from the more reliable tips.

The media continued to spiral out of control. As the death toll climbed, the media, from around the world, covered the incident ever more fervently. Criticisms of the police surfaced, and some demanded to have the tarot card made fully public. The police did not honor the request.

On Friday, 11 October, at 0930, Kenneth H. Bridges, a 53-year-old black father of six, was pumping gas at an Exxon station located at US-1 and Market Street, Fredericksburg, Virginia, when he was shot.[43,44] Much as with the Buchanan murder, a state trooper was about fifty yards away.[45] A witness reported seeing a white Astro van with ladder racks flee the area.[46,47] There was no evidence, no message, and no suspect.

The police had already created a dragnet plan whereby they would shut down the roadway system as they attempted to find the fleeing white van. The Bridges shooting was the first time it went live.[48] In response to the shooting, police across the area pulled over hundreds of white vans.[49] None were connected to the shooting. Traffic, however, ground to a halt.

On the same day, SNIPEMUR had another meeting. The status had not changed much; the investigators had very little evidence. They knew the same weapon was being used for each killing, but some worried that the killer might switch weapons. Some in attendance even began to raise concerns about the validity of the white van. One of the commanders of SNIPEMUR tried to encourage the investigators to "think three murders ahead."[50] Despite any initial internal dissent about the white van, investigators released a composite graphic of the vehicle based on reports from the 3 October shootings to the press.[51]

After two days without incident, at 2115 on Columbus Day, Monday, 14 October, Linda Franklin, a 47-year-old FBI analyst and mother of two, was shot and killed at a Home Depot located at 6210 Seven Corners Center, Falls Church, Virginia.[52,53] The ensuing dragnet shut down I-495, the George Washington Parkway, the American Legion Bridge, and the Woodrow Wilson Bridge. The police also had a witness with a criminal record who said he saw the shooting. The witness said that "it was a cream-colored Chevy Astro van with a silver ladder rack and a dead right taillight. The gunman had olive skin and a mustache and wore a denim jacket with a rifle similar to an AK-47."[54] With this information, the task force and dragnet focused even more on a white van. Once again, SNIPEMUR attempted to identify owners of white vans, this time Chevy Astros, who also owned .223 rifles.[55] As with the previous dragnet and attempt to match van and weapon to a suspect, nothing came of it.

On 16 October, it became clear the witness was lying. He had been inside the store when the shot was fired.[56] By 18 October, the police had arrested the witness "for providing false information to police."[57]

Leads continued to be tracked down but ultimately dismissed. There were more leads than the now massive task force could handle, but the investigators did their best. A few days went by without incident, and some began to wonder if the shooter had stopped. But on Saturday, 19 October, at 2000, Jeff Hopper, a 37-year-old white male, was leaving the Ponderosa Steak House located at 809 England Street, Ashland, Virginia, with his wife when he was shot in the same style as all the other victims. Like Seawell and Brown, he survived.[58,59] Still, no witness saw anything.

A Break in the Case

Just as in the Charlot shooting, investigators used dogs at the scene, and they found a note (Figure 8.3) with language similar to that used on the tarot card.[60] The media had misreported the tarot card language, so the use of similar language in the new note suggested to investigators that the message was authentic. The message contained references to past attempts to contact the police as well as a demand for $10 million to be deposited to a Platinum Visa credit card account.[61] The note contained threats of future killings if the demand was not met. According to the note, the police would receive a phone call with further instructions Sunday at 0600 at the Ponderosa. The problem was that by the time the letter had been processed and read, it was already 0800 on Sunday. There were other complications as well: the note had the wrong number for the Ponderosa, and the Ponderosa was not open at 0600 on

Sundays.[62] The note also said the money had to be deposited by Monday at 0900.

This note posed a number of issues for SNIPEMUR. There was debate about whether or not to proceed and deposit money into the account in the hopes of catching the shooter during a withdrawal. Some were concerned about the feasibility of catching the shooter this way and whether it was worth the risk. The card number provided had been stolen and therefore deactivated; although it could be reactivated, it did not appear that the use of the card could be reported fast enough in real time to ensure a capture.[63]

There was also debate about how to continue the dialogue with the shooter because the deadline to speak on the phone had passed. This issue caused significant discord in SNIPEMUR.

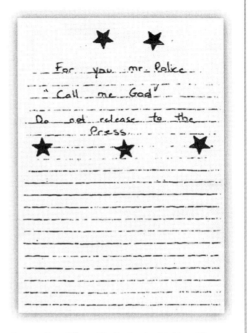

Figure 8.3 ▶ First Page of Letter Found at Ponderosa Steak House

Source: E-mail from Media Service Division, Montgomery County Department of Police, to Pherson Associates, 19 August 2009.

On the one hand, the trained negotiators wanted the police to take a very hard line with the shooter. They wanted to use strong language that would "call out" the sniper.[64] On the other hand, the profilers wanted a much more reserved approach. They wanted the police to engage the shooter in a non-threatening manner in order to draw out information that could help identify the sniper.

The task force managed to agree to put out a message via the media asking for the shooter to reattempt contact. On Sunday, the police issued the statement saying that they had been unable to comply but wanted to talk. Someone did call the task force the next day. Officers had been staged around the area of the Ponderosa in the belief the caller might still be around. When the call came in, police attempted to capture the caller, but it was too late—the caller was gone. Instead, police mistakenly picked up two illegal aliens.

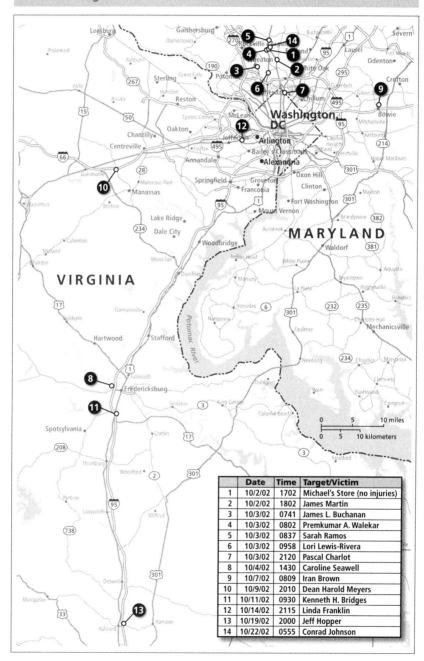

	Date	Time	Target/Victim
1	10/2/02	1702	Michael's Store (no injuries)
2	10/2/02	1802	James Martin
3	10/3/02	0741	James L. Buchanan
4	10/3/02	0802	Premkumar A. Walekar
5	10/3/02	0837	Sarah Ramos
6	10/3/02	0958	Lori Lewis-Rivera
7	10/3/02	2120	Pascal Charlot
8	10/4/02	1430	Caroline Seawell
9	10/7/02	0809	Iran Brown
10	10/9/02	2010	Dean Harold Meyers
11	10/11/02	0930	Kenneth H. Bridges
12	10/14/02	2115	Linda Franklin
13	10/19/02	2000	Jeff Hopper
14	10/22/02	0555	Conrad Johnson

The caller used the same phrases as were in the letter. Once again, threats were made if the demand was not met. But the caller ended the call quickly, and no further dialogue was possible. The person spoke with an accent most commonly described as Hispanic. The police once again released a message via the media asking the shooter to call back so they could better understand the demand.

On Tuesday, 22 October, at 0555, Conrad Johnson, a 35-year-old father of two, stood in the door of a public bus at Grand Pre Road and Connecticut Avenue in Aspen Hill, Maryland, when he was shot and killed.[65,66] Yet another death, and still no one saw the shooter. Investigators found another note. It reiterated the other messages and said, "Your incompetence has cost you another life."[67] Johnson's would be the last life lost. Map 8.1 details the locations of the sniper shootings.

The End of the Terror

Two days later, it all came to an end. At last, after three weeks of living a nightmare, the people in Maryland, Virginia, and the District of Columbia no longer had to fear being shot by a ghostlike gunman. All of the frustration and sleepless nights for the task force were replaced with a sense of accomplishment at ending the madness of the DC Sniper.

RECOMMENDED READING

Moose, Charles, and Charles Fleming. *Three Weeks in October: The Manhunt for the Serial Sniper.* New York: Signet, 2003.

Table 8.1 ▶ Case Snapshot: The DC Sniper		
Structured Analytic Technique Used	Heuer and Pherson Page Number	Analytic Family
Key Assumptions Check	p. 183	Assessment of Cause and Effect
Multiple Hypotheses Generator	p. 153	Hypothesis Generation and Testing
Quadrant Crunching	p. 111	Idea Generation

THE DC SNIPER
STRUCTURED ANALYTIC TECHNIQUES IN ACTION

In a crisis situation, using structured analytic techniques can help avoid a rush to judgment and ensure that no possibility has been prematurely discarded. Investigators in the case were challenged by the lack of hard evidence about the perpetrator, including the mode of transportation and motive for the crimes, the fast pace of the shooting spree, and a deluge of eye-witness information that overwhelmed the task force. The Key Assumptions Check in this case helps to explicate and challenge implicit assumptions about the sniper, while the Multiple Hypotheses Generator and Quadrant Crunching exercises systematically develop and assess a range of possible explanations.

Technique 1: Key Assumptions Check
The Key Assumptions Check is a systematic effort to make explicit and question the assumptions that guide an analyst's interpretation of evidence and reasoning about any particular problem. Such assumptions are usually necessary and unavoidable as a means of filling gaps in the incomplete, ambiguous, and sometimes deceptive information with which the analyst must work. They are driven by the analyst's education, training, and experience, including the organizational context in which the analyst works. It can be difficult to identify assumptions, because many are sociocultural beliefs that are held unconsciously or so firmly that they are assumed to be truth and not subject to challenge. Nonetheless, identifying key assumptions and assessing the overall impact should conditions change are critical parts of a robust analytic process.

Task 1. Conduct a Key Assumptions Check of the initial theory that the shooter most likely fits the profile of a classic serial killer—a lone, white male with some military experience.

STEP 1: Gather a small group of individuals who are working the issue along with a few "outsiders." The primary analytic unit already is working from an established mental model, so the "outsiders" are needed to bring other perspectives.

STEP 2: Ideally, participants should be asked to bring their list of assumptions when they come to the meeting. If not, start the meeting with a silent brainstorming session. Ask each participant to write down several assumptions on 3-by-5-inch cards.

STEP 3: Collect the cards and list the assumptions on a whiteboard for all to see. A simple template can be used, like the one shown in Table 8.2.

Table 8.2 ▶ Key Assumptions Check Template				
Key Assumption	Commentary	Supported	With Caveats	Unsupported
1.				
2.				
3.				
4.				

STEP 4: Elicit additional assumptions. Work from the prevailing analytic line back to the key arguments that support it. Use various devices to help prod participants' thinking. Ask the standard journalist questions: Who? What? When? Where? Why? and How? Phrases such as "will always," "will never," or "would have to be" suggest that an idea is not being challenged and perhaps should be. Phrases such as "based on" or "generally the case" usually suggest that a challengeable assumption is being made.

STEP 5: After identifying a full set of assumptions, critically examine each assumption. Ask:

▶ Why am I confident that this assumption is correct?
▶ In what circumstances might this assumption be untrue?
▶ Could this assumption have been true in the past but no longer be true today?
▶ How much confidence do I have that this assumption is valid?
▶ If this assumption turns out to be invalid, how much impact would it have on the analysis?

STEP 6: Using Table 8.2, place each assumption in one of three categories:

- ▶ Basically supported.
- ▶ Supported with some caveats.
- ▶ Unsupported or questionable—the "key uncertainties."

STEP 7: Refine the list, deleting those assumptions that do not hold up to scrutiny and adding new assumptions that emerge from the discussion.

STEP 8: Consider whether key uncertainties should be converted into collection requirements or research topics.

Analytic Value Added. Did the FBI investigators inherit any key assumptions when they took over the case that had an impact on how effectively they pursued the case? What is the value of conducting a Key Assumptions Check at the beginning of a major investigation? What impact did key assumptions have on how the investigation was conducted?

Technique 2: Multiple Hypotheses Generator

The Multiple Hypotheses Generator is a useful tool for broadening the spectrum of plausible hypotheses. It is particularly useful when there is a reigning lead hypotheses—in this case, the FBI profile—and there are few facts to prove or disprove it. The most important aspect of the tool is the discussion it generates among analysts about the range of plausible hypotheses, especially about the relative credibility of each permutation. It is important to remember that the credibility score is meant to illuminate new, credible hypotheses for further examination. And while the process encourages analysts to focus on the hypotheses with the highest credibility scores, hypotheses with low credibility scores should not be entirely discarded because new evidence could emerge that could make a hypothesis more credible.

Task 2. Use the Multiple Hypotheses Generator (see Table 8.3) to create and assess alternative hypotheses. Contact Pherson Associates at ThinkSuite@pher son.org or go to www.pherson.org to obtain access to the software if it is not available on your system.

STEP 1: Identify the lead hypothesis and its component parts.

STEPS 2 & 3: Identify plausible alternatives for each key component and strive to keep them mutually exclusive. Discard any "given" factors such as the How (shooting) that will be the same for all hypotheses.

Table 8.3 ▶ Multiple Hypotheses Generator Template		
Lead Hypothesis: A white male is driving a white van and killing to extort money.		
Components	Lead Hypothesis	Alternatives Brainstormed
Who?		
What?		
Why?		

STEPS 4, 5, & 6: Generate a list of possible permutations, discard any permutations that simply make no sense, and evaluate the credibility of the remaining hypotheses on a scale of 1 to 5, where 1 is low credibility and 5 is high credibility.

STEP 7: Re-sort the remaining hypotheses from most to least credible.

STEP 8: Restate the permutations as hypotheses.

STEP 9: Select from the top of the list those alternative hypotheses most deserving of attention and note why these hypotheses are most interesting.

Analytic Value Added. In light of your findings, how should investigators in the DC Sniper case have used this information? What new suspects should they have pursued?

Technique 3: Quadrant Crunching

Quadrant Crunching combines the methodology of a Key Assumptions Check with Multiple Scenarios Generation to generate an array of alternative scenarios or stories. This process is particularly helpful in the DC Sniper case because of embedded assumptions in the FBI profile, witness reports of white vans, and the contents of the demand note. This technique allows the user to look at and challenge those key assumptions. When combined with the Multiple Hypotheses Generator, this technique provides a strong basis for developing and considering alternative explanations and scenarios.

Task 3. Use Quadrant Crunching to challenge the key assumptions in the case that is listed below.

STEPS 1 & 2: State your lead hypothesis or key assumption and break it down into its component parts. For the purposes of this exercise: A **lone white male** is conducting the shootings from a **white van to extort money**.

Table 8.4 ▶ Quadrant Crunching Sample Matrix		
Key Assumptions	Contrary Assumptions	Contrary Dimensions

STEP 3: Identify contrary assumptions and at least two contrary dimensions in a template like that shown in Table 8.4.

STEP 4: Array combinations of these contrary assumptions in a set of 2 × 2 matrices.

STEP 5: Generate scenarios for each quadrant.

STEP 6: Select those scenarios (cells) deserving the most attention.

STEP 7: Develop indicators for the selected scenarios.

Analytic Value Added. Which alternative scenarios should investigators have pursued, and why?

NOTES

1. "2002 Area Sniper Shootings," *Washington Post,* August 4, 2009, http://www.washingtonpost.com/wp-srv/metro/daily/oct02/snipershootings.htm.

2. Sari Horwitz and Michael E. Ruane, *Sniper: Inside the Hunt for the Killers Who Terrorized the Nation* (New York: Random House, 2003), 15–16.

3. "Profiles of Those Killed," Fox News Online, October 23, 2002, http://www.foxnews.com/story/0,2933,65519,00.html.

4. "2002 Area Sniper Shootings," *Washington Post.*

5. Horwitz and Ruane, *Sniper: Inside the Hunt for the Killers Who Terrorized the Nation,* 11.

6. Ibid.

7. Charles Moose and Charles Fleming, *Three Weeks in October: The Manhunt for the Serial Sniper* (New York: Signet, 2003), 6.

8. Horwitz and Ruane, *Sniper: Inside the Hunt for the Killers Who Terrorized the Nation,* 14.

9. "Profiles of Those Killed," Fox News Online.

10. "2002 Area Sniper Shootings," *Washington Post.*

11. "Profiles of Those Killed," Fox News Online.

12. "The Hunt for a Sniper: Death by the Highway; Fatal Shooting of Driver at Gasoline Station Intensifies Hunt for Suburban Sniper," *New York Times,* October 12, 2002, http://www.nytimes.com/2002/10/12/us/hunt-for-sniper-death-highway-fatal-shooting-driver-gasoline-station-intensifies.html.

13. "Quarterly Crime Report Year End 2002," Montgomery County Department of Police, April 29, 2003, http://www.montgomerycountymd.gov/content/Pol/crimestats/pdfs/2002_YearEnd.pdf.

14. "Profiles of Those Killed," Fox News Online.

15. "2002 Area Sniper Shootings," *Washington Post.*

16. Ibid.

17. "Profiles of Those Killed," Fox News Online.

18. "2002 Area Sniper Shootings," *Washington Post.*

19. Moose and Fleming, *Three Weeks in October,* 32.

20. "2002 Area Sniper Shootings," *Washington Post.*

21. "Profiles of Those Killed," Fox News Online.

22. Moose and Fleming, *Three Weeks in October,* 39.

23. A conflict exists between Chief Moose's account, which says the car was found abandoned and burned out, and the book by Horwitz and Ruane, which says the car that fled the scene was a red Toyota and that the driver was identified and discounted. Neither book mentions why the car was discounted, and we have used the more detailed version by Chief Moose here.

24. Moose and Fleming, *Three Weeks in October,* 32.

25. Ibid., 72–74.

26. Ibid., 74.

27. The description of the dark-colored car with New Jersey tags appears in the book by Horwitz and Ruane, but Chief Moose, in his book, reported no eyewitnesses. The Horwitz and Ruane book does not make it clear whether the police were informed of the vehicle despite two witnesses claiming they saw it.

28. Horwitz and Ruane, *Sniper: Inside the Hunt for the Killers Who Terrorized the Nation,* 104.

29. Moose and Fleming, *Three Weeks in October,* 86.

30. Horwitz and Ruane, *Sniper: Inside the Hunt for the Killers Who Terrorized the Nation,* 111.

31. A conflict regarding the phrase on the tarot card exists between the account in the book by Horwitz and Ruane and the account by Chief Moose (p. 131). The version by Horwitz and Ruane has been used here because it matches the wording on the image of the tarot card from the FBI.

32. Horwitz and Ruane, *Sniper: Inside the Hunt for the Killers Who Terrorized the Nation,* 119.

33. "Man Killed at Suburban D.C. Gas Station," CNN, October 10, 2002, http://edition.cnn.com/2002/US/South/10/09/shootings.maryland/index.html.

34. Moose and Fleming, *Three Weeks in October,* 141.

35. Ibid., 144–45.

36. Horwitz and Ruane, *Sniper: Inside the Hunt for the Killers Who Terrorized the Nation,* 102

37. Ibid.

38. Moose and Fleming, *Three Weeks in October,* 150.

39. Ibid.

40. "Profiles of Those Killed," Fox News Online.

41. "2002 Area Sniper Shootings," *Washington Post.*

42. Horwitz and Ruane, *Sniper: Inside the Hunt for the Killers Who Terrorized the Nation,* 130–31.

43. "Profiles of Those Killed," Fox News Online.

44. "2002 Area Sniper Shootings," *Washington Post.*

45. Horwitz and Ruane, *Sniper: Inside the Hunt for the Killers Who Terrorized the Nation,* 140.

46. "2002 Area Sniper Shootings," *Washington Post.*

47. Horwitz and Ruane, *Sniper: Inside the Hunt for the Killers Who Terrorized the Nation,* 141.

48. The book by Horwitz and Ruane and the account of Chief Moose offer conflicting information about when the first dragnet occurred. Chief Moose specifically says a dragnet was first used in the Franklin murder, but Horwitz and Ruane refer to a Virginia dragnet that occurred after the Bridges murder. Moose may be referring to the first dragnet by the task force itself instead of the first instance of a dragnet.

49. Horwitz and Ruane, *Sniper: Inside the Hunt for the Killers Who Terrorized the Nation,* 141.

50. Ibid., 145.

51. Ibid.

52. "Profiles of Those Killed," Fox News Online.

53. "2002 Area Sniper Shootings," *Washington Post.*

54. Horwitz and Ruane, *Sniper: Inside the Hunt for the Killers Who Terrorized the Nation,* 153.

55. Ibid., 156.

56. Ibid., 162.

57. "Timeline: Tracking the Sniper's Trail," Fox News Online, October 2, 2002, http://www.foxnews.com/story/0,2933,66630,00.html.

58. "2002 Area Sniper Shootings," *Washington Post.*

59. Horwitz and Ruane, *Sniper: Inside the Hunt for the Killers Who Terrorized the Nation,* 167.

60. Dogs had been used at all the scenes since the Charlot killing.

61. Moose and Fleming, *Three Weeks in October,* 246.

62. Ibid.

63. Ibid., 253.

64. Ibid., 255.

65. "Profiles of Those Killed," Fox News Online.

66. "2002 Area Sniper Shootings," *Washington Post.*

67. Horwitz and Ruane, *Sniper: Inside the Hunt for the Killers Who Terrorized the Nation,* 188.

▶ If Colombia's leading narco-insurgent group, the Revolutionary Armed Forces of Colombia (known by its Spanish acronym, the FARC), is planning to attack the US homeland, how would they go about it?

▶ What are the major factors that would influence the type of attack the FARC would launch? Who and what would be the most likely targets?

▶ What capabilities and resources could the FARC draw on internally to launch an attack against the United States?

▶ Would the FARC look to other groups for assistance in launching an attack?

▶ What events or activities would best signal that a FARC attack on the US homeland may be imminent?

9 Colombia's FARC Attacks the US Homeland

CASE NARRATIVE

The Revolutionary Armed Forces of Colombia—known by the Spanish acronym FARC—is Latin America's largest, oldest, and currently most capable insurgent organization. Its history of kidnappings, assassinations, and indiscriminate acts of violence makes the FARC one of the most despised groups in Colombia and has landed it on the US State Department's list of foreign terrorist organizations.[1] In recent years, the FARC has cultivated relationships with foreign states, such as Venezuela and Ecuador, and terrorist groups, such as the Spanish Basque separatist group ETA and the Irish Republican Army, reportedly to gain access to military materiel and terrorist expertise. Since 2003, the Colombian government—with help from the US military—has cracked down on the FARC and its main source of income: the drug trade. While this has led to operational successes, including the deaths of many FARC leaders, it has also raised the specter of increased violence against not only the Colombian government but also the United States, as the FARC seeks to regroup and assert its revolutionary credentials.

Revolutionary Roots

The FARC was formally established in 1965 after Colombia's two major political parties ended more than a decade of political violence, a period known as *La Violencia,* which resulted in over 200,000 deaths. Under this agreement, known as the National Front, the two leading political parties agreed to share power, end the violence, and return the country to civilian rule.

The period from the late 1960s to the mid-1970s was the height of armed rebellion throughout Latin America. Funded in part by Cuba, leftist revolutionary groups operated throughout the continent. Since then, almost all of the groups have been eliminated, legitimized, or disbanded—but not the FARC. Several factors account for the FARC's ability to survive when almost all other armed communist insurgencies in Latin America have disappeared. Much of Colombia's territory is beyond the central government's control. Large parts of the Amazon region have provided safe haven to the FARC and other outlaw groups for decades. The FARC also has developed significant military capability and experience over forty years of armed struggle. But the most important factor contributing to the FARC's longevity has been a sustainable business model based on kidnapping for ransom, extortion, and, increasingly, the drug trade.

According to the Colombian government, the FARC had about 16,000 insurgents in 2001. The head of the United States Southern Command (USSOUTHCOM) testified in March 2008 that the FARC had been reduced to about 9,000 fighters. FARC forces are well equipped, and the group is known to use highly sophisticated technology. Its forces are mostly self-trained and self-supplied, although FARC has recently received some external assistance.

The FARC is made up of about seventy-seven distinct military units, called Fronts, organized by geographic location. These in turn are grouped into seven "blocs." The FARC is led by a seven-member Secretariat and a twenty-seven-member Central General Staff or *Estado Major*. FARC is most active in the southern and eastern portions of the country, which are mostly jungle. [2,3] It also has an International Commission with representatives in Latin America, Europe, Canada, and the United States. [4,5] The FARC maintains a series of Web sites to post its messages and attract followers within Colombia and overseas.

In 1999, Colombian President Andres Pastrana tried to engage the FARC in peace negotiations. As part of this initiative, he gave them control over a 42,000-square-mile swath of jungle, which was called the *despeje* or the "demilitarized zone." After three years of unsuccessful negotiations and in the wake of a series of high-profile terrorist attacks, Pastrana ended peace talks and ordered his troops to retake the *despeje*. When President Alvaro Uribe came to power in 2002, he ordered a major military campaign against the FARC and its sister insurgency the National Liberation Army (ELN). In 2007, several members of the FARC leadership were killed; in the following year, the FARC Secretariat's chief spokesperson, Raul Reyes, was killed during a Colombian incursion into

Ecuador. The FARC suffered another major setback in July 2008 when Eastern Front Commander Gerardo Aguilar Ramirez, aka "Cesar," was captured as part of an operation to rescue three American hostages who had been held in captivity by the FARC since their plane crashed in February 2003.

FARC rebels stand in formation during a practice ceremony.

FARC's Terrorist Acts

FARC is responsible for most of the ransom kidnappings in Colombia. It targets wealthy landowners, politicians, foreign tourists, and prominent Colombian and foreign officials. Notable FARC operations include the following:

- The March 1999 murder of three US missionaries working in Colombia.
- The October 2001 kidnapping and murder of a former Minister of Culture.
- The February 2002 kidnapping of presidential candidate Ingrid Betancourt, who was traveling in guerrilla territory.
- The November 2005 kidnapping of sixty people, holding them hostage until the government agreed to release hundreds of FARC insurgents and sympathizers serving prison sentences.[6]

FARC is renowned for its reliance on assassinations and its use of mortar-like devices, called *rompas,* which the rebels fashion from empty natural gas canisters. In part because of its history of kidnappings, assassinations, and

Former Colombian presidential candidate Ingrid Betancourt is seen during her captivity in this image taken from television 31 August 2003.

indiscriminate violent acts, FARC is one of the most despised groups in Colombia. Opinion polls show just 1 percent of Colombians hold a favorable view of the FARC.[7]

FARC Builds Its Foreign Connections

When President Uribe launched his crackdown on the FARC and the ELN in 2003, both groups sought refuge across the border in Venezuela and Ecuador. The border areas have traditionally been hard to govern and thus ideal places for arms smugglers and drug traffickers to operate. When Raul Reyes was killed in 2008, the Colombian government said it had found documents on a rebel laptop that indicated that Venezuela and Ecuador were providing material support to the FARC.

In August 2009, the *New York Times* reported that evidence taken from an insurgent laptop documented Venezuelan aid to the FARC. The messages describe FARC plans to purchase surface-to-air missiles, sniper rifles, and radios in Venezuela in 2008. The messages appear to corroborate the assertion that Venezuela helped the FARC acquire Swedish-made rocket launchers. The rocket launchers were purchased by the Venezuelan Army in the late 1980s but were captured in Colombia in combat operations against the FARC in 2008.[8]

In 2009 Venezuelan President Hugo Chavez denied providing such assistance and expressed concern over US plans to increase its military presence on Colombian military bases, claiming it would lead to the destabilization of the region.[9]

The FARC's ties to Venezuela and Spain's Basque separatist group ETA became a major issue in March 2010 when a Spanish judge charged thirteen members of ETA and FARC with planning to assassinate visiting senior Colombian officials, including President Uribe. The judge said a FARC member had carried out surveillance on the Colombian embassy in Madrid and the routes taken by former Colombian president Pastrana, who lives in Spain. The FARC then asked ETA to follow Pastrana, as well as the former ambassador to Spain Noemi Sanin, current Vice President Francisco Santos, the former mayor of Bogota Antanas Mockus "with the aim of assassinating one of them when they were in Spain." Uribe was added later to that list. Six ETA members and seven FARC members were charged in the plot.[10]

Members of the Irish Republican Army (IRA) have also been accused of supporting the FARC. In April 2002, the US House Committee on International Relations issued a summary of a nine-month investigation that stated links between the IRA and the Colombian guerrillas went back to 1998. The study noted that three IRA members were arrested in Colombia in August 2001 and accused of teaching bomb-making methods to FARC insurgents. According to the report, the training helped the rebels become proficient in urban terror techniques used by the IRA in Northern Ireland; two of the Irish were the IRA's leading explosives and mortar experts.[11]

FARC's Role in the Drug Trade

Experts estimate that the FARC takes in roughly $500 million annually from the illegal drug trade.[12] The FARC also profits from kidnappings, extortion schemes, and an unofficial "tax" it levies in the countryside for protection and social services.

About half of FARC's operational units are involved in some aspects of the drug trade, with most of this activity relating to managing local drug production.[13] (Map 9.1 shows the presence of FARC across Colombia along with areas of coca cultivation.) The nature of FARC's drug involvement varies from region to region, and the group's control of population and territory in rural areas "has allowed it to dictate terms for coca growth, harvest, and processing."[14]

Map 9.1 ▶ FARC Presence in Colombia and Coca Cultivation Areas

A press release issued by the US Department of Justice (DoJ) when Ramirez was extradited to the United States in July 2009 asserted that "the FARC is responsible for the production of more than half the world's supply of cocaine and nearly two-thirds of the cocaine imported into the United States." The press announcement stated that by the late 1990s, FARC became the exclusive buyer of raw cocaine paste used to make cocaine in all areas of

FARC operations.[15] A 2009 report by the US Government Accountability Office says the FARC accounts for 60 percent of the total cocaine exported from Colombia to the United States.[16]

The DoJ press release also states that in the late 1990s, the FARC leadership met and voted unanimously in favor of expanding coca production, expanding the FARC's international distribution routes, and appointing members within each Front to be in charge of coca production. The press release states that the FARC leadership, recognizing that the FARC could not survive without drug revenue, directed its members to disrupt coca fumigation efforts, shoot down fumigation aircraft, and attack Colombian infrastructure to force the government to divert its resources from fumigation. In addition, the leaders ordered FARC members to kidnap and murder US citizens in order to dissuade the United States from fumigating coca and disrupting the FARC's cocaine-manufacturing and distribution activities. In late 2001 and early 2002, FARC leaders participated in a meeting at which they voted unanimously to encourage the kidnapping of US citizens for that purpose. They also called on FARC to increase cocaine exports to the United States (see Figure 9.1).

Figure 9.1 ▶ Chronology of Key Events in Colombia

Date	Event
1958	Conservatives and Liberals agree to form the National Front in a bid to end a civil war that has caused over 200,000 deaths.
1965	Founding of National Liberation Army (ELN) and Maoist People's Liberation Army (EPL).
1966	Founding of Revolutionary Armed Forces of Colombia (FARC).
1971	Emergence of left-wing M-19 Movement.
1978	President Julio César Turbay (Liberal) begins intensive fight against the drug traffickers.
1982	President Belisario Betancur (Conservative) grants guerrillas amnesty and frees political prisoners.
1985	M-19 guerrillas kill eleven judges and ninety other people in attack on Palace of Justice.
1989	M-19 becomes legal party after concluding peace agreement.
1993	Medellin drug cartel leader Pablo Escobar killed while trying to evade arrest.

(Figure continues)

Figure 9.1 ▶ Chronology of Key Events in Colombia *(Continued)*

1998	President Andres Pastrana (Conservative) initiates peace talks with guerrillas, grants FARC safe haven in the *despeje,* an area the size of Switzerland in the southeast.
1999	FARC kills three US Indian rights activists kidnapped in Colombia.
January 1999	Pastrana and FARC leader Manuel "Sureshot" Marulanda meet.
July 2000	Pastrana and the United States launch Plan Colombia with almost $1 billion in aid.
April 2001	A report issued by the US House of Representatives Committee on International Relations notes that fifteen IRA members traveled to Colombia over three years to provide military training to the FARC in return for $2 million in drug money.
October 2001	Pastrana and FARC sign the San Francisco agreement, committing to negotiate a cease-fire and extend life of the *despeje* until January 2002.
August 2001	A FARC insurgent and two IRA urban warfare specialists are arrested with explosives in their possession; three more IRA members are arrested and charged with training FARC guerrillas to make bombs.
January 2002	Pastrana accepts FARC's cease-fire timetable and extends safe haven to April.
February 2002	Pastrana breaks off three years of peace talks following an aircraft hijacking and orders rebels out of safe haven.
May 2002	The FARC kills 119 civilians in the Choco Department using *rompas,* homemade propane gas mortars.
August 2002	FARC attacks rock Bogotá as President Alvaro Uribe (Independent) is sworn in; Uribe promises to crack down hard on insurgents.
June 2004	Uribe launches the "Patriot Plan" and deploys 15,000 troops to search for and capture the FARC leadership.
May 2006	President Uribe wins second term in office.
June 2007	Colombian government releases dozens of jailed FARC guerrillas to spur a dialogue, but FARC rejects move.
September 2007	Venezuelan President Hugo Chavez in his role as mediator invites FARC for talks on a possible hostage release deal.
November 2007	Chavez withdraws his country's ambassador to Bogotá in a row over his role in negotiations between FARC and Colombian government.
January 2008	FARC agrees to release two high-profile hostages as part of Chavez mediation.
March 2008	Colombian cross border strike into Ecuador results in death of senior FARC rebel leader Raul Reyes and sparks diplomatic crisis with both Ecuador and Venezuela.
May 2008	FARC announces the death of its leader and founder, Manuel Marulanda.

Figure 9.1 ▶ (Continued)

July 2008	Colombian army rescues highest-profile hostage, Ingrid Betancourt, held in captivity for six years.
February 2009	FARC releases six high-profile hostages, including former provincial governor.
February 2009	Syrian arms dealer Monzer al-Kassar is sentenced to thirty years in prison for trying to sell surface-to-air missiles, grenades, assault rifles, and C-4 explosives to FARC for a profit of more than $1 million.
March 2009	FARC releases Swedish man, Erik Larsson, thought to be last foreign hostage.
March 2009	President Uribe offers peace talks if FARC halts criminal activities.
August 2009	Relations with Venezuela deteriorate; Venezuela withdraws its ambassador after Colombia accuses it of supplying arms to FARC.
October 2009	Colombia signs deal with US military giving United States access to seven Colombian military bases.
November 2009	Venezuelan President Chavez orders 15,000 troops to the Colombian border and urges his armed forces to prepare for war.
December 2009	FARC and the ELN announce they will stop fighting each other and concentrate on attacking the Colombian military.
December 2009	FARC kills the governor of the southern state of Caquetá after abducting him.
March 2010	Spain's High Court says Venezuela facilitated contacts between FARC and Spain's ETA terrorists and that FARC had asked ETA for logistical help with an attempted assassination attempt on Colombian officials visiting Spain.

The Role of US Military Support

Although the FARC has sustained itself as a potent insurgent threat for decades in Colombia, the loss of many of its key leaders and the Uribe administration's aggressive military tactics have taken their toll on FARC's overall capabilities. US military support to the Colombian armed forces has contributed to the Colombian military's success. The US military supports counterdrug operations from several bases in the United States, most notably US Southern Command in Miami, Florida (see Table 9.1).[17] It also has forces assigned to seven Colombian military bases.[18] US Southern Command assistance to Colombia's armed forces, for example, has included the following:[19]

▶ Training and equipping elite units.

▶ Assisting in joint operations.

Table 9.1 ▶ US Military Support to Colombia
Key US Military Bases That Support Counterdrug Operations in Colombia
US Southern Command (USSOUTHCOM), Miami, Florida
Joint Interagency Task Force-South (JIATF-South), Key West, Florida
US Army South (USARSO), Fort Sam Houston, Texas
12th Air Force Southern (AFSOUTH), Davis-Monthan Air Force Base, Arizona
Special Operations Command South (USSOCSOUTH), Homestead Air Reserve Base, Miami, Florida

▶ Providing training teams to work with Colombian military commanders and their staffs to improve their operational planning.

▶ Supplying helicopters, intelligence platforms, rations, fuel, and munitions to Colombian military units engaged in operations against high-ranking insurgent leaders.

▶ Aiding social and civic support programs in communities previously controlled by guerrilla groups.

This mutually beneficial relationship has allowed both countries to pursue important objectives; for the Colombians, it has allowed them to pursue guerrilla forces far more aggressively throughout the country and, for the United States, it has helped stem the flow of cocaine from the Andes. But the growing success of US and Colombian military and intelligence operations against FARC could come at a price of more aggressive and desperate actions by the FARC. The FARC prides itself on being one of the most long-lived insurgencies in South America, and it is well financed through extensive networks that stretch far beyond the Andes. For US decision makers, a key question is whether they can say confidently that war with the FARC is slowly but steadily being won. Or should they be concerned that the FARC might decide out of necessity that it must shift the battlefield and target US interests more directly, both in Colombia and, possibly, within the United States?

RECOMMENDED READINGS

Brittain, James J. *Revolutionary Social Change in Colombia: The Origin and Direction of the FARC-EP.* London: Pluto Press, London.

Gonsalves, Mark, Tom Howes, Keith Stansell, and Gary Brozek. *Out of Captivity: Surviving 1,967 Days in the Colombian Jungle.* New York: HarperCollins, 2010.

Kirk, Robin. *More Terrible Than Death: Drugs, Violence, and America's War in Colombia.* New York: Public Affairs 2003.

Table 9.2 ▶ Case Snapshot: Colombia's FARC Attacks the US Homeland		
Structured Analytic Technique Used	Heuer and Pherson Page Number	Analytic Family
Red Hat Analysis and Structured Brainstorming	pp. 197, 92	Assessment of Cause and Effect, Idea Generation
Multiple Scenarios Generation	p. 128	Scenarios and Indicators
Indicators	p. 132	Scenarios and Indicators
Indicators Validator	p. 140	Scenarios and Indicators

COLOMBIA'S FARC ATTACKS THE US HOMELAND
STRUCTURED ANALYTIC TECHNIQUES IN ACTION

While no analyst has a crystal ball, it is incumbent upon analysts to help policy makers anticipate how adversaries will behave, outline the range of possible futures that could develop, and recognize the signs that a particular future is beginning taking shape. Red Hat Analysis, Multiple Scenarios Generation, Indicators, and Indicators Validator can help analysts accomplish each of these tasks. The fictional "Future Scenario" (Box 9.1) augments the fact-based case study by providing additional narrative to set the stage for employing the techniques.

Technique 1: Red Hat Analysis and Structured Brainstorming

Analysts frequently endeavor to forecast the actions of an adversary or a competitor. In doing so, they need to avoid the common error of mirror imaging, the natural tendency to assume that others think and perceive the world in the same way as they do. Red Hat Analysis is a useful technique for trying to perceive threats and opportunities as others see them, but this technique alone is of limited value without significant understanding of the cultures of other countries, groups, or the people involved. There is a great deal of truth to the maxim that "where you stand depends on where you sit." By imagining the situation as the target perceives it, an analyst can gain a different and usually more accurate perspective on a problem or issue. Reframing the problem typically changes the analyst's perspective from that of an

Box 9.1 TENSIONS MOUNT: A FUTURE SCENARIO

With momentum increasingly on their side, Colombian military commanders and their US advisors decide to launch a combined major offensive against one of the FARC's most important military fronts. After six months of intense planning, a coordinated attack against the FARC's Third Front begins, and most major combat operations are concluded within two weeks. The attack is heralded as a major success: the Third Front's military commander is killed, at least a thousand FARC insurgents are killed or captured, and two members of the FARC's seven-member political Secretariat are captured. Experts are quoted in the press saying the attack might be a tipping point presaging the final demise of the insurgency.

The captured Secretariat members had been indicted previously by the US Attorney in Miami on cocaine importation conspiracy charges. Four weeks after the military operation, the Colombian government agrees to extradite both Secretariat members to Miami to face prosecution in US courts.

In Colombia, the remaining members of the Secretariat announce that their movement has suffered major losses but will regroup and live to fight another day "even more deeply committed to the revolutionary struggle." Their public statements are particularly critical of the role played by US military forces in supporting the operation. The FARC posting on the Internet states: "If the United States is determined to bring the fight to us, then we have no choice but to bring it to them. There is a price that all American soldiers—and even their friends and families—now must pay for intervening in the internal affairs of Colombia."

US intelligence learns that in internal deliberations, the FARC leadership is concerned that the attacks are seriously eroding morale within the movement. Moreover, US counterdrug initiatives aimed at the FARC and Colombia are doing serious damage to their drug production, export, and distribution infrastructure. They are overheard saying: "If they go after our infrastructure, then we must go after theirs." Intelligence analysts interpret this and other statements as indicative of FARC's intent to launch a spectacular, retaliatory attack against US persons and places within the borders of the United States.

analyst observing and forecasting an adversary's behavior to that of someone who must make difficult decisions within that operational culture. This reframing process often introduces new and different stimuli that might not have been factored into a traditional analysis.

Brainstorming is a group process that follows specific rules and procedures designed to generate new ideas and concepts. (See Box 9.2.) The stimulus for creativity comes from two or more analysts bouncing ideas off each other. A brainstorming session usually exposes an analyst to a greater range of ideas and perspectives than the analyst could generate alone, and this broadening of views typically results in a better analytic product.

Structured Brainstorming is a systematic 12-step process for conducting group brainstorming. It requires a facilitator, in part because participants are not allowed to talk during the brainstorming session. Structured Brainstorming

---

Box 9.2 SEVEN RULES FOR SUCCESSFUL BRAINSTORMING

1. Be specific about the purpose and the topic of the brainstorming session.

2. Never criticize an idea, no matter how weird, unconventional, or improbable it might sound. Instead, try to figure out how the idea might be applied to the task at hand.

3. Allow only one conversation at a time and ensure that everyone has an opportunity to speak.

4. Allocate enough time to complete the brainstorming session.

5. Try to include one or more "outsiders" in the group, usually someone who does not share the same body of knowledge or perspective as other group members but has some familiarity with the topic.

6. Write it down! Track the discussion by using a whiteboard, an easel, or sticky notes.

7. Summarize key findings at the end of the session. Ask the participants to write down the most important thing they learned on a 3-by-5-inch card as they depart the session. Then, prepare a short summary and distribute the list to the participants (who may add items to the list) and to others interested in the topic (including those who could not attend).

is most often used to identify key drivers or all the forces and factors that may come into play in a given situation.

Task 1. Conduct a Red Hat/Structured Brainstorming exercise to identify the forces and factors that would most influence a FARC decision to attack the US homeland.

STEP 1: Gather a group of analysts with knowledge of the target and its operating culture and environment.

STEP 2: Pass out sticky notes and markers to all participants. Inform the team that there is no talking during the sticky-notes portion of the brainstorming exercise.

STEP 3: Present the team with the following question: What are all the things the FARC Secretariat would think about when planning an attack on the US homeland?

STEP 4: Ask them to put themselves in the FARC's shoes and simulate how its leaders would respond. Emphasize the need to avoid mirror imaging. The question is not "What would you do if you were in their shoes?" but "How would the FARC leadership approach this problem, given their background, past experience, and the current situation?"

STEP 5: Ask the group to write down responses to the question using a few key words that will fit on a sticky note. After a response is written down, the participant gives it to the facilitator, who then reads it out loud. Marker-type pens are used so that people can easily see what is written on the sticky notes when they are posted on a wall or whiteboard.

STEP 6: Stick all the sticky notes on a wall in the order in which they are called out. Treat all ideas the same. Encourage participants to build on one another's ideas. Usually there is an initial spurt of ideas followed by pauses as participants contemplate the question. After five or ten minutes there is often a long pause of a minute or so. This slowing down suggests that the group has "emptied the barrel of the obvious" and is now on the verge of coming up with some fresh insights and ideas. Do not talk during this pause, even if the silence is uncomfortable.

STEP 7: After two or three long pauses, conclude this divergent thinking phase of the brainstorming session.

STEP 8: Ask all participants (or a small group) to go up to the wall and rearrange the sticky notes by affinity groups (groups that have some common characteristics). Some sticky notes may be moved several times; some may also be copied if the idea applies to more than one affinity group.

STEP 9: When all sticky notes have been arranged, ask the group to select a word or phrase that best describes each grouping.

STEP 10: Look for sticky notes that do not fit neatly into any of the groups. Consider whether such an outlier is useless noise or the germ of an idea that deserves further attention.

STEP 11: Assess what the group has accomplished. Can you identify four or five key factors, forces, themes, or dimensions that are most likely to influence how the FARC leadership would mount an attack?

STEP 12: Present the results and describe the key themes or dimensions of the problem that were identified. Consider less conventional means of presenting the results by engaging in a hypothetical conversation in which the leaders discuss the issue in the first person.

Analytic Value Added. Were we careful to avoid mirror imaging when we put ourselves "in the shoes" of the FARC Secretariat? Did we explore all the possible forces and factors that could influence how the FARC might launch an attack on the US homeland? Did our ideas group themselves into coherent affinity groups? How did we treat outliers or sticky notes that seemed to belong in a group all by themselves? Did the outliers spark new lines of inquiry? Did the labels we generated for each group accurately capture the essence of that set of sticky notes?

Technique 2: Multiple Scenarios Generation

In the complex, evolving, uncertain situations that intelligence analysts and decision makers must deal with, the future is not easily predicable. The best an analyst can do is to identify the driving forces that may determine future outcomes and monitor those forces as they interact to become the future. Scenarios are a principal vehicle for doing this. Scenarios are plausible and sometimes provocative stories about how the future might unfold. When alternative futures have been clearly outlined, decision makers can mentally rehearse these futures and ask themselves, "What should I be doing now to prepare for these futures?"

Scenarios Analysis provides a framework for considering various plausible futures. Trying to divine or predict a single outcome typically is a disservice to senior officials and decision makers. Generating several scenarios helps focus attention on the key underlying forces and factors most likely to influence how a situation develops. Multiple Scenarios Generation creates a large number of possible scenarios. This is desirable to make sure nothing has been overlooked. Once generated, the scenarios can be screened quickly without detailed analysis of each one. Once sensitized to these different scenarios, analysts are more likely to pay attention to outlying data that would suggest that events are playing out in a way not previously imagined.

Task 2. Use Multiple Scenarios Generation to identify the most plausible attack scenarios the FARC would consider in launching a retaliatory attack on the US homeland.

STEP 1: Clearly define the focal issue and the specific goals of the futures exercise.

STEP 2: Brainstorm to identify the key forces, factors, or events that are most likely to influence how the issue will develop over a specified time period. In this case, use the four or five key drivers, themes, or dimensions that emerged from Task 1, the Red Hat/Structured Brainstorming exercise.

STEP 3: For each of these key drivers, define the two ends of the spectrum.

STEP 4: Pair the drivers in a series of 2 × 2 matrices. If you have four drivers, they can be combined into six pairs, generating six different matrices. Five drivers would generate ten different matrices.

STEP 5: Develop a story or two for each quadrant of each 2 × 2 matrix.

STEP 6: From all the scenarios generated, select three or four that are the most deserving of attention because they best illustrate the range of attacks FARC is most likely to contemplate.

STEP 7: Consider whether one of the final scenarios you select might be described as a "wild card" (low-probability/high-impact) or "nightmare" scenario.

Analytic Value Added. Did the technique help us generate a robust set of potential scenarios to consider? Did we discover new scenarios that we probably would not have imagined if we had not used this particular technique? Did similar themes emerge from different matrices even though different pairs of drivers were being considered? Were the final scenarios selected both plausible and the most deserving of attention?

Technique 3: Indicators

Indicators are observable or deduced phenomena that can be periodically reviewed to help track events, distinguish between competing hypotheses, spot emerging trends, and warn of unanticipated change. An indicators list is a preestablished set of actions, conditions, facts, or events whose simultaneous occurrence would argue strongly that a phenomenon is present or a hypothesis is correct. The identification and monitoring of indicators are fundamental tasks of intelligence analysis, as they are the principal means of avoiding surprise. In intelligence analysis, indicators are often described as forward-looking or predictive indicators. In the law enforcement community, indicators are used to assess whether a target's activities or behavior is consistent with an established pattern or lead hypothesis. These are often described as backward-looking or descriptive indicators.

Preparation of a detailed indicator list by a group of knowledgeable analysts is usually a good learning experience for all participants. It can be a useful medium for an exchange of knowledge between analysts from different organizations or those with different types of expertise—for example, counterterrorism or counter drug analysis, infrastructure protection, and country expertise. The indicator list can become the basis for conducting an investigation or directing collection efforts and routing relevant information to all interested parties. Identification and monitoring of indicators or signposts that a scenario is emerging can provide early warning of the direction in which the future is heading, but these early signs are not obvious. The human mind tends to see what it expects to see and to overlook the unexpected. Indicators take on meaning only in the context of a specific scenario with which they have been identified. The prior identification of a scenario and associated indicators can create an awareness that prepares the mind to recognize and prevent a bad scenario from unfolding or help a good scenario to come about.

Task 3. Create separate sets of indicators for each alternative scenario that was generated in Task 2.

STEP 1: Work alone, or preferably with a small group, to brainstorm a list of indicators for each scenario.

STEP 2: Review and refine each set of indicators, discarding any that are duplicative within any given scenario and combining those that are similar.

STEP 3: Examine each indicator to determine if it meets the following five criteria. Discard those that are found wanting.

1. **Observable and collectible.** There must be some reasonable expectation that, if present, the indicator will be observed and reported by a reliable source. If an indicator will be used to monitor change over time, it must be collectible over time.

2. **Valid.** An indicator must be clearly relevant to the end state the analyst is trying to predict or assess, and it must be inconsistent with all or at least some of the alternative explanations or outcomes. It must accurately measure the concept or phenomenon at issue.

3. **Reliable.** Data collection must be consistent when comparable methods are used. Those observing and collecting data must observe the same things. Reliability requires precise definition of the indicators.

4. **Stable.** An indicator must be useful over time to allow comparisons and to track events. Ideally, the indicator should be observable early in the evolution of a development so that analysts and decision makers have time to react accordingly.

5. **Unique.** An indicator should measure only one thing and, in combination with other indicators, should point only to the phenomenon being studied. Valuable indicators are those that are not only consistent with a specified scenario or hypothesis but are also inconsistent with all other alternative scenarios.

Analytic Value Added. What new or otherwise implicit criteria did the indicators process expose? Do the indicators prompt additional areas for collection?

Technique 4: Indicators Validator

The Indicators Validator is a simple tool for assessing the diagnostic power of indicators. Once an analyst has developed a set of attention-deserving alternative scenarios or competing hypotheses, the next step is to generate indicators for each scenario or hypothesis that would appear if that particular scenario were beginning to emerge or that particular hypothesis were true. A critical question that is not often asked is whether a given indicator would appear only for the scenario or hypothesis to which it is assigned or also in one or more alternative scenarios or hypotheses. Indicators that could appear under several are not considered diagnostic, suggesting that they are not particularly useful in determining whether a specific scenario is beginning to emerge or a particular hypothesis is true. The ideal indicator is highly likely for the scenario to which it is assigned and highly unlikely for all others.

Task 4. Use the Indicators Validator to assess the diagnosticity of your indicators.

STEP 1: Create a matrix similar to that used for Analysis of Competing Hypotheses.[20] This can be done manually or by using the Indicators Validator software. Contact Pherson Associates at ThinkSuite@pherson .org or go to www.pherson.org to obtain access to the Indicators Validator software if it is not available on your system. List the alternative scenarios along the top of the matrix and the indicators that have been generated for each of the scenarios down the left side of the matrix.

STEP 2: Moving across the indicator rows, assess whether the indicator for each scenario:

> ▶ is highly likely to appear.
> ▶ is likely to appear.
> ▶ could appear.
> ▶ is unlikely to appear.
> ▶ is highly unlikely to appear.

Indicators developed for their particular scenario, the home scenario, should be either highly likely or likely.

If the software is unavailable, you can do your own scoring. If the indicator is highly likely in the home scenario, then in the other scenarios,

> ▶ highly likely is 0 points.
> ▶ likely is 1 point.
> ▶ could appear is 2 points.
> ▶ unlikely is 4 points.
> ▶ highly unlikely is 6 points.

If the indicator is likely in the home scenario, then in the other scenarios,

▶ highly likely is 0 points.

▶ likely is 0 points.

▶ could appear is 1 point.

▶ unlikely is 3 points.

▶ highly unlikely is 5 points.

STEP 3: Tally up the scores across each row and then rank order all the indicators.

STEP 4: Re-sort the indicators, putting those with the highest total scores at the top of the matrix and those with the lowest scores at the bottom. The most discriminating indicator is highly likely to emerge under the home scenario and highly unlikely to emerge under all other scenarios. The least discriminating indicator is highly likely to appear in all scenarios. Most indicators will fall somewhere in between.

STEP 5: The indicators with the most highly unlikely and unlikely ratings are the most discriminating and should be retained.

STEP 6: Indicators with no highly unlikely or unlikely ratings should be discarded.

STEP 7: Use your judgment as to whether you should retain or discard indicators that score fewer points. Generally you should discard all indicators that have highly unlikely or unlikely ratings. In some cases, an indicator may be worth keeping if it is useful when viewed in combination with several other indicators.

STEP 8: Once nondiscriminating indicators have been eliminated, regroup the indicators under their home scenario.

STEP 9: If a large number of indicators for a particular scenario have been eliminated, develop additional—and more diagnostic—indicators for that scenario.

STEP 10: Check the diagnostic value of any new indicators by applying the Indicators Validator to them as well.

Analytic Value Added. Does each scenario have a robust set of highly diagnostic indicators? Do these indicator lists provide useful leads for alerting FBI field offices and state and local fusion centers of plausible, potential emerging threats? Are they focused enough to generate specific collection requirements, giving federal, state, local, and tribal officials a more concrete idea of what to look for?

NOTES

1. Stephanie Hanson, "FARC, ELN: Colombia's Left-Wing Guerrillas," Council of Foreign Relations Backgrounder, August 19, 2009, http://www.cfr.org/publication/9272/farc_eln.html.

2. Ibid., 4.

3. Farhan Daredia, "FARC Front Leader Extradited to US" [Department of Justice press release], July 17, 2009, http://www.mainjustice.com/2009/07/17/farc-front-leader-extradited-to-us/.

4. US Department of the Treasury, "Designation of FARC International Commission Members" [press release], September 30, 2008, http://www.america.gov/st/texttrans-english/2008/October/20081002123000eaifas0.7901575.html.

5. Eric Green, "FARC Terrorist Group in Colombia Diminished but Still Dangerous," October 2, 2008, http://www.america.gov/st/democracy-english/2008/October/20 0810021603451xeneerg0.7314112.html.

6. Hanson, "FARC, ELN: Colombia's Left-Wing Guerrillas."

7. Simon Romero, "Manuel Marulanda, Top Commander of Colombia's Largest Guerrilla Group, Is Dead," *New York Times*, May 26, 2008, http://www.nytimes.com/2008/05/26/world/americas/26marulanda.html.

8. Simon Romero, "Venezuela Still Aids Colombia Rebels, New Material Shows," *New York Times*, August 2, 2009, http://www.nytimes.com/2009/08/03/world/americas/03venez.html.

9. Hanson, "FARC, ELN: Colombia's Left-Wing Guerrillas."

10. Agence France Press, "Spain Charges 13 over ETA-FARC Plot to Kill Colombian President," Expatica.com, March 1, 2010, http://www.expatica.com/es/news/spanish-rss-news/spain-charges-19-over-eta-farc-plot-to-kill-colombian-president_27346.html.

11. Warren Hoge, "Adams Delays Testifying in US About IRA Action in Colombia," *New York Times*, April 24, 2002, http://www.nytimes.com/2002/04/24/world/adams-delays-testifying-in-us-about-ira-action-in-colombia.html.

12. International Crisis Group, "Colombia: Making Military Progress Pay Off," Latin America Briefing no. 17, April 29, 2008, http://www.crisisgroup.org/~/media/Files/latin-america/colombia/b17_colombia_making_military_progress_pay_off.ashx.

13. Ibid.

14. Ibid., 8.

15. MainJustice: Just Anti-Corruption, "FARC Front Leader Extradited to US" [Department of Justice press release], July 17, 2009, http://www.mainjustice.com/2009/07/17/farc-front-leader-extradited-to-us/.

16. Hanson, "FARC, ELN: Colombia's Left-Wing Guerrillas."

17. United States Southern Command Web site, http://www.southcom.mil/AppsSC/pages/team.php.

18. "Supplemental Agreement for Cooperation and Technical Assistance in Defense and Security Between the Governments of the United States of America and the Republic of Colombia," March 11, 2009, http://justf.org/content/supplemental-agreement-cooperation-and-technical-assistance-defense-and-security-between-gov.

19. United States Southern Command, "Fact Sheet: SOUTHCOM Support to Colombia," http://www.southcom.mil/AppsSC/factFiles.php?id=35.

20. For a full explanation of Analysis of Competing Hypotheses, see Richards J. Heuer Jr. and Randolph H. Pherson, *Structured Analytic Techniques for Intelligence Analysis* (Washington, DC: CQ Press, 2011), 160.

Key Questions

▶ What are the most likely terrorist targets in Mumbai?

▶ What type of attack would the terrorists most likely mount?

▶ How would they gain access to the city?

▶ What can be done to deter future terrorist attacks?

10 Defending Mumbai from Terrorist Attack

CASE NARRATIVE

The teeming sprawl of modern Mumbai's more than 18 million residents had humble beginnings.[1] Poised on a peninsula jutting into the Arabian Sea, the city formerly known as Bombay began its life as a small fishing village populated by native Koli people.[2] Portuguese sailors later claimed the Koli's seven swampy islands but did not see much value in them. In 1661, the Portuguese government gifted the islands to Britain as part of the dowry for Charles II's marriage to Catherine of Braganza. The city's gradual transformation into a bustling hub of world commerce began when the East India Company recognized the potential of the location's natural harbor and leased the islands from the British crown. The subsequent colonization of India by Britain and the development of the textile industry in the mid-nineteenth century solidified the city's importance to Asia and the rest of the world.

By 2008, Mumbai had become the epicenter of India's booming economy. The city hosts India's stock exchange and boasts a population density four times greater than that of New York City.[3] A recent Global Cities Index rated Mumbai as the world's 4th most populous city, with the 25th highest GDP.[4] Mumbai's modern docking facilities, rail connections, and international airport make it India's gateway to the world's globalized economy.[5] The city is also home to the popular Bollywood film industry, which churns out movies whose financial success is only eclipsed by that of their American counterparts. A virtual kaleidoscope of colors and cultures, Mumbai is both a playground for the fantastically wealthy and a congested shantytown for the urban poor. Local residents boast that it is a city that never sleeps with streets that are never empty.[6]

Map 10.1 ▶ Mumbai Peninsula

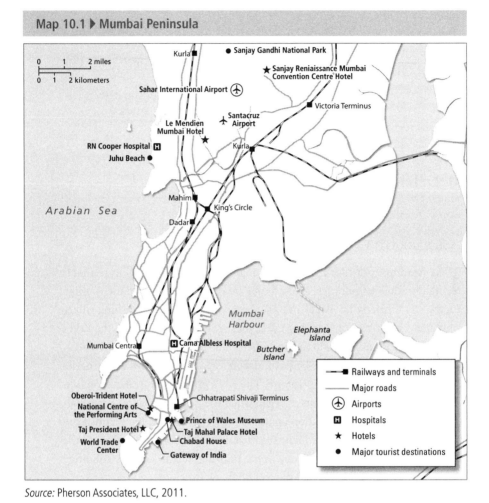

Source: Pherson Associates, LLC, 2011.

It was not Mumbai's spectacular growth and increasing globalization that was foremost on the minds of Indian security officials in the fall of 2008, however. In mid-October, the United States had quietly told the Indian government that intelligence collected in Pakistan warned of an "oncoming attack that will be launched by terrorists against hotels and business centers in Mumbai (formerly Bombay)."[7,8] The source of the warning made it credible, but it lacked specificity about the attackers and their methods, weapons, and targets. Absent such details, it would be difficult to assign priorities in defending the vast city. It fell to Indian intelligence and law enforcement officials to identify the most likely whens, wheres, and hows of an attack.

A History of Violence

Mumbai already had long experience as a target of terrorism. Between 1993 and 2008, terrorists conducted numerous bomb attacks in and around the city (see Table 10.1). Several of the incidents involved simultaneous attacks on multiple targets. In all, 544 died and 1,774 sustained injuries in the attacks. The assailants' weapons of choice included bombs—often hidden or thrown from motor scooters—and grenades. During this period there were no reports of suicide bombings.

Table 10.1 ▶ Bomb Blasts in Mumbai, 1993–2008*			
Date	Place	Killed	Injured
12 March 1993	Thirteen attacks throughout city	257	700
23 January 1998	Kanjurmarg Station	unknown	unknown
24 January 1998	Goregaon and Malad Railway tracks	0	2
27 February 1998	Three bombings at Virar, Santa Cruz, and Kandivali Railway Stations	9	22
2 December 2002	Bus in Ghatokpar at railway station	3	34
6 December 2002	Air-conditioning vent in McDonald's, Central Railway Station	0	25
27 January 2003	Bicycle near Vile Parle Railway Station	1	25
13 March 2003	Train car at Mulund Station	10	70
14 April 2003	Parcel at V.N. Jewelers in Bandra	1	0
28 July 2003	Bus in Ghatkopar near a telephone exchange	4	32
25 August 2003	Two taxis at Gateway of India and Zaveri Bazaar	50	150
11 July 2006	Seven trains around the city	209	714
	Total Casualties	544	1,774

*No attacks were recorded in 2007 and 2008.

The most notable of these attacks occurred in 1993, when Islamic terrorists exploded devices at thirteen locations throughout Mumbai, causing extensive casualties. The targets ranged from hotels to the airport to bazaars. The modus operandi was a staged vehicle with RDX bombs (see Box 10.1 on RDX bombs),

---

Box 10.1 RDX BOMBS

RDX, commonly known as cyclonite, was widely used during World War II, often in explosive mixtures with TNT.[i] During World War II, the British termed cyclonite "Research Department Explosive" (R.D.X.) for security reasons and used it as a more powerful form of TNT for attacking German U-boats.[ii] It was one of the first plastic explosives and has been used in many terrorist plots.[iii] Outside of military applications, RDX is used in controlled demolition to raze structures. Ahmed Ressam, the Al-Qaeda "Millenium Bomber," used a small quantity of RDX as one of the components in the explosives that he prepared to bomb Los Angeles International Airport on New Year's Eve 1999/2000; the combined explosives could have produced a blast forty times greater than that of a devastating car bomb.[iv,v]

---

i. Tenney L. Davis, *The Chemistry of Powder and Explosives*, Vol. II (New York: John Wiley & Sons, 1943).

ii. MacDonald and Mack Partnership, *Historic Properties Report: Newport Army Ammunition Plant; Newport Indiana*, AD-A175 818, prepared for National Park Service (Minneapolis, MN: McDonald and Mack Partnership, 1984), 18. Available at http://www.dtic.mil/cgi-bin/GetTRDoc?AD=ADA175818.

iii. John Sweetman, *The Dambusters Raid* (London: Cassell Military Paperbacks, 2002), 144.

iv. *US v. Ressam*, US Court of Appeals for the Ninth Circuit (February 2, 2010), http://www.nefafoundation.org/miscellaneous/US_v_Ressam_9thcircuit appeals0210.pdf.

v. *US v. Ressam*, US District Court, Western District of Washington at Seattle, December 1999, http://nefafoundation.org/miscellaneous/FeaturedDocs/U.S._v_Ressam_Complaint.pdf.

---

although the assailants also threw grenades at some of the targets.[9] The attack was orchestrated by Dawood Ibrahim, a well-known organized crime leader, in response to ongoing violence between Hindus and Muslims in prior months and, more specifically, as retaliation for the destruction of a sixteenth-century Mosque in late 1992.[10,11] Hinduism is the dominant religion in India; only 12 percent of the population is Muslim. Perceived inequities have been a major factor sparking intercommunal violence in the country.

Five years later, a series of bombings occurred at train stations across the city and in the suburbs. Over a two-month period, assailants conducted successful attacks at six different train stations in three separate incidents.[12] The terrorists targeted railway stations, platforms, and tracks. During the trial of the accused men, the prosecutor argued the attack was conducted at the behest of the Pakistani Inter-Services Intelligence (ISI). Some of the blasts occurred the night before parliamentary elections.[13]

From December 2002 through August 2003, seven violent incidents occurred. Although all the attacks involved bombings, these incidents had the most variation in attack method. In the first attack on 2 December, a bomb was placed on a bus at the Ghatkopar train station.[14] Four days later, a bomb exploded in an air-conditioning vent inside a McDonald's fast-food restaurant at the central railway station.[15] Roughly a month and a half later on 27 January, a bomb attached to a bicycle exploded at the Vile Parle train station.[16] About two weeks later on 13 March, a bomb exploded inside a train car at the Mulund train station.[17] The most unusual attack occurred a month later on 14 April, when a parcel exploded inside a jeweler's store.[18] No attacks were recorded in May or June, but on 28 July a bus at Ghatkopar train station was destroyed by

Wreckage from 25 August 2003 terrorist bombing attacks at Zaveri Bazaar in Bombay.

a bomb.[19] The final and deadliest attack in this series occurred on 25 August. Two taxis exploded at the Gateway of India and at the Zaveri Bazaar, killing 50 people and injuring 150.[20]

Most of the attacks were traced back to radical Islamic groups; most of these were based in Pakistan. Authorities believed the Student Islamic Movement of India (SIMI) was responsible for the 6 December 2002 and 25 August 2003 attacks; Laškar-ĕ-Taiba (LeT) was suspected in the 25 August 2003 attack as well.[21,22]

Almost three years passed until the next incident, which came to be called 7/11. On 11 July 2006, seven explosions occurred on seven trains along the western rail line in Mumbai between 1824 and 1835 hours.[23] The explosions occurred at or near the Khar, Mahim, Matunga, Jogeshwari, Borivili, and Bhayandra-Mira Road train stations and between the Khar and Santa Cruz stations. Each bomb consisted of a pressure cooker filled with 2.5 kg of RDX and ammonium nitrate; the bombs were placed inside first-class train compartments.[24,25] Indian officials claimed that SIMI and LeT conducted the attacks on behalf of the Pakistani ISI.[26]

Recent Major Terrorist Attacks in India

Mumbai has not been the only target of attack for Muslim and separatist groups. From 2001 to 2008, twenty-one major incidents occurred elsewhere in India.[27,28,29] Some 550 people died in these attacks, most of which involved bombs.

Assailants used a vehicle-borne improvised explosive device (VBIED) to blow up the front gate of the Jammu and Kashmir state assembly complex on 1 October 2001. Two attackers entered the complex and opened fire until security forces shot and killed them.[30,31] Two months later, on 13 December 2001, five individuals attacked the National Parliament in New Delhi using AK-47s and grenades.[32] At least one of the attackers was wearing a suicide vest, but it exploded after he was shot and did not harm anyone.[33] The terrorist group Jaish-e-Mohammed (JEM) claimed responsibility for the October attack, and some of its members were convicted; authorities also suspected LeT of involvement.[34,35]

On 24 September 2002, terrorists launched a similar attack on the Hindu temple complex in Gandhinagar. Two terrorists entered the complex and opened fire with AK-47s; they also threw hand grenades before being killed by Indian commandos.[36,37] Another attack using similar tactics occurred on 14 May 2002 when three attackers fired at a bus and then attacked the Kalu Chak

Map 10.2 ▶ India, Mumbai, and Previous Attack Sites

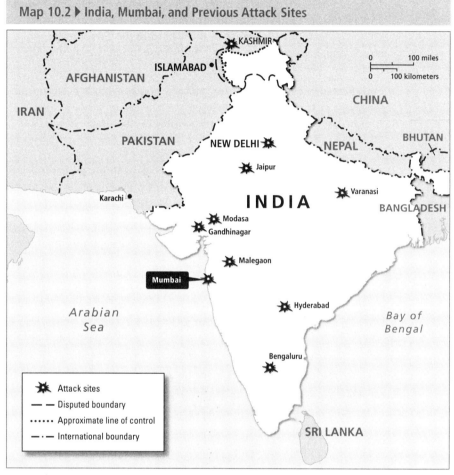

Source: Pherson Associates, LLC, 2011.

army camp in Jammu.[38] LeT was suspected of conducting the attack, and press reports raised the specter of Pakistani support.[39]

Sporadic bombings continued for several years.

▶ On 15 August 2004, a bomb exploded in Assam during the Independence Day parade.[40] The attack was attributed to the United Liberation Front of Asom (ULFA),[41] a terrorist group with the goal of "establishing a 'sovereign socialist Assam' through armed struggle."[42]

▶ On 29 October 2005, three bombs exploded during the festival of lights in New Delhi[43] at two marketplaces and on a bus.[44] Police suspected that a group connected to LeT, called Inquilab, was responsible for the attack.[45]

▶ Terrorists detonated bombs at the Sankat Mochan temple and a train and hall in the Cantonmen railway station in Varanasi on 7 March 2006. The tactics were similar to those used in the Gandhinagar attack, and as many as ten other bombs were found throughout the city.[46]

▶ On 8 September 2006, two or three bicycle bombs exploded at a Muslim graveyard near a Mosque just before prayers began on Shab-e-Barat.[47] Although it is not clear who was responsible for the attack, one person arrested for the incident had ties to LeT.[48]

In 2007, the frequency of attacks began to escalate. In the past, almost all attacks on trains in India had occurred at or near a primary rail station. On 19 February 2007, however, two crude briefcase bombs were detonated on a train near the village of Dewana and set the train on fire. The train was heading to the Pakistani-Indian border when it caught fire. Officials found two unexploded briefcases in other cars on the train. The attack took place the day before scheduled India-Pakistan peace talks began.[49]

Only three months later, on 18 May 2007, a bomb exploded during prayers at the Mecca Masjid in Hyderabad, a city populated mostly by Muslims.[50] In addition to the bomb that detonated, police found two unexploded bombs with cell phone triggers inside the mosque that had failed to explode. Following the blast, Muslim protestors at the site became unruly, and police fired into the crowd, killing some of the protestors.[51] Hyderabad was the site of violence again when two bombs exploded in the early evening of 25 August 2007. The terrorists targeted the Lumbini Amusement Park and the restaurant Gokul Chat Bhandar.[52] Authorities discovered nineteen other bombs hidden throughout the city.[53]

On 11 October, a blast at a Sufi mosque in Ajmer killed three people. A few days later on 14 October, a theater in Ludhiana was rocked with an explosion that killed seven people. Three simultaneous bombs on 23 November in judicial complexes in Lucknow, Varanasi, and Faizabad killed thirteen.[54]

The number of terrorist attacks escalated even further beginning in May 2008. On 13 May, seven bombs exploded in Jaipur at several markets and Hindu temples. On 25 July 2008, eight bombs exploded in Bengaluru (formerly Bangalore). The next day, sixteen bombs exploded in Ahmedabad. Then on 13 September, five bombs exploded in the markets of New Delhi. Suspicion for the Jaipur, Bengaluru, and New Delhi attacks fell on SIMI, LeT, and Harkat-ul-Jehad-al-Islami (HUJI), a Sunni terrorist group.[55,56,57] SIMI was also associated with the Ahmedabad attack.[58] A group called the Indian Mujahideen, however, claimed responsibility for the Jaipur, Ahmedabad, and New Delhi attacks.[59]

Two weeks after the explosions in New Delhi, another bomb went off in the city on 24 September 2008. Two terrorists dropped the bomb in a bag from their motorcycle, and a 10-year-old boy was trying to return it to them when the bomb exploded.[60] Two days later in the towns of Modasa and Malegaon, two bombs exploded nearly simultaneously after being dropped from motorcycles.[61] The attack in Modasa occurred in a Muslim-dominated market.[62] In Malegaon, the blast occurred near a building previously used by SIMI before it was banned.[63]

Three attacks occurred in the following month. The first occurred in Kanpur when a bomb on a bicycle exploded on 14 October.[64] The next attack occurred a week later on 21 October in Imphal. The bomb had been placed on a motor scooter[65] and may have been targeting a nearby police complex. Authorities suspected a separatist group called the People's Revolutionary Party of Kangleipak based out of Myanmar (Burma) of conducting the bombing.[66] The deadliest of the attacks that month occurred on 30 October in Assam. As with the attacks in Jaipur, Ahmedabad, and Bengaluru and the first New Delhi attack in September 2008, multiple bombs—eighteen—using RDX[67] exploded throughout the city nearly simultaneously. Authorities suspected HUJI and ULFA of carrying out the attacks.[68]

Countering the Threat

Responsibility for defending Mumbai from terrorist attack is shared by several law enforcement and intelligence organizations at both the local and national levels. At the national level, in addition to military intelligence, two main civilian intelligence services as well as other ministries share an intelligence mandate. At the local level, the police respond to and share information based on national-level guidance regarding terrorist activities.

The Research and Analysis Wing (RAW) and the Intelligence Bureau are the two main civilian intelligence services. The RAW is the country's foreign intelligence unit and focuses primarily on issues outside India's borders, mostly in the neighboring countries of Pakistan and Bangladesh.[69] The Intelligence Bureau concentrates primarily on domestic security.[70] Both services are routinely engaged in collecting intelligence on and assessing the threat posed by militant Pakistani Islamist groups. Along with RAW, the Army's Signals Intelligence Directorate collects signals intelligence that has the potential to reveal terrorist planning and operations.[71]

India's Ministry of Home Affairs has several armed units it can task to assist in internal security matters. The Border Security Force is a paramilitary service dedicated to monitoring the country's international frontiers.[72] The Indian Home Guard is a paramilitary force capable of serving as an auxiliary to the Indian Police Service—a nationwide law enforcement unit. The National Security Guard, also known as the "Black Cats," is a highly trained counterterrorism force capable of preventing or responding to large-scale terror assaults.[73]

In addition to these national resources, the Mumbai Police Department has had extensive experience trying to counter terrorist attacks. In 2004, the Mumbai Police Department created an elite Anti-Terrorism Squad to exchange information on terrorist threats and coordinate its activities with national intelligence agencies. Members of the squad receive special weapons and tactics training.[74]

Recommended Readings

Rabasa, Angel, et al. *The Lessons of Mumbai.* Santa Monica, CA: RAND Corporation, 2009. http://www.rand.org/pubs/occasional_papers/2009/RAND_OP249.pdf.

Rotella, Sebastian. "On the Trail of a Terrorist." *Washington Post*, November 14, 2010. http://www.washingtonpost.com/wp-dyn/content/article/2010/11/13/AR2010111304345.html.

Table 10.2 ▶ Case Snapshot: Defending Mumbai from Terrorist Attack		
Structured Analytic Technique Used	Heuer and Pherson Page Number	Analytic Family
Structured Brainstorming	p. 92	Idea Generation
Red Hat Analysis	p. 197	Assessment of Cause and Effect
Quadrant Crunching	p. 111	Idea Generation
Indicators	p. 132	Scenarios and Indicators
Indicators Validator	p. 140	Scenarios and Indicators

DEFENDING MUMBAI FROM TERRORIST ATTACK
STRUCTURED ANALYTIC TECHNIQUES IN ACTION

It is mid-October 2008. You are an analyst working in the Mumbai Police Department, and you just received the US warning about the threat to Mumbai from the Intelligence Bureau in New Delhi. Analysis of the threat has to be done quickly in order to develop guidance to help authorities anticipate and detect the type of attack that is being planned. While no analyst has a crystal ball, it is incumbent upon analysts to help law enforcement officials and policy makers anticipate how adversaries will behave, outline the range of possible futures that could develop, and recognize the signs that a particular future is beginning to take shape. The techniques in this case—Structured Brainstorming, Red Hat Analysis, Quadrant Crunching, Indicators, and the Indicators Validator—can help analysts tackle each part of this task.

Technique 1: Structured Brainstorming
Brainstorming is a group process that follows specific rules and procedures designed for generating new ideas and concepts. The stimulus for creativity comes from two or more analysts bouncing ideas off each other. A brainstorming session usually exposes an analyst to a greater range of ideas and perspectives than the analyst could generate alone, and this broadening of views typically results in a better analytic product. (See seven rules for successful brainstorming in Box 10.2.)

Structured Brainstorming is a more systematic 12-step process for conducting group brainstorming. It requires a facilitator, in part because participants

---

Box 10.2 SEVEN RULES FOR SUCCESSFUL BRAINSTORMING

1. Be specific about the purpose and the topic of the brainstorming session.

2. Never criticize an idea, no matter how weird, unconventional, or improbable it might sound. Instead, try to figure out how the idea might be applied to the task at hand.

3. Allow only one conversation at a time and ensure that everyone has an opportunity to speak.

4. Allocate enough time to complete the brainstorming session.

5. Try to include one or more "outsiders" in the group, usually someone who does not share the same body of knowledge or perspective as other group members but has some familiarity with the topic.

6. Write it down! Track the discussion by using a whiteboard, an easel, or sticky notes.

7. Summarize key findings at the end of the session. Ask the participants to write down the most important thing they learned on a 3-by-5-inch card as they depart the session. Then, prepare a short summary and distribute the list to the participants (who may add items to the list) and to others interested in the topic (including those who could not attend).

---

are not allowed to talk during the brainstorming session. Structured Brainstorming is most often used to identify key drivers or all the forces and factors that may come into play in a given situation.

Task 1. Conduct a Structured Brainstorming exercise to identify all the various modes of transport the assailants might use to enter Mumbai.

STEP 1: Gather a group of analysts with knowledge of the target and its operating culture and environment.

STEP 2: Pass out sticky notes and marker-type pens to all participants. Inform the team that there is no talking during the sticky-notes portion of the brainstorming exercise.

STEP 3: Present the team with the following question: What are all the various modes of transport the assailants might use to enter Mumbai?

STEP 4: Ask them to pretend they are Muslim terrorists and simulate how they would expect the assailants to think about the problem. Emphasize the need to avoid mirror imaging. The question is not "What would you do if you were in their shoes?" but "How would the assailants think about this problem?"

STEP 5: Ask the group to write down responses to the question with a few key words that will fit on a sticky note. After a response is written down, the participant gives it to the facilitator, who then reads it out loud. Marker-type pens are used so that people can easily see what is written on the sticky notes when they are posted on the wall.

STEP 6: Stick all the sticky notes on a wall in the order in which they are called out. Treat all ideas the same. Encourage participants to build on one another's ideas. Usually an initial spurt of ideas is followed by pauses as participants contemplate the question. After five or ten minutes there is often a long pause of a minute or so. This slowing down suggests that the group has "emptied the barrel of the obvious" and is now on the verge of coming up with some fresh insights and ideas. Do not talk during this pause, even if the silence is uncomfortable.

STEP 7: After two or three long pauses, conclude this divergent-thinking phase of the brainstorming session.

STEP 8: Ask all participants (or a small group) to go up to the wall and rearrange the sticky notes by affinity groups (groups that have some common characteristics). Some sticky notes may be moved several times; some may also be copied if an idea applies to more than one affinity group.

STEP 9: When all sticky notes have been arranged, ask the group to select a word or phrase that best describes each grouping.

STEP 10: Look for sticky notes that do not fit neatly into any of the groups. Consider whether such an outlier is useless noise or the germ of an idea that deserves further attention.

STEP 11: Assess what the group has accomplished. How many different ways have you identified that the assailants could transport a team to Mumbai?

STEP 12: Present the results, describing the key themes or dimensions of the problem that were identified. Consider less conventional means of presenting the results by engaging in a hypothetical conversation in which terrorist leaders discuss the issue in the first person.

Analytic Value Added. Were we careful to avoid mirror imaging when we put ourselves "in the shoes" of Muslim terrorist planners? Did we explore all the possible forces and factors that could influence how the terrorists might gain access to Mumbai to launch their attack? Did we cluster the ideas into coherent affinity groups? How did we treat outliers or sticky notes that seemed to belong in a group all by themselves? Did the outliers spark any new lines of inquiry?

Technique 2: Red Hat Analysis
Analysts frequently endeavor to forecast the actions of an adversary or a competitor. In doing so, they need to avoid the common error of mirror imaging, the natural tendency to assume that others think and perceive the world in the same way as they do. Red Hat Analysis is a useful technique for trying to perceive threats and opportunities as others see them, but this technique alone is of limited value without significant understanding of the cultures of other countries, groups, or people involved. There is a great deal of truth to the maxim that "where you stand depends on where you sit." By imagining the situation as the target perceives it, an analyst can gain a different and usually more accurate perspective on a problem or issue.

Reframing the problem typically changes the analyst's perspective from that of an analyst observing and forecasting an adversary's behavior to that of someone who must make difficult decisions within that operational culture. This reframing process often introduces new and different stimuli that might not have been factored into a traditional analysis.

Task 2. Use Red Hat Analysis to prioritize the list of various modes of transport the terrorists might use to enter Mumbai.

STEP 1: Develop a list of criteria that most likely would guide the terrorists planning the attack as they decide their preferred mode of transport to enter Mumbai.

STEP 2: Use this list to prioritize the ideas that were generated for each affinity group, placing the most likely choice for that group at the top of the list and the least likely at the bottom.

STEP 3: After prioritizing the ideas in each affinity group, generate a master list combining all of the lists. The most likely ideas overall should be at the top of the list and the least likely overall at the bottom.

Analytic Value Added. Was your list of criteria comprehensive? Did some criteria deserve greater weight than others? Did you reflect this when you rated the various ideas?

Technique 3: Quadrant Crunching

Quadrant Crunching combines the methodology of a Key Assumptions Check[75] with Multiple Scenarios Generation[76] to generate an array of alternative scenarios or stories. This process is particularly helpful in the Mumbai case because little is known about the actual plans and intentions of the attackers. This technique helps the analyst identify and challenge key assumptions that may underpin the analysis while generating an array of credible alternative scenarios to help law enforcement focus on the most likely types of attacks to anticipate.

Task 3. Use Quadrant Crunching to brainstorm all the possible ways terrorists might launch an attack on Mumbai. List the scenarios from most to least likely.

STEP 1: State your lead hypothesis.

STEP 2: Break the lead hypothesis down into its component parts based on the journalist's list of Who? What? When? Where? Why? and How?

STEP 3: Identify which of these components are most critical to the analysis.

STEP 4: For each of the critical components, identify at least two contrary dimensions in a table (a sample template is provided in Table 10.3).

Table 10.3 ▶ Quadrant Crunching Matrix Template	
Key Components of the Lead Hypothesis	Contrary or Alternative Dimensions

STEP 5: Array combinations of these contrary assumptions in sets of 2 × 2 matrices.

STEP 6: Generate one or two credible scenarios for each quadrant.

STEP 7: Array all the scenarios generated in a single list with the most credible scenario at the top of the list and the least credible at the bottom.

Analytic Value Added. Which scenario is the most deserving of attention? Should attention focus on just one scenario, or could several scenarios play out simultaneously? Are any key themes present when reviewing the most likely set of attention-deserving scenarios? Does this technique help one determine where to devote the most attention in trying to deter the attack or mitigate the potential damage of the attack?

Technique 4: Indicators

Indicators are observable or deduced phenomena that can be periodically reviewed to track events, anticipate an adversary's plan of attack, spot emerging trends, distinguish among competing hypotheses, and warn of unanticipated change. An indicators list is a pre-established set of actions, conditions, facts, or events whose simultaneous occurrence would argue strongly that a phenomenon is present or about to be present or that a hypothesis is correct. The identification and monitoring of indicators are fundamental tasks of intelligence analysis, as they are the principal means of avoiding surprise. In the law enforcement community, indicators are used to assess whether a target's activities or behavior is consistent with an established pattern or lead hypothesis. These are often described as backward-looking or descriptive indicators. In intelligence analysis, indicators are often described as forward-looking or predictive indicators.

Preparation of a detailed indicator list by a group of knowledgeable analysts is usually a good learning experience for all participants. It can be a useful medium for an exchange of knowledge between analysts from different organizations or those with different types of expertise—for example, counterterrorism or counter drug analysis, infrastructure protection, and country expertise. The indicator list can become the basis for conducting an investigation or directing collection efforts and routing relevant information to all interested parties. Identification and monitoring of indicators or signposts that a scenario is emerging can provide early warning of the direction in which the future is heading, but these early signs are not obvious. The human mind tends to see what it expects to see and to overlook the unexpected. Indicators take on meaning only in the context of a specific scenario with which they have been identified. The prior identification of a scenario and associated indicators can create an awareness that prepares the mind to recognize and prevent a bad scenario from unfolding or help a good scenario to come about.

Task 4. Create separate sets of indicators for the most attention-deserving scenarios, including those that were generated in Task 3, the Quadrant Crunching exercise.

STEP 1: Create a list of the most attention-deserving scenarios to track for this case.

STEP 2: Work alone, or preferably with a small group, to brainstorm a list of indicators for each scenario.

STEP 3: Review and refine each set of indicators, discarding any that are duplicative and combining those that are similar.

STEP 4: Examine each indicator to determine if it meets the following five criteria. Discard those that are found wanting.

  ▸ **Observable and collectible**. There must be some reasonable expectation that, if present, the indicator will be observed and reported by a reliable source. If an indicator is to monitor change over time, it must be collectible over time.

  ▸ **Valid**. An indicator must be clearly relevant to the end state the analyst is trying to predict or assess, and it must be inconsistent with all or at least some of the alternative explanations or outcomes. It must accurately measure the concept or phenomenon at issue.

  ▸ **Reliable**. Data collection must be consistent when comparable methods are used. Those observing and collecting data must observe the same things. Reliability requires precise definition of the indicators.

  ▸ **Stable**. An indicator must be useful over time to allow comparisons and to track events. Ideally, the indicator should be observable early in the evolution of a development so that analysts and decision makers have time to react accordingly.

  ▸ **Unique**. An indicator should measure only one thing and, in combination with other indicators, should point only to the phenomenon being studied. Valuable indicators are those that not only are consistent with a specified scenario or hypothesis but also are inconsistent with all other alternative scenarios.

Analytic Value Added. Are the indicators mutually exclusive and comprehensive? Have a sufficient number of high-quality indicators been generated for each scenario to enable an effective analysis? Can the indicators be used to help detect a planned attack or deter a possible hostile course of action?

Technique 5: Indicators Validator

The Indicators Validator is a simple tool for assessing the diagnostic power of indicators. Once an analyst has developed a set of attention-deserving alternative scenarios or competing hypotheses, the next step is to generate indicators for each scenario or hypothesis that would appear if that particular scenario were beginning to emerge or that particular hypothesis were true. A critical question that is not often asked is whether a given indicator would appear only for the scenario or hypothesis to which it is assigned or also in one or more alternative scenarios or hypotheses. Indicators that could appear under several scenarios or hypotheses are not considered diagnostic; that is, they are not particularly useful in determining whether a specific scenario is beginning to emerge or a particular hypothesis is true. The ideal indicator is highly likely for the scenario to which it is assigned and highly unlikely for all others.

Task 5. Use the Indicators Validator to assess the diagnosticity of your indicators.

STEP 1: Create a matrix similar to that used for Analysis of Competing Hypotheses.[77] This can be done manually or by using the Indicators Validator software. Contact Pherson Associates at ThinkSuite@pherson .org or go to www.pherson.org to obtain access to the Indicators Validator software if it is not available on your system. List the alternative scenarios along the top of the matrix and the indicators that have been generated for each of the scenarios down the left side of the matrix.

STEP 2: Moving across the indicator rows, assess whether the indicator for each scenario:

▶ is highly likely to appear.

▶ is likely to appear.

▶ could appear.

▶ is unlikely to appear.

▶ is highly unlikely to appear.

Indicators developed for their particular scenario, the home scenario, should be either highly likely or likely.

If the software is unavailable, you can do your own scoring. If the indicator is highly likely in the home scenario, then in the other scenarios,

▶ highly likely is 0 points.
▶ likely is 1 point.
▶ could is 2 points.
▶ unlikely is 4 points.
▶ highly unlikely is 6 points.

If the indicator is *likely* in the home scenario, then in the other scenarios,

▶ highly likely is 0 points.
▶ likely is 0 points.
▶ could is 1 point.
▶ unlikely is 3 points.
▶ highly unlikely is 5 points.

STEP 3: Tally up the scores across each row and then rank order all the indicators.

STEP 4: Re-sort the indicators, putting those with the highest total score at the top of the matrix and those with the lowest score at the bottom. The most discriminating indicator is highly likely to emerge under the home scenario and highly unlikely to emerge under all other scenarios. The least discriminating indicator is highly likely to appear in all scenarios. Most indicators will fall somewhere in between.

STEP 5: The indicators with the most highly unlikely and unlikely ratings are the most discriminating and should be retained.

STEP 6: Indicators with no highly unlikely or unlikely ratings should be discarded.

STEP 7: Use your judgment as to whether you should retain or discard indicators that score fewer points. Generally you should discard all indicators that have no highly unlikely or unlikely ratings. In some cases, an indicator may be worth keeping if it is useful when viewed in combination with several other indicators.

STEP 8: Once nondiscriminating indicators have been eliminated, regroup the indicators under their home scenarios.

STEP 9: If a large number of indicators for a particular scenario have been eliminated, develop additional—and more diagnostic—indicators for that scenario.

STEP 10: Recheck the diagnostic value of any new indicators by applying the Indicators Validator to them as well.

Analytic Value Added. Does each scenario have a robust set of highly diagnostic indicators? Do these indicator lists provide useful leads for alerting local officials and businesspeople, such as hotel and restaurant owners, of plausible attack scenarios? Are the indicators focused enough to generate specific collection requirements or follow-on tasking by giving local officials and businesspeople a more concrete idea of what to look for?

NOTES

1. "Introduction to Mumbai" (from *Frommer's India,* 3rd ed.), *New York Times* Web site, 2009, http://travel.nytimes.com/frommers/travel/guides/asia/india/mumbai/frm_mumbai_3476010001.html.

2. The Municipal Corporation of Greater Mumbai, "Mumbai Travel Guide," http://www.mcgm.gov.in/irj/portal/anonymous/qlmumbaitravelguide (accessed December 5, 2010).

3. "Introduction to Mumbai" (from *Frommer's India,* 3rd ed.).

4. *Foreign Policy,* "The Global Cities Index," *Foreign Policy,* September/October 2010, 124.

5. "Introduction to Mumbai" (from *Frommer's India,* 3rd ed.).

6. The Municipal Corporation of Greater Mumbai, "Mumbai Travel Guide" (accessed December 5, 2010).

7. "US Warned India 'Twice' About Sea Attack: Report," *Indian Express,* December 2, 2008, http://www.indianexpress.com/news/us-warned-india-twice-about-sea-attack-re/393184/.

8. Richard Esposito, Brian Ross, and Pierre Thomas, "US Warned India in October of Potential Terror Attack," *ABC World News,* December 1, 2008, http://abcnews.go.com/Blotter/story?id=6368013.

9. Express News Service, "100 Guilty," Mumbai Newsline, May 18, 2007, http://cities.expressindia.com/fullstory.php?newsid=236913.

10. " '93 Mumbai Blasts: 3 Get Death Sentence," *Times of India,* July 18, 2007, archived at http://web.archive.org/web/20071213221400/http://timesofindia.indiatimes.com/India/93_Mumbai_blasts_3_get_death_sentence/articleshow/2213717.cms.

11. "Mumbai Bombing Sentencing Delay," BBC News, September 13, 2006, http://news.bbc.co.uk/2/hi/south_asia/5340660.stm.

12. " '98 Blasts: Guilty to Be Sentenced on Wednesday," *Times of India*, July 3, 2004, http://timesofindia.indiatimes.com/articleshow/763146.cms.

13. "Mumbai's Trains under Attack for More Than a Decade," *Times of India*, March 14, 2003, http://timesofindia.indiatimes.com/articleshow/40207873.cms.

14. "3 Killed, 32 Injured in Mumbai Bomb Blast," *Times of India*, December 2, 2002, http://timesofindia.indiatimes.com/articleshow/30087211.cms.

15. Tarun (India), "Major Islamic Terror Attacks in India: India Is Being Attacked by Islamists from Inside as Well as Outside," *Daniel Pipes* (blog), October 8, 2006, http://www.danielpipes.org/comments/59319/.

16. Vijay Singh, "Blast Near Vile Parle Station in Mumbai, One Killed, 25 Injured," *Rediff India Abroad*, January 28, 2003, http://www.rediff.com/news/2003/jan/27mum2.htm.

17. Vijay Singh, "Blast in Mumbai Train, 10 Killed," *Rediff India Abroad*, March 14, 2003, http://www.rediff.com/news/2003/mar/13mum.htm.

18. "Parcel Bomb Kills Bandra Security Guard," *Times of India*, April 15, 2003, http://timesofindia.indiatimes.com/articleshow/43402607.cms.

19. Vijay Singh and Syed Firdaus Ashraf, "Blast in Ghatkopar in Mumbai, 4 Killed and 32 Injured," *Rediff India Abroad*, updated July 29, 2003, http://www.rediff.com/news/2003/jul/28blast.htm.

20. "A Chronology of the 2003 Mumbai Twin Blasts Case," *Rediff India Abroad*, July 27, 2007, http://news.rediff.com/report/2009/jul/27/a-chronology-of-the-2003-mumbai-twin-blasts-case.htm.

21. Tarun (India), "Major Islamic Terror Attacks in India."

22. "Bombay Blasts Revenge for Gujarat Riots—Indian State," *China Daily*, August 27, 2003, http://www.chinadaily.com.cn/en/doc/2003–08/27/content_258711.htm.

23. "At Least 174 Killed in Indian Train Blasts," CNN, July 11, 2006, http://www.cnn.com/2006/WORLD/asiapcf/07/11/mumbai.blasts/index.html.

24. "Small, Logical Steps Cracked Case: Roy," *Times of India*, October 2, 2006, http://timesofindia.indiatimes.com/articleshow/2062187.cms.

25. "India Police: Pakistan Spy Agency behind Mumbai Bombings," CNN, October 1, 2006, http://www.cnn.com/2006/WORLD/asiapcf/09/30/india.bombs/index.html.

26. Ibid.

27. "Major Attacks and Blasts in India since 2001," Reuters, August 25, 2007, http://in.reuters.com/article/topNews/idINIndia-29149720070825/.

28. "Major Attacks since 2003," *Times of India*, November 27, 2008, http://timesofindia.indiatimes.com/India/India_a_major_terror_target/articleshow/3761676.cms (site discontinued).

29. "India: A Major Terror Target," *Hindustan Times* (New Delhi, India), September 13, 2008, http://www.hindustantimes.com/storypage/storypage.aspx?sectionName=&id=e0a7ae2d-e33c-4eac-b5e8–41d2b78df73a&&Headline=Major+attacks+since+2003 (site discontinued).

30. "Fidayeen Storm J&K House, Kill 29," *Tribune* (Chandigarh, India), October 2, 2001, http://www.tribuneindia.com/2001/20011002/main1.htm.

31. *Times* Wire Reports, "31 Killed in Attack on Kashmir Legislature," *Los Angeles Times*, October 2, 2001, http://articles.latimes.com/2001/oct/02/news/mn-52360/.

32. "Terrorists Attack Parliament; Five Intruders, Six Cops killed," *Rediff India Abroad*, December 13, 2001, http://www.rediff.com/news/2001/dec/13parl1.htm.

33. Kanchana Suggu, "The Militants Had the Home Ministry and Special Parliament Label," *Rediff India Abroad*, December 13, 2001, http://www.rediff.com/news/2001/dec/13parl14.htm.

34. US Department of State, "Terrorist Organizations," chap. 6 in *Country Reports on Terrorism 2008*, April 30, 2009, http://www.state.gov/s/ct/rls/crt/2008/122449.htm.

35. Anjali Mody, "4 Accused in Parliament Attack Case Convicted," *Hindu* (Chennai, India), December 17, 2002, http://www.hinduonnet.com/2002/12/17/stories/2002121705260100.htm.

36. Amy Waldman, "Gunmen Raid Hindu Temple Complex in India, Killing 29," *New York Times,* September 25, 2002, http://www.nytimes.com/2002/09/25/world/gunmen-raid-hindu-temple-complex-in-india-killing-29.html.

37. CNN-IBN, "Akshardham Attack Verdict Today," *IBN Live*, July 1, 2006, http://ibnlive.in.com/news/akshardham-attack-verdict-today/14271–3.html.

38. Mukhtar Ahmad, "33 Killed in Attack on Army Camp in Jammu," *Rediff India Abroad*, May 14, 2002, http://www.rediff.com/news/2002/may/14jk.htm.

39. "Pakistan Army Masterminded Jammu Attack," Rediff, May 16, 2002, http://www.rediff.com/news/2002/may/16jk3.htm.

40. Wasbir Hussain, "A Deathly Reminder," *Outlook India,* August 16, 2004, http://outlookindia.com/article.aspx?224789.

41. "Incidents Involving United Liberation Front of Asom (ULFA): 2010–2011," South Asia Terrorism Portal, updated June 19, 2011, http://www.satp.org/satporgtp/countries/india/states/assam/terrorist_outfits/ULFA_tl.htm.

42. "United Liberation Front of Asom (ULFA)—Terrorist Group of Assam," South Asia Terrorism Portal, http://www.satp.org/satporgtp/countries/india/states/assam/terrorist_outfits/Ulfa.htm.

43. "Blasts in New Delhi Kill 55," CNN, October 30, 2005, http://www.cnn.com/2005/WORLD/asiapcf/10/29/india.explosion/index.html.

44. "55 Killed in Three Blasts in Delhi," *Rediff India Abroad*, October 29, 2005, http://www.rediff.com/news/2005/oct/29delhi.htm.

45. "Police Say Blasts Work of Single Outfit," *Rediff India Abroad*, October 30, 2005, http://www.rediff.com/news/2005/oct/30dblast3.htm.

46. "Serial Blasts in Varanasi," *Telegraph* (Calcutta, India), March 8, 2006, http://www.telegraphindia.com/1060308/asp/frontpage/story_5941755.asp.

47. "Blasts Kill 37 in India Graveyard," BBC News, September 8, 2006, http://news.bbc.co.uk/2/hi/south_asia/5326730.stm.

48. "Police Arrest Malegaon Blasts 'Conspirator,' " *Times of India,* November 6, 2006, http://timesofindia.indiatimes.com/articleshow/334758.cms.

49. "Indian, Pakistani Leaders Pledge to Continue Talks Despite Deadly Train Bombing," *PBS NewsHour*, February 19, 2007, http://www.pbs.org/newshour/updates/asia/jan-june07/train_02–19.html.

50. "Bomb Hits Historic India Mosque," BBC News, May 18, 2007, http://news.bbc.co.uk/2/hi/south_asia/6668695.stm.

51. Syed Amin Jafri, "9 Killed in Hyderabad Blast; 5 in Police Firing," *Rediff India Abroad*, updated May 19, 2007, http://www.rediff.com/news/2007/may/18blast.htm.

52. "Death Toll in Hyderabad Serial Blasts Rises to 44," IBN Live, updated August 26, 2007, http://ibnlive.in.com/news/death-toll-in-hyderabad-serial-blasts-rises-to-41/47450–3.html.

53. "19 Bombs Found after Fatal Blasts in India," *New York Times,* August 26, 2007, http://www.nytimes.com/2007/08/26/world/asia/26iht-india.4.7259786.html.

54. Department of State, *Country Reports on Terrorism 2007* (Washington, DC: Department of State, 2008), http://www.state.gov/s/ct/rls/crt/2007/.

55. Abhishek Sharan, "HuJI, SIMI Stamp on Attacks," *Hindustan Times* (New Delhi, India), May 14, 2008, http://www.hindustantimes.com/News/india/HuJI-SIMI-stamp-on-attacks/310684/Article1–310633.aspx.

56. Neha Singh, "Eight Small Blasts Hit Bangalore," Reuters, July 25, 2008, http://uk.reuters.com/article/idUKISL16912820080725.

57. "SIMI, LeT May Be Behind Bangalore Blasts: IB," *Times of India,* July 25, 2008, http://timesofindia.indiatimes.com/SIMI_LeT_may_be_behind_Bangalore_blasts_IB__/articleshow/3279993.cms.

58. "Ahmedabad Blasts Carried Out on the Direction of Pak's Amir Raza Khan," *Times of India,* November 20, 2008, http://timesofindia.indiatimes.com/India/Ahmedabad_blasts_carried_out_on_the_direction_of_Paks_Amir_Raza_Khan/articleshow/3738211.cms.

59. "There Will Be More Bomb Attacks, Warns Indian Mujahideen," *Economic Times* (India), September 14, 2008, http://economictimes.indiatimes.com/articleshow/3480529.cms.

60. Gethin Chamberlain, "Boy Killed in Terrorist Bomb Attack in Delhi," *Guardian* (London), September 28, 2008, http://www.guardian.co.uk/world/2008/sep/28/india/. (Initially published in *The Observer.*)

61. "3 Blown Dead: This Terror Run Isn't Over Yet," *Hindustan Times* (New Delhi, India), September 29, 2008, http://www.hindustantimes.com/This-terror-run-isn-t-over-yet/H1-Article1–341363.aspx.

62. Associated Press, "Explosion Kills 1, Wounds 15 in Western India," MSNBC, September 29, 2008, http://www.msnbc.msn.com/id/26946171/.

63. Mateen Hafeez and Yogesh Naik, "Blasts in Maharashtra, Gujarat; 8 Killed," *Times of India,* September 30, 2008, http://timesofindia.indiatimes.com/Blasts_in_Maharashtra_Gujarat_8_killed/articleshow/3542011.cms.

64. "Explosion in Kanpur, Seven Injured," *Indian Express,* October 14, 2008, http://www.indianexpress.com/news/explosion-in-kanpur-seven-injured/373293/.

65. "Imphal Blast Near Police Hub Kills 17," *Telegraph* (Calcutta, India), October 21, 2008, http://www.telegraphindia.com/1081022/jsp/nation/story_10002920.jsp.

66. "India Wants to Seal Border with Myanmar after Blast," Reuters, October 22, 2008, http://www.reuters.com/article/latestCrisis/idUSDEL42232/.

67. Biswajyoti Das, "India Suspects Islamists, Separatists in Assam Attack," Reuters, October 31, 2008, http://www.reuters.com/article/newsOne/idUSTRE49U20V20081031/.

68. "One Arrested for Assam Serial Blasts," *Times of India,* October 31, 2008, http://timesofindia.indiatimes.com/Assam_blasts_toll_rises_to_77_curfew_in_Ganeshguri/articleshow/3658239.cms.

69. Padma Rao Sundarji, "India's Lack of Preparedness Raised Mumbai's Death Toll," McClatchy Newspapers, December 3, 2008, http://www.mcclatchydc.com/2008/12/03/57012/indias-lack-of-preparedness-raised.html.

70. Steven Aftergood, "India Intelligence and Security Agencies: Intelligence Bureau," Federation of American Scientists, updated December 2006, http://www.fas.org/irp/world/india/ib/index.html.

71. "Why Politicians Won't Get Off the Line," *Hindustan Times* (New Delhi, India), April 24, 2010, http://www.hindustantimes.com/Why-politicians-won-t-get-off-the-line/Article1–535365.aspx.

72. Border Security Force, "History," http://bsf.gov.in/Pages/History.aspx.

73. Sundarji, "India's Lack of Preparedness Raised Mumbai's Death Toll."

74. Mumbai Police, "Anti Terrorism Squad," http://www.mumbaipolice.org/special/anit_terror_squad.htm.

75. Richards J. Heuer Jr. and Randolph H. Pherson, *Structured Analytic Techniques for Intelligence Analysis*, Washington, DC: CQ Press, 2011, 183.

76. Ibid., 128.

77. For a full explanation of Analysis of Competing Hypotheses, see Richards J. Heuer Jr. and Randolph H. Pherson, *Structured Analytic Techniques for Intelligence Analysis* (Washington, DC: CQ Press, 2011), 160.

11 Shades of Orange in Ukraine

CASE NARRATIVE

On 18 March 2004, analysts in Washington, D.C., awoke to the news that Ukrainian politics had moved in two contrasting directions. The Rada, Ukraine's parliament, voted that day to establish 31 October 2004 as the date for the country's presidential election, setting the stage for a historic transfer of power through the ballot box.[1] A few blocks away at the Constitutional Court, however, justices took an important step toward emasculating that transfer by validating President Leonid Kuchma's constitutional reform bill aimed at shifting the power to appoint Ukraine's government from the president to the legislature (see Box 11.1). Ukraine's opposition cried foul, accusing the unpopular Kuchma and his allies of scheming to retain power even if they were unable to win reelection. Presidential hopeful Viktor Yushchenko reacted to the Court's ruling by announcing that his opposition bloc would use "all available means," including "taking people to the street and blocking the parliamentary rostrum," to prevent adoption of the constitutional reform bill.[2]

In Washington, D.C., US policy makers wondered about the implications of these dual developments. The US relationship with Ukraine was arguably at its lowest point since Ukrainian independence in 1991. A series of shocking revelations about Kuchma's administration—including tape recordings that pointed to Kuchma's involvement in the killing of an investigative journalist and in illegal arms sales to Iraqi leader Saddam Hussein—had badly frayed US-Ukrainian ties, leading Washington to restrict its dealings with Kuchma to a minimum.[3,4] The scheduling of elections raised the prospect that a new

Map 11.1 ▶ Ukraine

president could assume office and turn the page on the relationship's problems. But Kuchma's maneuverings on constitutional reform begged questions about his willingness to let go of power. As they considered how best to chart a course toward more productive relations with Kiev, Washington policy makers turned to analysts for help in understanding how Ukraine's presidential transition might unfold in the fall.

Origins of a Transition

The events of 18 March were but the latest twists in a long-running Ukrainian saga that mixed modern electoral politics with Byzantine court intrigue. Leonid Kuchma was just the second president in Ukraine's short history of post-Soviet independence, and his tenure had been marked by near constant political ferment. A former Soviet-era industrialist from Ukraine's east, Kuchma had won office in 1994 by amassing 52 percent of the vote in a runoff election against incumbent Leonid Kravchuk, which had divided largely along geographic lines: voters in the Ukrainian-speaking west and center of Ukraine

Box 11.1 KUCHMA'S PROPOSED CONSTITUTIONAL CHANGES

Constitutional reform had been a priority issue for President Leonid Kuchma since his election in 1994. He succeeded in winning approval of a new constitution in 1996—Ukraine's first since the 1978 model that governed the Ukrainian Soviet Socialist Republic—which tilted the balance of power from the legislature to the presidency, and for several years thereafter he continued to press for amendments that would further enhance presidential powers at the expense of the Rada. As Kuchma's popularity declined, however, he became intent on reversing that course, and in March 2003 he proposed a series of amendments that would transform Ukraine into what was termed a European-style "parliamentary-presidential state," with several powers transferring from the executive to the Rada:

▶ The prime minister and most government ministers would be appointed by parliament and not by the president.

▶ The legislature's term of office would be extended to five years, and its elections would be held simultaneously with presidential elections.

▶ The unicameral 450-seat Rada would be replaced by a bicameral parliament with a 300-seat lower chamber and an upper chamber comprised of 3 representatives from each of Ukraine's 27 regions.

▶ All seats in the lower chamber would be elected from party lists, as opposed to half from party lists and half from single-seat constituencies.

▶ The president would be elected by popular ballot in October 2004, but as of 2006 would be elected by a vote in the legislature.[i]

These provisions were slightly modified over the course of the next year, and the version ruled constitutional by the court in March 2004 provided for the prime minister to appoint most government ministers, subject to legislative approval, and for continued popular election of the president.[ii]

---

i. Oleg Varfolomeyev, "Kuchma's Reform Draft: A Trap for the Opposition?" *Russia Eurasia Review* 2, no. 7 (2003), http://www.jamestown.org/single/?no_cache=1&tx_ttnews[tt_news]=28407&tx_ttnews[backPid]=226.
ii. Jan Maksymiuk, "Ukraine Faces Radical Changes in Its Constitutional System," *Ukraine Weekly*, January 11, 2004, http://www.ukrweekly.com/old/archive/2004/020404.shtml.

Figure 11.1 ▶ The Rada and the Constitutional Court Split, 18 March 2004

The Rada, Ukraine's parliament, votes to establish 31 October 2004 as the date for the country's presidential election, setting the stage for a historic transfer of power through the ballot box.

Meanwhile, the Constitutional Court takes an important step toward emasculating that transfer by approving President Leonid Kuchma's constitutional reform bill, which is aimed at shifting the power to appoint Ukraine's government from the president to the legislature.

had opted for Kravchuk, while those in the Russian-speaking east and south of the country backed Kuchma. Kuchma's first years in office featured rapid progress in implementing monetary, trade, fiscal, deregulatory, and privatization reforms, with significant assistance from the International Monetary Fund, European Union, US Agency for International Development, and American financier-philanthropist George Soros.[5] Kuchma and his team of technocrats—including then-chair of Ukraine's National Bank, Viktor Yushchenko—succeeded in stabilizing the country's currency, easing national debt levels, and privatizing significant portions of the economy. Monthly inflation fell from the hyperinflationary level of 91 percent per month in December 1993 to 2.1 percent in the summer of 1994.[6]

As Ukraine's economy stabilized, however, the struggles for dominance among the country's three power centers—president, prime minister, and legislature—grew more acute. To bolster his power, Kuchma made constitutional reform his next priority, and in 1996 he succeeded in winning approval for a new constitution that gave the presidency the power to nominate the prime minister—subject to legislative approval—and to appoint all government min-isters and regional governors. With reinforced executive powers, Kuchma dis-played decreasing interest in responding to popular sentiment, and his administration focused less and less on driving reforms and more and more on intrigue and old-fashioned political patronage.[7]

Pipeline Politics

That patronage focused heavily on Ukraine's lucrative natural gas trade. The country had some gas of its own, and it also hosted an extensive network of gas pipelines constructed during the Soviet era that linked Russia's massive gas reserves to markets in Europe. Nearly a quarter of Europe's natural gas con-sumption—accounting for a large portion of the Russian government's reve-nues—flowed through pipelines in Ukraine.[8] This made Ukraine a vital strategic factor in both the European and Russian economies (see Box 11.2). At the same time, as a legacy of the Soviet period, the price of Russian gas flowing into Ukraine varied widely for different customers. Ukraine's residential customers were graced with a highly subsidized price; Ukraine's industry—based largely in its eastern region and heavily dependent on Russian gas to fuel operations—paid a second, higher price; and European customers further down the pipeline paid a third, much higher set of prices. For unscrupulous and politically connected operators in Ukraine, this multitiered pricing scheme allowed the import of cheap gas allegedly for residential use and its subsequent illegal re-export at enormous profit.[9]

Accordingly, control over the energy industry and its attendant revenues became Ukraine's most powerful political currency, eagerly sought by rival clans inside Ukraine and by powerful players in Russia and the West.

The parties who control the Ukrainian oil and gas sector use their positions to block development, to extract economic rent, and to pick commercial winners and losers for their personal convenience. For example, only some projects get governmental approvals; only some companies get sought-after contracts. Consequently, control over the sector is a major prize in political contests. When one political bloc is uppermost in national politics, no proj-ect proceeds without the blessing of, and benefits for, people connected with that bloc. When that group loses the political upper hand, deals are often subject to renegotiation. At the same time, it becomes the job of each succes-sive political opposition to block all policy proposals, even the sensible ones, because the opposition is not profiting.[10]

Box 11.2 UKRAINE THROUGH RUSSIAN EYES

Ukraine at the turn of the millennium was arguably the most important country in the world from the Russian perspective. A series of official Russian foreign policy documents had defined the newly independent former Soviet republics along Russia's periphery as Moscow's top foreign policy priority.[i] Ukraine's large population, deeply rooted historical and cultural ties to Russia, and centrality to Russia's economy made it by far the most prominent state in this category. Almost a quarter of Moscow's state revenues derived from oil and gas exports to Europe, and some 80 percent of its gas exports to the lucrative European market depended on pipelines crossing Ukraine.[ii] Short of physical ownership of the pipelines, the Kremlin anxiously sought a regime in Kyiv that would respect vital Russian energy interests. It was not therefore surprising that Moscow had selected one of its most powerful energy titans, ex–prime minister and erstwhile Gazprom chair Viktor Chernomyrdin, as its ambassador to Ukraine in 2001.

Beyond these energy concerns, the unsettled question of Ukraine's geopolitical orientation was a matter of great emotional and practical import for Russia. NATO's inclusion of Poland, Hungary, and the Czech Republic in 1999 troubled Moscow, which believed the enlargement to be inconsistent with assurances at the time of Germany's unification that NATO would not move eastward. The Russians were

Russian President Vladimir Putin (right) with Ukrainian President Leonid Kuchma, March 2002.

powerless to prevent the move, however, and gradually accepted it. By early 2004, NATO was moving rapidly to incorporate seven additional members, including the former Soviet republics of Latvia, Lithuania, and Estonia, and Ukraine was beginning to figure prominently in discussions about a potential third tranche of new members. Russia's relations with

> **Box 11.2** *(Continued)*
>
> the United States—which had warmed following the 9/11 attacks as Washington sought help against terrorist groups and their supporters in Iraq, Iran, and elsewhere—began once again to sour after Moscow refused to back the Iraq war and Washington celebrated the triumph of pro-NATO nationalists in Georgia's "Rose Revolution" (see Box 11.3). The possibility that the NATO alliance could move into the heartland of Moscow's former empire and assume control of the all-important Ukrainian pipelines prompted deep anxiety in both the security and business establishments in Russia.
>
> ---
>
> i. "The Foreign Policy Concept of the Russian Federation," June 28, 2000, reprinted at http://www.fas.org/nuke/guide/russia/doctrine/econcept.htm.
> ii. Radio Free Europe/Radio Liberty, "Factbox: Russian Gas Export Pipelines, Projects," January 6, 2009, http://www.rferl.org/content/Russian_Gas_Export_Pipelines_Projects/1366873.html.

The high stakes attached to the control of Ukraine's gas sector made the country's electoral politics far more than a simple battle for voter support. Behind a facade of party platforms and coalition building, Ukrainian elections intertwined powerful business owners, organized crime, and raw geopolitical maneuvering from abroad with what appeared to be only nominal regard for the legal and ethical norms that constrain electoral behavior in the West. In the run-up to the 1998 parliamentary elections, corrupt industrialists ("oligarchs") based in the eastern cities of Dnepropetrovsk (including Kuchma's billionaire son-in-law Viktor Pinchuk) and Donetsk rose to prominence, much to the chagrin of liberals and nationalists in Ukraine's west.[11] Just as Russian businesspeople had used their wealth and media control to ensure Russian President Boris Yeltsin's reelection in 1996, so, too, did Ukrainian businesspeople—working with Viktor Medvedchuk, another prominent oligarch and leader of the Social Democratic United Party—orchestrate Kuchma's reelection in 1999. He won by a vote of 56 percent to 37 percent in a runoff against Communist Party leader Petro Symonenko.[12] Office of Democratic Institutions and Human Rights (OSCE) election monitors criticized that election for numerous improprieties, including "widespread and systematic" campaigning by state officials

Box 11.3 GEORGIA'S "ROSE REVOLUTION"

In early November 2003, less than a year before Ukraine's presidential election was scheduled to take place, Georgia, another former Soviet republic, held legislative elections. The elections were widely viewed as a key test of the strength of contending political factions prior to the Georgian presidential election slated for the spring of 2005, when the increasingly unpopular president Shevardnadze was due to leave office.

The election pitted government loyalists, who controlled Georgia's commerce and media, against self-proclaimed liberals attempting to exploit the public's growing unhappiness with perceived bureaucratic corruption. Official results indicated that Shevardnadze's ruling party triumphed, but opposition groups alleged massive fraud in the vote tabulation. Citing independent exit polls, Mikheil Saakashvili, a US-educated former Georgian official who had gone into political opposition after a falling out with Shevardnadze, claimed that his party had in fact won the elections, and he urged Georgians to undertake a campaign of public

Box 11.3 *(Continued)*

demonstrations and nonviolent civil disobedience against Shevardnadze's regime.

Rallying around Saakashvili's claims, Georgia's main opposition parties united to demand Shevardnadze's ouster and the rerun of the elections. In mid-November, massive antigovernmental demonstrations erupted in the central streets of Tbilisi, and they soon spread to nearly all of Georgia's major cities. A youth organization called *Kamara* ("Enough!") and several prominent nongovernmental organizations (NGOs) helped to organize the protests, which reached their peak on 22 November, when Shevardnadze attempted to open the new session of parliament. Led by Saakashvili, protesters burst into the session with roses in their hands, prompting Shevardnadze to flee the building. He declared a state of emergency and attempted to mobilize military and security forces, but they refused to support the government. Recognizing the inevitable, Shevardnadze reached out to opposition leaders Saakashvili and Zurab Zhvania on 23 November in a meeting arranged by then Russian Foreign Minister Igor Ivanov. After the meeting, Shevardnadze announced his resignation. New presidential elections were held in January 2004, in which Saakashvili won an overwhelming victory.

NGOs had played a significant role in monitoring the parliamentary elections, organizing opposition groups and protesters, and financing their activities. A former Georgian parliamentarian claimed that in the three months prior to the Rose Revolution, the Soros foundation had spent some $42 million in support of Georgian NGOs.[i] Soros himself downplayed the role of his foundation in the Rose Revolution, however, saying that he was "pleased and proud of the work of the foundation in preparing Georgian society for what became a Rose Revolution," but that "the role of the foundation has been greatly exaggerated."

---

i. K. R. Bolton, "Russo-Georgian Conflict Originates with Soros Subversion," August 14, 2008, http://www.rense.com/general83/soros.htm.

for Kuchma, violations of Ukraine's election laws, and comprehensive failure to ensure balanced media coverage.[13] Medvedchuk eventually became Kuchma's chief of staff during the latter's second term, and oligarchs based in Ukraine's east tightened their grip on both politics and commerce.

A House Divided

The rough and tumble of gas politics produced an array of victims as well as victors, however. Viktor Yushchenko became prime minister under Kuchma at the end of 1999, but following his attempts to reform the energy sector, he was removed in 2001 by a Rada vote of no confidence that was initiated by Kuchma's oligarchic allies; his firing transformed him from mere technocrat into an opposition politician with a strong public base.[14,15] Similarly, Yulia Tymoshenko made millions from the gas trade in the 1990s through a shady alliance with then Deputy Prime Minister Pavel Lazarenko (whom the United States subsequently convicted of money laundering), and she parlayed her wealth into political prominence as deputy prime minister for fuel and energy in the early years of Kuchma's second term.[16] But after tangling with some powerful oligarchs, she found herself fired from the government in 2001 and then briefly jailed on charges of corruption levied by both Ukrainian and Russian prosecutors.[17] Emerging from prison after the Kuchma government dropped the charges, she entered opposition politics with a vengeance, leading a series of popular demonstrations against the Kuchma regime's corruption and cozy dealings with Russia.[18]

The opposition's criticisms resonated with significant portions of Ukraine's public. In late 2000, a former Kuchma bodyguard released a series of tapes that he claimed to have secretly recorded. The tapes documented Kuchma's involvement in the killing of an investigative journalist and in the illegal sale of arms to Iraqi leader Saddam Hussein. The tapes became a sensation, and they fed a growing perception that there was little that Kuchma and his oligarchic allies would not do to amass and protect their wealth and political power.[19] Several prominent businesspeople broke with the Kuchma regime, fed up with the government's heavy-handed efforts to control their operations.[20] A study by the US-based nonprofit International Foundation for Election Systems conducted at the end of 2003 found that 85 percent of Ukrainians were either very or somewhat dissatisfied, and a similar percentage felt that corruption was a common and serious problem; 70 percent had little or no confidence in Kuchma.[21]

These perceptions redounded to the advantage of Ukraine's political opposition. Determined to capitalize on popular discontent and avoid the squabbling that had plagued oppositionists in the past, former prime minister Viktor Yushchenko formed a broad umbrella group, "Our Ukraine," that united centrist and rightist opposition forces and swept to victory in the 2002 parliamentary elections, amassing nearly a quarter of the vote.[22] Kuchma chief of staff Medvedchuk employed numerous tactics to thwart the opposition—for example denying Yushchenko coverage by state-controlled media and hiring Russian political consultants to set up fake parties to draw support from actual opposition groups—but the pro-government bloc won a paltry 11.8 percent of the vote.[23]

Marshalling of Forces

Defeat in the 2002 parliamentary elections sent a jolt through Kuchma's administration. As his second term as president neared its end, Kuchma and his team of political operators suddenly faced the danger of losing not only their offices but also their freedom, should the next president prosecute them for any of the numerous crimes that they had allegedly committed. To address this danger, they pursued several options. Immediately following the elections, Medvedchuk moved quickly and effectively to bribe or intimidate legislators into supporting the regime, and Kuchma subsequently initiated a new round of constitutional reforms designed to transfer several executive authorities from the presidency to the Rada, where his allies could presumably continue to wield power behind the scenes.[24,25] Following the Constitutional Court's ruling on 18 March 2004 that the reform bill was constitutional, the bill faced just one more hurdle: approval by a two-thirds majority in the legislature.

In addition to pursuing constitutional reform, Kuchma also attempted to engineer the election of a loyal successor. After much deliberation, Kuchma settled on Viktor Yanukovych, the hardscrabble governor of the crime-ridden Donetsk region, leader of the Regions of Ukraine party, and reputed protégé of Ukraine's richest and most brutal oligarchic clan, headed by Rinat Akhmetov.[26] Kuchma named Yanukovych as prime minister in November 2002, signaling all but explicitly that he would be the regime's preferred candidate in the 2004 presidential election. In support of Yanukovych's candidacy, Medvedchuk tightened the regime's control over broadcast media and the Central Electoral Commission.[27] Together with Ukraine's top oligarchic clan leaders, Medvedchuk began planning the most expensive presidential campaign in Ukraine's history, funded heavily by Akhmetov.[28]

Meanwhile, the other "Viktor"—Yushchenko—emerged as Yanukovych's primary opposition for the presidency. Handsome and articulate, Yushchenko

Figure 11.2 ▶ Ukrainian Presidential Election 2004: Players and Parties

The Ballot

Yulia Tymoshenko
(Yulia Tymoshenko Bloc)

Viktor Yushchenko
Former Premier
(Our Ukraine)

Viktor Yanukovych
Former Premier
(Party of Regions)

Leonid Kuchma
Incumbent President
(For a United Ukraine)

Viktor Medvedchuk
Head of Presidential Administration
(Social Democratic Party of Ukraine)

Viktor Pinchuk
(Head of Dnipropetrovs'k Clan)

Oleksandr Moroz
Former Chair of Rada
(Socialist Party of Ukraine)

Petro Symonenko
Former Premier
*(Communist Party
of Ukraine)*

Rinat Akhmetov
Billionaire
(Sponsor of Party of Regions)

stood in sharp contrast to the hulking and poorly spoken Yanukovych, and opinion polls consistently ranked him as Ukraine's most popular politician. Still, he faced a formidable battle to succeed Kuchma. Denied the airwaves, he focused on organizing large public rallies, covered by Ukraine's newly emerging Internet newspapers.[29] Uniting centrist and nationalist opposition groups behind him, Yushchenko targeted the support of Ukraine's "multi-millionaires"—conceding that its billionaires would back Yanukovych—and centered his campaign on the themes of good government, good values, private property, and European integration.[30] As Ukraine's long winter melted into the spring of 2004, analysts weighed his prospects for success against the combined efforts of Ukraine's wealthiest and most powerful forces.

RECOMMENDED READINGS

International Foundation for Election Systems. "Attitudes and Expectations: Public Opinion in Ukraine 2003." http://www.ifes.org/~/media/Files/Publications/Survey/2004/142/Ukraine_Survey_2003_English.pdf.

Office of Democratic Institutions and Human Rights (OSCE). "Ukraine Presidential Elections 31 October and 14 November 1999 Final Report." Warsaw, Poland: March 7, 2000.

Pifer, Steven. "Ukraine's Future and US Interest." House International Relations Committee Subcommittee on Europe, May 12, 2004. http://2001–2009.state.gov/p/eur/rls/rm/32416.htm.

Table 11.1 ▶ Case Snapshot: Shades of Orange in Ukraine		
Structured Analytic Technique Used	Heuer and Pherson Page Number	Analytic Family
Structured Brainstorming	p. 92	Idea Generation
Outside-In Thinking	p. 201	Assessment of Cause and Effect
Simple Scenarios	p. 125	Scenarios and Indicators

SHADES OF ORANGE IN UKRAINE
STRUCTURED ANALYTIC TECHNIQUES IN ACTION

The exercises in this case require you to put yourself in the shoes of an analyst who has just been tasked by the US National Security Council to provide an assessment of the factors that will determine who the next Ukrainian president will be. Policy makers often call on analysts in this manner to support policy deliberations in advance of major policy initiatives. In this case, the Ukrainian election is still months away, and US policy makers are grappling with how best to ensure that Ukraine holds a free and fair election. Analysts can add tremendous value by helping policy makers understand the full complement of factors that will determine who will be the next Ukrainian president. This type of analysis can help policy makers identify opportunities for pursuing US interests and avoid potential pitfalls.

Techniques 1 & 2: Structured Brainstorming and Outside-In Thinking
Brainstorming is a group process that follows specific rules and procedures designed for generating new ideas and concepts (see Box 11.4). The stimulus for creativity comes from two or more analysts bouncing ideas off each other. A brainstorming session usually exposes an analyst to a greater range of ideas and perspectives than the analyst could generate alone, and this broadening of views typically results in a better analytic product.

Outside-In Thinking helps analysts who are familiar with issues related to their own field of specialization consider how factors external to their area of expertise could affect their analysis. This technique is most helpful when considering all the factors at play at the beginning of an analytic process. Outside-In Thinking can reduce the risk of analytic failure by helping analysts identify

---

Box 11.4 SEVEN RULES FOR SUCCESSFUL BRAINSTORMING

1. Be specific about the purpose and the topic of the brainstorming session.

2. Never criticize an idea, no matter how weird, unconventional, or improbable it might sound. Instead, try to figure out how the idea might be applied to the task at hand.

3. Allow only one conversation at a time and ensure that everyone has an opportunity to speak.

4. Allocate enough time to complete the brainstorming session.

5. Try to include one or more "outsiders" in the group, usually someone who does not share the same body of knowledge or perspective as other group members but has some familiarity with the topic.

6. Write it down! Track the discussion by using a whiteboard, an easel, or sticky notes.

7. Summarize key findings at the end of the session. Ask the participants to write down the most important thing they learned on a 3-by-5-inch card as they depart the session. Then, prepare a short summary and distribute the list to the participants (who may add items to the list) and to others interested in the topic (including those who could not attend).

---

external factors and uncover new interrelationships and insights that otherwise would be overlooked.

Using these two techniques together prompts analysts to consider the full range of factors that could shape the outcome of the election.

Task 1. Conduct a Structured Brainstorming of the factors that will determine the outcome of the Ukrainian election.

STEP 1: Pass out sticky notes and markers to all participants. Inform the team that there will be no talking during the sticky-notes portion of the brainstorming exercise.

STEP 2: Display the following focal question for the team: What are all the factors that will determine who will be the next Ukrainian president?

STEP 3: Ask the group to respond to the question by writing a few key words on their sticky notes. After a response is written down, the participant gives it to the facilitator, who then reads it out loud. Marker-type pens are used so that people can easily see what is written on the sticky notes when they are posted on the wall. Urge participants to use short phrases rather than long sentences.

STEP 4: Place all the sticky notes on a wall in the order in which they are called out. Treat all ideas the same. Encourage participants to build on one another's ideas. Usually there is an initial spurt of ideas followed by pauses as participants contemplate the question.

STEP 5: After five or ten minutes there is often a long pause of a minute or so. This slowing down suggests that the group has "emptied the barrel of the obvious" and is now on the verge of coming up with some fresh insights and ideas. Do not talk during this pause even if the silence is uncomfortable.

STEP 6: After two or three long pauses, encourage Outside-In Thinking by asking the group specifically to focus on identifying external factors that could affect the outcome of the Ukrainian election. Use the mnemonic STEEP +2 (Social, Technological, Economic, Environmental, Political plus Military and Psychological) to catalyze the process.

Give the students a few minutes of brainstorming and pauses to think about the issue and jot down a few ideas. Then go around the room and collect the sticky notes. Read the responses slowly and stick them on the wall or the whiteboard in random order as you read them.

STEP 7: Ask all participants (or a small group) to go up to the wall and rearrange the sticky notes by affinity groups (groups that have some common characteristics). Some sticky notes may be moved several times; some may also be copied if an idea applies to more than one affinity group.

STEP 8: When all sticky notes have been arranged, ask the group to select a word or phrase that best describes each grouping.

STEP 9: Assess specifically how each of these forces and factors could have an effect on the problem and, using this list of forces and factors, generate a list of areas for additional collection and research.

Analytic Value Added. What key factors will influence the outcome of the election? What gaps deserve additional attention?

Technique 3: Simple Scenarios

The Simple Scenarios technique helps analysts develop an understanding of the multiple ways in which a situation might evolve. The technique can be used by an individual analyst or a group of analysts. In either situation, the analytic value added of Simple Scenarios lies not in the specifics of the scenarios themselves but in the analytic discussion of which drivers will affect a particular scenario, the implications of each scenario for policy makers, and the indicators that will alert policy makers to the fact that such a future is unfolding.

Task 2. Conduct a Simple Scenarios analysis to consider the range of possible outcomes and driving factors that will shape the outcome of the Ukrainian election.

STEP 1: Clearly define the focal issue and the specific goals of the Simple Scenarios exercise.

STEP 2: Make a list of forces, factors, and events that are likely to influence the future.

STEP 3: Organize the forces, factors, and events that are related to each other into five to ten affinity groups that are expected to be the driving forces in how the focal issue will evolve.

STEP 4: Write a brief description of each or use the descriptions previously developed.

STEP 5: Generate a matrix of scenarios with the list of drivers down the left side, as shown in Table 11.2.

Table 11.2 ▶ Simple Scenarios Template				
	Best Case	Worst Case	Mainline	Additional
Driver 1				
Driver 2				
Driver 3				
Driver 4				
Driver 5				

STEP 6: Generate at least four different scenarios—a best case, a worst case, mainline, and at least one other.

STEP 7: The columns of the matrix are used to describe the scenarios. Each scenario is assigned a positive or negative value for each driver. The values are strong or positive (+), weak or negative (−), and blank if neutral or no change. An easy way to code the matrix is to assume that the scenario occurred and ask, "Did driver A exert a strong, weak, or neutral influence on the outcome?"

STEP 8: This is a good time to reconsider both the drivers and the scenarios. Is there a better way to conceptualize and describe the drivers? Have any important forces been omitted? Look across the matrix to see the extent to which each driver discriminates among the scenarios. If a driver has the same value across all scenarios, it is not discriminating and should be deleted or further defined. To stimulate thinking about other possible scenarios, consider the key assumptions that were made when deciding on the most likely scenario. What if some of these assumptions turn out to be invalid? If they are invalid, how might that might affect the outcome, and are such alternative outcomes included within the available set of scenarios?

STEP 9: For each scenario, write a one-page story to describe what the future looks like and/or how it might come about. The story should illustrate the interplay of the drivers.

STEP 10: For each scenario, describe the implications for the decision maker. The implications should be focused on variables that the United States could influence to shape the outcome.

STEP 11: Generate a list of indicators for each scenario that would help you discover that events are starting to play out in the way envisioned by the scenario.

STEP 12: Monitor the list of indicators on a regular basis.

Analytic Value Added. What judgments should analysts highlight in response to US policy makers' questions about what will influence the outcome of the Ukrainian election?

NOTES

1. Radio Free Europe/Radio Liberty, *Newsline*, March 18, 2004, http://www.rferl.org/content/article/1143120.html.

2. Radio Free Europe/Radio Liberty, *Newsline*, March 19, 2004, http://www.rferl.org/content/article/1143121.html.

3. Tara Kuzio, "US-Ukraine Relations Will Not Revive under Kuchma," *Kyiv Post*, March 13, 2003, http://www.taraskuzio.net/media21_files/18.pdf.

4. Tara Kuzio, "Ukraine's Relations with the West: Disinterest, Partnership, Disillusionment," *European Security* 12, no. 2 (2003): 21–44, http://www.taraskuzio.net/International%20Relations_files/ukraine_west_relations.pdf.

5. Anders Äslund, "Leonid Kuchma's Reforms: 1994–96," chap. 3 in *How Ukraine Became a Market Economy and Democracy* (Washington, DC: Peter G. Peterson Institute for International Economics, 2009), 59–90.

6. Ibid., 73.

7. Ibid., 86.

8. Radio Free Europe/Radio Liberty, "Factbox: Russian Gas Export Pipelines, Projects," January 6, 2009, http://www.rferl.org/content/Russian_Gas_Export_Pipelines_Projects/1366873.html.

9. Edward Chow and Jonathan Elkind, "Where East Meets West: European Gas and Ukrainian Reality," *Washington Quarterly* 32, no. 1 (2009): 77–92, http://www.twq.com/09winter/docs/09jan_ChowElkind.pdf.

10. Chow and Elkind, "Where East Meets West," 81.

11. Taras Kuzio, "How the Gas Issue Plays in Ukrainian Politics and How Ukrainian Politicians Play the Gas Issue," transcript from lecture at Harvard University, March 7, 2008, http://www.taraskuzio.net/conferences2_files/Ukrainian_Politics_Energy.pdf.

12. Ibid.

13. Organization for Security and Co-operation in Europe (OSCE) Office of Democratic Institutions and Human Rights (ODIHR), *Ukraine Presidential Elections 31 October and 14 November 1999: Final Report* (Warsaw, Poland: OSCE ODIHR, 2000), http://www.osce.org/odihr/elections/ukraine/presidential_1999/.

14. Taras Kuzio, "Ukraine Steps Up the Struggle against Organized Crime and Corruption—or Does It?" *Radio Free Europe/Radio Liberty Organized Crime and Terrorism Watch* 3, no. 10 (2003), http://www.taraskuzio.net/media11_files/4.pdf.

15. Adrian Karatnycky, "Ukraine's Orange Revolution," *Foreign Affairs*, March–April 2005, http://www.foreignaffairs.com/articles/60620/adrian-karatnycky/ukraines-orange-revolution/.

16. Irena Chalupa, "Ukraine's Gold-Plaited Comeback Kid," Radio Free Europe/Radio Liberty, September 23, 2008, http://www.rferl.org/content/Tymoshenko_Profile/1291005.html.

17. Roman Woronowycz, "Yulia Tymoshenko Arrested," *Ukraine Weekly*, February 18, 2001, http://www.ukrweekly.com/old/archive/2001/070107.shtml.

18. Chalupa, "Ukraine's Gold-Plaited Comeback Kid."

19. Äslund, *How Ukraine Became a Market Economy and Democracy*, 154.

20. Ibid.

21. Rakesh Sharma and Nathan Van Dusen, *Attitudes and Expectations: Public Opinion in Ukraine 2003* (Washington, DC: International Foundation for Election Systems,

2004), http://www.ifes.org/~/media/Files/Publications/Survey/2004/142/Ukraine_Survey_2003_English.pdf.

22. Central Election Commission of Ukraine, http://www.cvk.gov.ua/.

23. Äslund, *How Ukraine Became a Market Economy and Democracy*, 155–56.

24. Olexiy Haran and Rostyslav Pavlenko, "Political Reform or a Game of Survival for President Kuchma?" PONARS (Program on New Approaches to Russian Security) Policy Memo 294, November 2003, http://www.gwu.edu/~ieresgwu/assets/docs/ponars/pm_0294.pdf.

25. Äslund, *How Ukraine Became a Market Economy and Democracy*, 158–59.

26. Taras Kuzio, "From Kuchma to Yushchenko," *Problems of Post-Communism* (March/April 2005), 8, http://www.taraskuzio.net/Comparative%20Politics_files/electionsorangerevolution.pdf.

27. Äslund, *How Ukraine Became a Market Economy and Democracy*, 180.

28. Ibid.

29. Ibid., 178.

30. Ibid., 179.

Key Questions

▶ Who targeted the US presence in Belgrade and why?

▶ What could increase or decrease the threat of future violence?

▶ What competing interests must the United States weigh in deciding how to respond to anti-American violence?

12 Violence Erupts in Belgrade

CASE NARRATIVE

On the evening of Sunday, 17 February 2008, an angry crowd of several hundred Serbian protesters converged on the US embassy building—or Chancery—in Belgrade, Serbia. The mob threw stones at the building, chanted nationalist slogans, and vented anger at US support for Kosovo's declaration of independence from Serbia earlier in the day.[1] With some difficulty, Serbian police repelled the attacks, but not before the rioters had assaulted and damaged the US, Croatian, and Slovenian embassies, as well as McDonald's and Nike stores nearby.[2] Serbian officials downplayed the attacks and emphasized Serbia's commitment to peaceful resolution of the situation surrounding Kosovo.[3] But violence in the Serbian capital, coupled with sporadic eruptions in neighboring Kosovo, forced US officials to make difficult assessments about the prospective threat to US interests in the region and how the United States should respond. Did these attacks presage greater violence against Americans, and should US officials count on Serbian authorities to protect the US diplomatic presence?

Another Chapter in an Epic Struggle

The violence on 17 February was but the latest episode in the bloody and emotion-laden conflict over Kosovo that has waxed and waned for centuries. Albanians have deep roots in the region, claiming to be direct descendants of the earliest known inhabitants of Kosovo, the Illyrians. For Serbs, Kosovo has long had great symbolic importance as the host of several revered Orthodox shrines.

Serbian riot police block a street during clashes with protesters in front of the US Embassy in Belgrade, 17 February 2008.

It is also the site of Serbia's defeat at the hands of the Turks in the "Battle of Kosovo Polje" in 1389, which led to Serbia's subjugation to the Ottoman Empire until its independence in 1898. Under Ottoman rule, the Albanian population in Kosovo grew dominant and the majority converted to Islam, while much of the Orthodox Serbian population moved northward toward Belgrade in the so-called "Great Migration."[4]

In the course of the seventeenth, eighteenth, and nineteenth centuries, Kosovo and the rest of the Balkans became an arena for conflict between empires (Ottoman, Austro-Hungarian, and Russian) and religions (Islam, Catholicism, and Orthodox Christianity). By the turn of the twentieth century, these conflicts had assumed an ethnic character, as both Serbian and Albanian nationalists struggled to carve new nation-states out of the decaying Ottoman Empire and assert control over Kosovo. Vicious fighting between Serbs and Albanians broke out repeatedly, with multiple allegations of massacres by each side against the other. After changing hands numerous times prior to the end of World War II, Kosovo became an integral part of the republic of Serbia within Yugoslavia.[5]

During Communist rule under Yugoslav leader Josip Broz Tito, the Albanian population of Kosovo grew rapidly until it exceeded three-quarters of the region's inhabitants, while the Slav population dwindled to less than a sixth.

Map 12.1 ▶ Serbia and the Breakaway Republic of Kosovo

A powerful Albanian national movement prompted Tito to grant Kosovo autonomy in 1974, fueling Serbian nationalist resentment that Serbian Communist Party chief Slobodan Milosevic rode to power. In 1989, he revoked Kosovo's autonomy, and as Yugoslavia disintegrated in the early 1990s, he banned the Albanian language from official use and fired Albanians employed in public institutions who would not take an oath of allegiance to the Federal Republic of Yugoslavia (FRY). Kosovar Albanians responded with numerous protests, strikes, and the establishment of extra-legal parallel government institutions, setting the stage for direct confrontation between Kosovar Albanians and Serbian authorities in what was then the FRY.[6]

By 1998, this confrontation had escalated into de facto civil war between Kosovar Albanians and Serbs. An increasingly well-armed and well-funded underground Albanian guerrilla movement, the Kosovo Liberation Army, emerged from the shadows and launched a series of operations against Serbian officials and civilians in Kosovo. Milosevic responded ruthlessly, killing more than 1,500 Kosovar Albanians, driving more than 400,000 from their homes, and engaging in what the Organization for Security and Cooperation in Europe (OSCE) called "a pattern of human rights and humanitarian law violations on a staggering scale, often committed with extreme and appalling violence."[7]

Diplomatic efforts to resolve the conflict by the United Nations (UN), OSCE, and six-nation "Contact Group" (United States, Russia, France, Italy, United Kingdom, and Germany) had little impact, in part due to Russia's reluctance to enforce international dictates on what it regarded as a domestic Yugoslav affair. As the fighting continued to escalate, the North American Treaty Organization (NATO) alliance issued a warning to both sides and announced its willingness to use air strikes if necessary to end the fighting. NATO's initiative culminated in negotiations in Rambouillet near Paris in February and March 1999, where the Kosovar Albanian delegation signed a proposed peace agreement but the Serbian delegation refused. Immediately afterward, FRY military and police forces stepped up operations against ethnic Albanians in Kosovo.[8]

Having failed to persuade Milosevic to stop the attacks, NATO commenced air strikes on 23 March 1999. The bombing—which targeted not only the Yugoslav military but also strategic assets such as electrical grids, water facilities, and communications infrastructure—continued until 10 June, when, with Russian mediation, NATO and Yugoslav authorities announced a military-technical agreement to end hostilities. This was followed in short order by the passage of UN Security Council Resolution (UNSCR) 1244, which placed Kosovo under interim UN administration, authorized a NATO-led peacekeeping force (KFOR), affirmed the territorial integrity and sovereignty of the FRY (now Serbia), and initiated a political process to determine Kosovo's future status. Although the UN resolution effectively ended the fighting, it did not end the dispute over Kosovo: violence between the remaining Serbian enclaves and Kosovar Albanians flared periodically, and in 2004 riots erupted that resulted in widespread attacks by crowds of Albanians on Serb communities and cultural sites.[9]

The hard task of reconciling competing Albanian and Serbian claims over Kosovo's status fell to the respected Finnish politician and diplomat, Martti Ahtisaari, who in late 2005 was appointed UN Special Envoy for Kosovo. After more than a year of status negotiations, Ahtisaari produced a draft settlement proposal that could serve as the basis for an eventual agreement. The package he presented to the UN Security Council in April 2007 included a recommendation that Kosovo become independent subject to a period of international supervision. Kosovar Albanians accepted the proposal; Serbia rejected it as a violation of its legal sovereignty over Kosovo, which it argued was reaffirmed by UNSCR 1244. The United States and European Union (EU) supported the Ahtisaari plan and Kosovo's push for independence. Russia backed Belgrade's position, rejected a draft UN Security Council Resolution based on the Ahtisaari plan, and called for new negotiations to produce a settlement acceptable to both sides.[10,11]

February 2008: Tense Final Days of the Impasse

By February 2008, Kosovar Albanian patience with the impasse was reaching its end (see Figure 12.1). A unilateral declaration of independence by Kosovo appeared imminent. In Kosovo, posters emblazoned with the US, British, and EU flags expressed thanks "to all the countries [that] are contributing [to] and supporting the independence of Kosovo."[12] Other posters around the capital of Pristina urged Kosovar Albanians to "celebrate with dignity."[13] Serbian Prime Minister Vojislav Koštunica—amid reports that the EU was considering a plan to send a police force to Kosovo post-independence—reiterated that Serbia would never accept Kosovo's independence, and he accused Europe, "under strong outside pressure from the US" of "trampling [on] the fundamental principles" of the UN as the EU "yielded to a policy of force." Serbian President Boris Tadic, however, in a nod toward Serbian hopes for EU membership, tempered his comments, saying, "I will never give up the fight for our Kosovo, and with all my strength, I will fight for Serbia to be in the European Union."[14] Ethnic tensions inside Kosovo seemed to mount; police in Kosovo's ethnically divided city of Mitrovica reported an explosion behind a building that housed the advance team for the EU mission.[15] The next day, the EU approved a plan to send a 1,800-person police and judicial mission to help Kosovo's nascent government.[16]

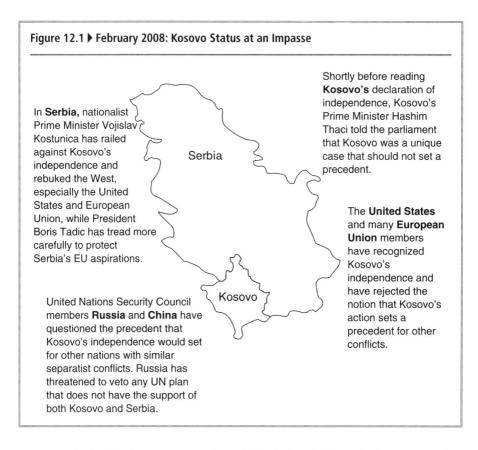

Figure 12.1 ▶ February 2008: Kosovo Status at an Impasse

In **Serbia,** nationalist Prime Minister Vojislav Kostunica has railed against Kosovo's independence and rebuked the West, especially the United States and European Union, while President Boris Tadic has tread more carefully to protect Serbia's EU aspirations.

Shortly before reading **Kosovo's** declaration of independence, Kosovo's Prime Minister Hashim Thaci told the parliament that Kosovo was a unique case that should not set a precedent.

The **United States** and many **European Union** members have recognized Kosovo's independence and have rejected the notion that Kosovo's action sets a precedent for other conflicts.

United Nations Security Council members **Russia** and **China** have questioned the precedent that Kosovo's independence would set for other nations with similar separatist conflicts. Russia has threatened to veto any UN plan that does not have the support of both Kosovo and Serbia.

In Serbia, the government braced for the inevitable and adopted an action plan pledging no violence and a resolution preemptively declaring any unilateral act by Kosovo's ethnic Albanian leadership to be invalid and illegal. Koštunica enjoined Serbians to reject Kosovo's independence, saying, "We shall not allow such a creation to exist for a minute. It has to be legally annulled the moment it is illegally proclaimed by a leadership of convicted terrorists."[17] Its annulment was planned to be the centerpiece of a "Thursday of rejection" planned for 14 February.[18]

Reports surfaced about an alleged Serbian "secret action plan" to be implemented upon Kosovo's declaration of independence, which reportedly included retaliatory steps to keep Kosovo under Serbian control.[19,20] Publicly, however, Serbian Foreign Minister Vuk Jeremic told the UN Security Council that while Serbia would never accept a violation of its territorial integrity and would take diplomatic, political, and economic measures to impede Kosovo, Belgrade would not use force to keep Kosovo from seceding.[21]

The Day of the Attack

Braving heavy snow and freezing temperatures, Kosovar Albanians on 17 February took to the streets to celebrate their parliament's vote for independence with festive rallies, fireworks, and even a 100-foot birthday cake. Some revelers waved US flags and chanted "God Bless America."[22]

In Belgrade, the mood was far less joyous. In a fiery, nationally televised speech just minutes after Kosovo's declaration, Koštunica declared Kosovo's independence null and void and denounced the United States and EU for supporting Kosovo's secession.[23] In addition to accusing Washington of being "ready to violate the international order for its own interests," Koštunica singled out US President Bush for personal rebuke, saying that he "is responsible for this violation, [and] will be noted in black letters in Serbian history books, along with his European followers."[24,25] Despite the acerbic remarks, Serbian leaders pledged peaceful resistance after Kosovo's declaration.[26] In Kosovo, however, unidentified attackers threw grenades at EU and UN buildings, and Serbs who had gathered to protest the declaration said they were under orders from Belgrade to ignore the independence declaration and remain in Kosovo to keep the northern part of the territory under de facto Serbian control.[27]

The US Embassy building in Belgrade guarded by Serbian police, 17 February 2008.

Figure 12.2 ▶ Chronology of Selected Events

Date	Event
1974	Josip Broz Tito grants Kosovo autonomy.
1989	Slobodan Milosevic revokes Kosovo autonomy.
1990s	Yugoslavia disintegrates, but Kosovo remains integrated.
1998	Kosovar Albanians protest lack of independence and set up a parallel government. A de facto civil war breaks out between Kosovar Serbs and Albanians.
March 1999	NATO sponsors the Rambouillet Conference at which Kosovar Albanians sign a peace agreement, but the Serbs refuse. US-led NATO airstrikes mark beginning of war; Washington officially severs diplomatic relations with Serbia and closes its embassy.
June 1999	NATO and Serb authorities—with Russian mediation—announce a military-technical agreement to end hostilities, and the UN passes UN Security Council Resolution (UNSCR) 1244.
May 2001	The United States formally reopens Embassy Belgrade.
2005	Martti Ahtisaari is appointed UN Special Envoy for Kosovo.
April 2007	Ahtisaari presents a package to the UN Security Council that includes a recommendation that Kosovo become independent subject to a period of international supervision. Kosovar Albanians accept the proposal; Serbia rejects it as a violation of its legal sovereignty over Kosovo, which it argues was reaffirmed by UNSCR 1244.
13 February 2008	Serbian National Council meets and rejects in advance Kosovo independence, adopts action plan, and rules out nondiplomatic retaliatory steps such as military intervention or disruption of electricity.
15 February 2008	Boris Tadic is sworn in as Serbian president.
16 February 2008	EU announces plan to send 1,800-strong police and judicial force to Kosovo.
17 February 2008	Kosovo declares independence. Russia calls UN Security Council emergency session. Anti-independence rally in Belgrade turns violent, and "hooligans" attack US embassy.
18 February 2008	The United States recognizes Kosovo independence. Rallies and additional riots break out in Belgrade. Serbia recalls its ambassador from the United States.
19 February 2008	Attacks occur on UN-monitored border posts Jarinje and Banja in northern Kosovo.

By evening, violence threatened in Belgrade as well as protesters gathered at the US Chancery. Prepositioned Serbian riot police guarded the building—which directly abuts the sidewalk and a major thoroughfare—but the protesters grew quickly in numbers and fury. They chanted "Kosovo is the heart of Serbia," as they hurled paving stones, rocks, and bottles at police. The scene outside the Chancery grew particularly tense as the rioters threw incendiary devices at the building facade and tried to push past Serbian anti-riot police.[28,29,30]

The police eventually drove the rioters back from the building, but the angry mob only turned its attention to ransacking and burning a nearby McDonald's. The crowd also targeted other Western embassies, including those of NATO member Turkey and EU member Slovenia; the latter had recently taken over the EU chairmanship.[31] Although police prevented a group of rioters from approaching the Albanian embassy, and none of the seventy diplomats stationed at the US embassy were injured, over thirty people were wounded in the riots.[32] (See Box 12.1 for a discussion of US embassy security.)

The Aftermath

On 18 February 2008, despite fears that formal Western recognition of Kosovo's independence would spark a new round of violence in Belgrade and Kosovo, the United States formally recognized Kosovo's independence.[33, 34] France, the United Kingdom, Turkey and over a dozen other EU and NATO countries quickly followed suit.[35] Serbia protested the move by recalling its ambassador from Washington, D.C., and from other states that recognized Kosovo, but it did not sever diplomatic relations with the United States.[36]

On Monday and Tuesday, the celebrations in Pristina did not let up, but neither did the opposition and ensuing violence. Several thousand Serbs on Monday marched across the river dividing the ethnic Serbian northern portion of the city of Mitrovica from its ethnic Albanian south, chanting "Kosovo is Serbia." On Tuesday, Kosovo Serbs set fire to the Jarinje and Banja crossings on Kosovo's border with Serbia. The attack destroyed cars and burned small buildings, but there were no injuries. NATO and UN authorities closed the border in response.[37,38]

Observers' fears about further violence in Belgrade were proved at least partially correct when new protests resulted in small incidents of violence around the city on Monday. Police cordons prevented rioters from approaching Belgrade's "embassy row," where many Western embassies are located, and the protesters resorted to throwing stones at the officers. Elsewhere, rioters

Box 12.1 PROTECTING US DIPLOMATIC MISSIONS

The February 2008 attack on the US embassy building in Belgrade was not the first time that the United States has faced threats to its interests in Serbia. In March 1999, just before NATO commenced bombing, the United States severed diplomatic relations and completely closed its embassy in Serbia. The United States did not formally reopen the embassy until May 2001.[i]

In nonemergency situations, the downgrading of bilateral relations is often preceded by the political step of withdrawing the ambassador or highest-ranking diplomat, often at least initially "for consultations," to a country's home capital. But the severing of diplomatic relations and closing of an embassy are rare and usually are reserved for extraordinary circumstances such as war or serious civil instability. The United States instead works to maintain its representation abroad, even in dangerous locales. To protect the safety of its diplomats and their families, the United States often will designate a particularly dangerous environment an "unaccompanied post," where diplomats must live and work without their families. This is true for the wartime embassies in Baghdad, Iraq, and Kabul, Afghanistan. Under normal circumstances, however, the families of US diplomats do accompany their family member to the post, even if the security situation has been tenuous in the past.

In the face of a sudden change in the security environment, the United States must carefully calibrate its response to protect US interests, personnel, and property. For example, in 2010 the United States for several days temporarily closed, rather than evacuated, its embassy in Yemen in response to specific threats by Al-Qaeda in the Arabian Peninsula (AQAP) to attack American interests in Yemen.[ii] Closures such as these do not come without a financial cost, which must be weighed against the threat, but US officials at the time said the specificity of the threat warranted this "administrative closure" to protect US embassy personnel. Other countries, whose embassies in Yemen were not specifically threatened, such as France and Spain, also closed their embassies to public access but kept their administrative offices open.

There are some circumstances in which evacuation—ranging from voluntary through dependents-only, nonessential personnel, and full

Box 12.1 *(Continued)*

mandatory evacuation—are deemed necessary to protect US persons. Following a 2010 attack in Mexico in which US personnel and dependents were killed, the United States offered staff the option of voluntary temporary evacuation of dependents but kept its Chancery and consulates open.[iii]

Decisions about security are made by the ambassador, in consultation with embassy staff and the Department of State, particularly if a security issue threatens bilateral relations between the two countries. If the ambassador is absent, the deputy chief of mission is designated to act as charge d'affaires. An embassy's physical security is maintained by the Regional Security Officer (RSO) and the Marine Security Guard Detachment (MSG) assigned to the embassy. The MSG is responsible for interior security of the post, including access control, personnel protection, and protection of sensitive classified information and equipment.[iv] The MSG reports to the ambassador through the RSO. In times of heightened tension in which the embassy is temporarily closed, the MSG, RSO, and other core staff will continue to maintain on-site security. Exterior security is governed by the 1961 Vienna Convention on Diplomatic Relations, which established the inviolability of the foreign mission and the receiving state's "duty to take all appropriate steps to protect the premises of the mission against any intrusion or damage and to prevent any disturbance of the peace of the mission or impairment of its dignity."[v]

---

i. "Background Note: Serbia," US Department of State, http://www.state.gov/r/pa/ei/bgn/5388.htm (accessed December 22, 2010).

ii. Julian Borger, Hugh Macleod, Ed Pilkington, and Peter Walker, "US and UK keep Yemen Embassies Shut for Second Day," *Guardian* (London), January 4, 2010, http://www.guardian.co.uk/world/2010/jan/04/yemen-embassies-shut/.

iii. "3 People Associated with US Consulate Killed in Mexico," CNN, March 14, 2010. http://articles.cnn.com/2010–03–14/world/mexico.violence_1_detention-officer-police-officer-sheriff-s-office.

iv. Michael Coady, "A Salute to Marine Security Guards," *DIPNOTE* (US Department of State blog), November 11, 2009, http://blogs.state.gov/index.php/entries/salute_marine_security_guards/.

v. Vienna Convention on Diplomatic Relations, 1961, Article 22, http://untreaty.un.org/ilc/texts/instruments/english/conventions/9_1_1961.pdf.

vandalized another McDonald's and the Turkish embassy, and police evacuated a shopping mall after a bomb threat.[39]

Newspaper headlines in Belgrade on Tuesday morning trumpeted defiance and anger over international support for Kosovo's declaration. Reports indicated that Koštunica and other party leaders planned to address a government-supported protest rally on Thursday, but Tadic demurred and scheduled a trip to Bucharest to thank Romania for its refusal to recognize Kosovo. Tadic, who had just been in New York to address the UN Security Council, appealed for calm ahead of the rally, urging that "there must be no violence and endangering of human lives . . . [because] only peace and reasonable moves give us the right to defend Kosovo."[40] The United States acknowledged that "small demonstrations" in Belgrade continued and expressed gratitude to the Serbian government for "maintaining law and order . . . and security around [the US] Embassy."[41] Nevertheless, with the clock ticking on the state-sponsored "Kosovo is Serbia" rally, the United States scrambled to calculate whether the rally might turn violent and how the embassy should prepare for it.

RECOMMENDED READINGS

Glenny, Misha. *The Balkans: Nationalism, War, and the Great Powers, 1804–1999.* New York: Penguin, 1999.

Judah, Tim. *The Serbs: History, Myth, and the Destruction of Yugoslavia.* 3rd ed. New Haven, CT: Yale University Press, 2009.

Malcolm, Noel. *Kosovo: A Short History.* New York: New York University Press, 1998.

Vickers, Miranda. *The Albanians: A Modern History.* London: I. B. Tauris, 2006. Originally published 1995.

Vienna Convention on Diplomatic Relations, 1961. April 18, 1961; entered into force on April 24, 1964. *United Nations, Treaty Series,* vol. 500 (2005): 95.

Table 12.1 ▶ Case Snapshot: Violence Erupts in Belgrade		
Structured Analytic Technique Used	Heuer and Pherson Page Number	Analytic Family
Force Field Analysis	p. 281	Decision Support
Decision Matrix	p. 278	Decision Support
Pros-Cons-Faults-and-Fixes	p. 284	Decision Support

VIOLENCE ERUPTS IN BELGRADE
STRUCTURED ANALYTIC TECHNIQUES IN ACTION

Many of the most important decisions are made quickly and under tight time constraints. This does not mean that decision makers or those supporting them should sacrifice good thinking, because a logical and thorough thought process is a fundamental element of devising the best course of action, even when the circumstances in which the decision is being made are less than ideal. The following techniques and exercises provide a template for a solid decision process by using Force Field Analysis, a Decision Matrix, and Pros-Cons-Faults-and-Fixes to identify and assess the problem, consider a range of options, and troubleshoot the decision.

Technique 1: Force Field Analysis

A Force Field Analysis is a decision tool that can be used to identify and assess the key forces and factors that are driving or constraining a particular outcome. By exhaustively listing and weighting all the forces for and against an issue or outcome, analysts can more thoroughly define the forces at hand. In addition, the technique helps analysts assess the relative importance of each of the forces affecting the issue. A clearer understanding of these forces can in turn be used to fashion a course of action that augments particular forces to achieve a desired outcome or diminishes forces to reduce the chances of an undesirable outcome.

Task 1. Conduct a Force Field Analysis of the factors for and against additional violence directed at US interests in Belgrade.

STEP 1:   Define the problem, goal, or change clearly and concisely.

STEP 2:   Use a form of brainstorming to identify the main factors that will influence the issue.

STEP 3:   Make one list showing the strongest forces for and against additional violence.

STEP 4:   Array the lists in a table (see the template in Table 12.2).

Table 12.2 ▶ Force Field Analysis Template			
Forces For and Against Outcome			
Score	Driving Forces	Constraining Forces	Score
Score of 1–5	Driving Force 1	Constraining Force 1	Score of 1–5
Score of 1–5	Driving Force 2	Constraining Force 2	Score of 1–5
Sum of Driving Forces			**Sum of Constraining Forces**

STEP 5:   Assign a value to each factor to indicate its strength. Assign the weakest intensity scores a value of 1 and the strongest a value of 5. The same intensity score can be assigned to more than one factor if the factors are considered equal in strength.

STEP 6:   Calculate a total score for each list to determine whether the arguments for or against are dominant.

STEP 7:   Examine the two lists to determine if any of the factors balance out each other.

STEP 8:   Analyze the lists to determine how changes in factors might affect the overall outcome.

Task 2. Answer these questions:

▶ Which forces are the strongest?

▶ Do any assumptions underpin your intensity scores?

▶ Are there uncertainties that could affect your analysis, and if so, what are they?

Analytic Value Added. Is additional violence against US interests in Belgrade likely?

Technique 2: Decision Matrix

A Decision Matrix helps identify a course of action that maximizes specific goals or criteria. This technique breaks down a decision into its component parts by listing all the options or possible choices and the criteria for judging the options. It uses weights to help analysts determine the extent to which each option satisfies each of the criteria relative to the other options. Although the matrix results in a quantitative score for each option, the numbers do not make the decision. Instead, they should be used to guide a decision maker's understanding of the trade-offs among the various and often competing goals, or criteria, and how an option might be modified to best meet those goals.

Task 3. Use a Decision Matrix to assess how the US diplomats in Belgrade should respond to the threat of additional violence.

STEP 1: Identify the decision or question to be considered.

STEP 2: List the selection criteria and options. The number of criteria and options can vary from case to case.

STEP 3: Consolidate items within each list to eliminate overlap among the items.

STEP 4: Fill in a matrix like the example in Table 12.3 with the criteria and options you have generated.

STEP 5: Assign a weight to each criterion based on the relative importance of each. An easy way to do this is to divide 100 percentage points among the criteria.

STEP 6: Work across the matrix one row at a time to evaluate the relative ability of each of the options to satisfy each criterion. To do so, assign 10 points to each row and divide these points according to an assessment of the ability of each option to satisfy the selection criteria.

STEP 7: Assess the strength of each option against each criterion by multiplying the criterion weight by the assigned strength of the option from step 6. For example, *criterion 1 weight × option 1 points = score*. For ease of calculation, simply use the whole number weight rather than a percentage.

Table 12.3 ▶ Decision Matrix Template

Selection Criteria	% Weight (W)	Option 1 Value (V)	Option 1 Weighted Value (W × V)	Option 2 Value (V)	Option 2 Weighted Value (W × V)	Option 3 Value (V)	Option 3 Weighted Value (W × V)	Option 4 Value (V)	Option 4 Weighted Value (W × V)
Criterion 1	30	3.5	105	2.0	60	2.0	60	2.5	75
Criterion 2	10								
Criterion 3	40								
Criterion 4	20								
Weighted Value Totals			105		60		60		75

STEP 8: Determine the total score for each option and enter the sum in the "total" cell at the bottom of the column. The option with the highest total score is the quantitative selection.

STEP 9: Use a qualitative sanity check to help identify key issues, variables, or other observations that could further aid the decision-making process.

Analytic Value Added. Based on your findings, which option best protects US political and security interests in Belgrade, and why?

Technique 3: Pros-Cons-Faults-and-Fixes

Pros-Cons-Faults-and-Fixes (PCFF) is a simple strategy for evaluating many types of decisions, including policy options. In this case, US officials are presented with an immediate need to respond to violence directed against US interests in the Serbian capital. PCFF is particularly suited to situations in which decision makers must act quickly, because the technique helps to explicate and troubleshoot a decision in a quick and organized manner such that the decision can be shared and discussed by all decision-making participants.

Task 4. Use PCFF to evaluate the option you chose in Task 3 (see the template for this in Table 12.4). If you have not completed Task 3, use PCFF to evaluate a proposal for how the United States should protect its political and security

Table 12.4 ▶ Pros-Cons-Faults-and-Fixes Template

Faults	Pros	Cons	Fixes
Describe any faults for Pro 1.	Pro 1	Con 1	Describe any fixes for Con 1.
Describe any faults for Pro 2.	Pro 2	Con 2	Describe any fixes for Con 2.
Describe any faults for Pro 3.	Pro 3	Con 3	Describe any fixes for Con 3.

interests in Belgrade over the week following the February attack on the US embassy building.

STEP 1: Clearly define the proposed action or choice.

STEP 2: List all the Pros in favor of the decision. Think broadly and creatively and list as many benefits, advantages, or other positives as possible. Merge any overlapping Pros.

STEP 3: List all the Cons or arguments against what is proposed. Review and consolidate the Cons. If two Cons are similar or overlapping, merge them to eliminate redundancy.

STEP 4: Determine Fixes to neutralize as many Cons as possible. To do so, propose a modification of the Con that would significantly lower its risk of being a problem, identify a preventive measure that would significantly reduce the chances of the Con being a problem, conduct contingency planning that includes a change of course if certain indicators are observed, or identify a need for further research or to collect information to confirm or refute the assumption that the Con is a problem.

STEP 5: Fault the Pros. Identify a reason why the Pro would not work or the benefit would not be received, pinpoint an undesirable side effect that might accompany the benefit, or note a need for further research to confirm or refute the assumption that the Pro will work or be beneficial.

STEP 6: Compare the Pros, including any Faults, against the Cons and Fixes.

Analytic Value Added. Based upon your assessment of the Pros and Cons, how can the United States best refine its strategy to protect its political and security interests in Belgrade?

NOTES

1. Dejan Anastasijevic, "Joy in Kosovo, Anger in Serbia," *Time*, February 17, 2008, http://www.time.com/time/world/article/0,8599,1714164,00.html.

2. "Rioters Attack US Embassy in Belgrade after Kosovo Protest Rally," Radio Free Europe/Radio Liberty, February 21, 2008, http://www.rferl.org/content/article/1079512 .html.

3. Ellie Tzortzi, "Serbia Pledges Long-Haul Fight over Kosovo," Reuters, February 17, 2008, http://www.reuters.com/article/2008/02/17/idUSL17718644._CH_.2400.

4. Misha Glenny, *The Balkans: Nationalism, War, and the Great Powers, 1804–1999* (New York: Penguin, 1999).

5. Noel Malcolm, *Kosovo: A Short History* (New York: New York University Press, 1998).

6. Gordon N. Bardos, "Balkan History, Madeleine's War, and NATO's Kosovo," *Servian Studies: Journal of the North American Society for Serbian Studies* 15, no. 1 (2001): 77–102. Available at http://www.serbianstudies.org/publications/pdf/Vol15–1_Bardos .pdf.

7. Organization for Security and Co-operation in Europe (OSCE) Office for Democratic Institutions and Human Rights (ODHIR), *Kosovo/Kosova as Seen, as Told: An Analysis of the Human Rights Findings of the OSCE Kosovo Verification Mission, October 1998 to June 1999* (Warsaw, Poland: OSCE, 1999), cover memo. Available at http:// webcache.googleusercontent.com/search?q=cache:74_xAObauVMJ:www.osce.org/ odihr/17774e.

8. North Atlantic Treaty Organization (NATO), "NATO's Role in Relation to the Conflict in Kosovo," updated July 15, 1999, http://www.nato.int/kosovo/history.htm.

9. Miranda Vickers, *The Albanians: A Modern History* (London: I. B. Tauris, 2006). Originally published 1995.

10. Warren Hoge, "Russia Objects to UN Plan for Kosovo as 'One-Sided,'" *New York Times*, March 20, 2007, http://www.nytimes.com/2007/03/20/world/europe/20nations .html.

11. Judy Dempsey, "Diplomats to Increase Pressure on Serbia to Accept Kosovo Plan," *New York Times*, April 18, 2007, http://www.nytimes.com/2007/04/18/world/ europe/18kosovo.html.

12. "Thaci Refuses to Confirm Independence Date," France 24, February 16, 2008, http://www.france24.com/en/20080215-thaci-refuses-confirm-independence-date-serbia-kosovo/.

13. Ibid.

14. Reuters, "Tadic Vows to Preserve Kosovo," France 24, February 15, 2008, http:// www.france24.com/en/20080215-tadic-vows-preserve-kosovo-kosovo-serbia/.

15. "Thaci Refuses to Confirm Independence Date," France 24.

16. Dan Bilefsky, "Kosovo Declares Its Independence from Serbia," *New York Times*, February 18, 2008, http://www.nytimes.com/2008/02/18/world/europe/18kosovo.html.

17. "Serbia Planning Wholesale Rejection of Kosovo State," *Sydney Morning Herald* (Australia), February 13, 2008, http://www.smh.com.au/news/world/serbia-planning-wholesale-rejection-of-kosovo-state/2008/02/13/1202760333880.html.

18. Ibid.

19. Slobodan Lekic, "Serbia PM: West Seeks 'Slave-like' Status for Serbia," Associated Press, February 15, 2008.

20. Jovana Gec, "Serbia to Fight Kosovo Independence," Associated Press, February 16, 2008, http://www.boston.com/news/world/europe/articles/2008/02/16/serbia_to_fight_kosovo_independence/.

21. "Thaci Refuses to Confirm Independence Date," France24.

22. Bilefsky, "Kosovo Declares Its Independence from Serbia."

23. Anastasijevic, "Joy in Kosovo, Anger in Serbia."

24. Tzortzi, "Serbia Pledges Long-Haul Fight over Kosovo."

25. Anastasijevic, "Joy in Kosovo, Anger in Serbia."

26. Tzortzi, "Serbia Pledges Long-Haul Fight over Kosovo."

27. Bilefsky, "Kosovo Declares Its Independence from Serbia."

28. "Belgrade-Serbia," video of the attack on the US embassy 0:01:59, No Comment TV, February 17, 2008, http://www.youtube.com/watch?v=V6WnspPzWmo.

29. Tzortzi, "Serbia Pledges Long-Haul Fight over Kosovo."

30. "Rioters Attack US Embassy in Belgrade after Kosovo Protest Rally," Radio Free Europe/Radio Liberty.

31. Simon Roughneen, "Serbia, Ally Reject Sovereign Kosovo," *Washington Times*, February 18, 2008, http://www.washingtontimes.com/news/2008/feb/18/serbia-ally-reject-sovereign-kosovo/.

32. Anastasijevic, "Joy in Kosovo, Anger in Serbia."

33. Julian Borger and Peter Beaumont, "Angry but Pragmatic, Protesters Fly the Flag for Nationalism," *Guardian* (London), February 19, 2008, http://www.guardian.co.uk/world/2008/feb/19/kosovo.serbia1.

34. "US, European Powers Recognize Kosovo: Rift with Russia, China Apparent in Security Council Debate," MSNBC, February 18, 2008, http://www.msnbc.com/id/23219277/ns/world_news-europe/t/us-european-powers-recognize-kosovo/.

35. "Western States Hail Newcomer," Oxford Analytica, February 19, 2009.

36. "US, European Powers Recognize Kosovo," MSNBC News.

37. Elie Tzortzi, "Serbs Vent Ire on Kosovo, Western Backers," Reuters, February 18, 2008, http://www.reuters.com/article/2008/02/18/idUSL18637552/.

38. Nick Thorpe, "Tension on New Kosovan Border," BBC, February 21, 2008, http://www.bbc.co.uk/2/hi/europe/7256549.stm.

39. "Fresh Clashes Reported in Serbian Capital, Slovene Shopping Mall Evacuated," Radio B92, in translation at BBC Worldwide Monitoring, February 18, 2008, http://www.bbc.co.uk/ (site discontinued).

40. F. Berruyer, "NATO Troops Seal Kosovo Border," France 24, February 20, 2008, http://www.france24.com/en/20080220-nato-troops-seal-kosovo-border-kosovo-independence/.

41. "Special State Department Teleconference Briefing on Kosovo," Briefer: Under Secretary of State for Political Affairs R. Nicholas Burns, Federal News Service, February 18, 2008.

Image Credits

Chapter 1: Who Poisoned Karinna Moskalenko?
Page 9 (left and right): AP Photo/Efrem Lukatsky
Page 11: Matt Cardy/Getty Images

Chapter 2: Is Wen Ho Lee a Spy?
Page 25: AP Photo/LM Otero

Chapter 3: The Road to Tarin Kowt
Page 44: Capt. Claudia Peña Crossland
Page 46 (left and right): Capt. Claudia Peña Crossland

Chapter 4: Who Murdered Jonathan Luna?
Page 63: Reproduced with permission of the FBI
Page 64: Reproduced with permission of the FBI

Chapter 5: The Assassination of Benazir Bhutto
Page 82: AP Photo/Shakil Adil
Page 83: AP Photo/Lefteris Pitarakis
Page 87 (top and bottom): REUTERS/Reuters TV

Chapter 7: The Atlanta Olympics Bombing
Page 122: Reproduced with permission of the FBI
Page 127: AP Photo/Greg Gibson

Chapter 9: Colombia's FARC Attacks the US Homeland
Page 157: AP Photo/Scott Dalton
Page 158: AP Photo/APTN/Noticias Uno

Chapter 10: Defending Mumbai from Terrorist Attack
Page 183: AP Photo/Rajesh Nirgude

Chapter 11: Shades of Orange in Ukraine
Page 206 (left and right): Wikimedia Commons
Page 208: www.kremlin.ru
Page 210: Wikimedia Commons
Page 214 (all): Wikimedia Commons

Chapter 12: Violence Erupts in Belgrade
Page 224: AP Photo/Marko Drobnjakovic
Page 229: REUTERS/Nikola Solic